The Ethnographic Self as Resource

The Ethnographic Self as Resource

Writing Memory and Experience into Ethnography

Edited by
Peter Collins and Anselma Gallinat

Berghahn Books
NEW YORK • OXFORD

Published in 2010 by

Berghahn Books

www.berghahnbooks.com

©2010, 2013 Peter Collins and Anselma Gallinat
First paperback edition published in 2013

Library of Congress Cataloging-in-Publication Data

Collins, Peter, 1954-
  The ethnographic self as resource : writing memory and experience into
ethnography / Edited by Peter Collins and Anselma Gallinat.
      p. cm.
  Includes bibliographical references and index.
  ISBN 978-1-84545-656-6 (hbk.)--ISBN 978-1-78238-061-0 (pbk.)
  1. Ethnology--Authorship. 2. Ethnology--Biographical methods. 3.
Ethnology--Fieldwork. I. Gallinat, Anselma. II. Title.
  GN307.7.C65 2010
  305.8--dc22

                              2010006675

British Library Cataloguing in Publication Data

A catalogue record for this book is available
from the British Library

Printed in the United States on acid-free paper.

ISBN 978-1-78238-061-0 (paperback) -- ISBN 978-1-78238-062-7 (retail ebook)

CONTENTS

PROLOGUE

The primary objective of this book is to provoke a sustained consideration on the part of anthropologists of the ways in which the self can be a resource in doing ethnography, both in the field and in the study. The project began, as so many do, in the conversations between the two editors, who felt that, despite a plethora of writing on the periphery of this key issue, there was no text that addressed directly the question 'To what extent can the self of the anthropologist be used as a resource in doing ethnography?' We invited a number of scholars to contribute essays that would illuminate the key issues raised by asking and attempting to answer this question. Typically, we did not get the essays we expected. What we have is an extraordinarily diverse range of responses, each of which naturally reflects the interests, concerns and puzzlements of the author. In hindsight, and given our own proclivities, we should not have expected anything different. All of those who were invited to participate are included in the collection, except Nazalie Iqbal, who was attempting to complete her doctoral thesis. In order to generate further dialogue we organised a panel at the EASA Conference in September 2006, held at Bristol University. Most of the contributors presented a version of their chapter. We were also joined by Anne Larsen and Lynette Šikić-Mićanović, whose papers we incorporate in this final text. Tamar El Or also read a paper of very great interest but had already promised it to another editor. We would like to thank all of the scholars involved in this intensely dialogic project for their time and effort.

Peter Collins and Anselma Gallinat
Newcastle upon Tyne July 2009

Chapter 1

THE ETHNOGRAPHIC SELF AS RESOURCE: AN INTRODUCTION

Peter Collins and Anselma Gallinat

The purpose of this chapter is to provide, briefly, the disciplinary context in which the idea of the self as resource in doing ethnography has emerged. We will delineate the relevant developments in the discipline with particular regard to 'anthropology at home', the reflexive turn and auto-ethnography. We will briefly introduce the work of scholars who already apply the kind of integrative approach we propose and then go on to detail the implications of such research and writing for methodology and the discipline at large. These include issues such as authenticity, 'playing the native card', memory and memorisation, ethics and honesty, and the question of whether this may lead from an anthropological 'double vision' to a 'split personality'. Throughout we shall relate this volume's chapters to this discussion and the overall thesis.

Making Visible: the Ethnographer Brought into Focus

The assumption that we can better understand ourselves through understanding others has a long history. It suffices to say here that this apparently simple thought was the seed that slowly developed into what we now call anthropology. By 1900, intrepid individuals were leaving home with the intention of understanding other ways of life. To cast matters in black and white, there was a time, before 1970, when anthropology was almost entirely a matter of isolating the other. The person or self of the anthropologist remained unseen and mostly unheard. Like the movies, the conceit was that we (the viewer, the reader) had direct, unmediated access to the lives before us, that is, without the facilitating role of film crew, director, editor and so forth. The film gives us an objective representation of life itself.

But there's the rub – it was the realisation that ethnography is representation, or life at least once removed, that caused what was and continues to be a reappraisal of the anthropological enterprise. The present volume is set in that tradition of reappraisal.

The adage was that anthropology sought to understand the other – at least partly in order better to know oneself. This approach to anthropology was epistemologically grounded in a fairly straightforward scientism. Here was the anthropologist and over there, ontologically discrete and entirely separate from him or her, were the objects of his or her attention – the other. Anthropology was a science, maybe not quite like physics or chemistry but similar enough to claim, or at first assume, a measure of objectivity in its practice. Anthropological accounts of others were therefore fundamentally realist. The aim of the fieldworker was to collect, accumulate, classify and analyse social facts. Language was considered a neutral tool that enabled the anthropologist to identify social phenomena and describe them exactly and truthfully. The discipline overall should be the accumulation of these facts. The personal identity of the anthropologist was an unimportant detail, though best practice assumed that the anthropologist, commencing their observations from outside of the frame should ensure that they took precautions to stay out. This is not to say that they chose to remain separate from the action during fieldwork. After all, at least since Malinowski's work on the Trobriand Islands, anthropological practice involved more or less systematic participant observation: the anthropologists should live among those whose lives they were attempting to understand for an extended period of time. But this was a practical strategy and was understood as a principle that distinguished the modern anthropologist from the Victorian armchair scholar who sifted through data gleaned by those – soldiers, traders, missionaries, colonial administrators – who had travelled there instead. It was certainly not a part of Malinowski's plan that anthropologists should place themselves in the ethnographic frame and he was careful to erase, wherever possible, the traces of his own presence in the field.

This means that, on the one hand, the anthropological endeavour gained legitimacy from 'being there' so long as evidence of 'doing there' was eradicated. In the field it was necessary to be 'with' the other as only in that way might one contextualise beliefs and practices in a holistic account of another culture: 'to realise *his* vision of *his* world' (Malinowski 1961 [1922]: 25). But Malinowski did not consider it necessary to include himself in his academic presentation of Trobriand life and kept his personal feelings and observations to his diary. This diary, published posthumously in 1967, is one of the more significant waymarks of our current journey as it remains a painful reminder that *doing* ethnography is inevitably intertwined with the rather subjective and deeply human *being* in the field.

Even those with just a passing acquaintance with the recent history of anthropology will know that by the 1970s the character of ethnography had undergone considerable change. For a variety of more or less connected reasons, including the influence of the postmodern turn, anthropology began to take a growing interest in the self of the anthropologist, or at least in the relationship between self and other. The possibility that anthropologists – and anthropology as an increasingly institutionalised practice – may have had an impact on the representation of 'an other' culture gave rise to an increasing awareness of anthropologists' position in the field. There was a growing recognition that Radcliffe-Brown might have been wrong and that the anthropologist can never be an entirely neutral 'device' for describing and explaining other cultures. The time had come when anthropologists felt obliged to confront the uncomfortable fact that they were always already implicated in 'the field'; that they were, inevitably, constructing what they came to re-present.

Writing Culture

Making room for the self in ethnography depended partly upon the loosening of textual conventions. *Writing Culture* (Clifford and Marcus 1986) has become iconic of significant and identifiable tendencies within the discipline – including reflexivity as a necessary component of doing fieldwork, the importance of critique, a growing interest in the textuality of anthropology (the so-called 'literary turn'), and the further possibility of doing 'anthropology at home' by the time of its publication. Although it would be overstating the case to cite *Writing Culture* as the cause of a paradigm shift, the book undoubtedly presented the most concise and subsequently most influential position statement of a new self-conscious and critical anthropology. We will consider a number of these trends here: reflexivity, ethnography as a form of writing, anthropology at home and auto-ethnography, and the employment of anthropology as cultural critique. We would argue that in one way or another each of these tendencies relates more or less directly to the emergence of the anthropologist's self in their ethnography. The tendency among anthropologists to attend more explicitly to the self was not merely a product of anthropology. Giddens (1991) and others have shown that reflexivity has been a part of the ambient climate of late modernity, a practice that characterises the world view of not only scholars but also the public at large. Indeed it might be argued that this text itself is another example of the modern tendency to dwell reflexively on the self.

Jay Ruby's edited collection, A *Crack in the Mirror* (1982), preceded *Writing Culture* by four years and anticipated some of the themes found there. The chapters in Ruby expertly indicate the inevitability of subjectivity in the ethnographic account comparing this to the sphere of cultural production. As the book aims to make the data-gathering process transparent (1982: 18–19), there is the stark realisation that at the centre of every ethnography lies the self of the anthropologist. From the 1970s on, there has been a growing tendency to acknowledge this presence, to have the anthropologist's self step from behind the camera and acknowledge her presence, both to herself and others (see also Coffey 1999). However, as Dyck says in his chapter here, it is unfortunate that this reflexivity has become a kind of reflex that is all too often confined to a preface or introduction as the new badge of ethnographic legitimacy. The information provided is often eclectic, limited and little commented upon (Salzman 2002); the text proceeds as before and little is gained. The actuality of the influence of the anthropologist's self on data collection and writing therefore tends, all too often, to be ghettoised and its consideration not properly developed. As Kohn remarks, in this way reflexivity also often appears rather static pointing to the anthropologist as a similarly static filter of the observed culture. In this volume Collins and Kohn make the case for a more processual form of reflexivity.

There are several notable instances, however, in which the self-awareness of the anthropologist has radically reshaped the form of their ethnography. One thinks particularly of Rabinow's *Reflections on Fieldwork in Morocco* (1977), Dumont's *The Headman and I* (1978), Crapanzano's *Tuhami* (1980), Shostak's *Nisa* (1981), Dwyer's *Moroccan Dialogues* (1982). We should note Pratt's observation (1986) that such accounts are often secondary, following on from more standard objectivist texts – Rabinow, for example, published *Symbolic Domination* (1975) two years before *Reflections* (1977). It is also worth noting that earlier texts exist which point towards these more experimental works – Sydney Mintz's *Worker in the Cane* (1960), for example. In these cases, a concerted attempt is being made to foreground the dialogical nature of ethnography both as a fieldwork practice and as published text. On the one hand, the voice of the other is foregrounded and, on the other, the self of the anthropologist is made explicitly and constantly present. Whatever these texts achieve, they certainly confirm the impossibility of objectively representing, ethnographically, an unproblematic other. In this volume Šikić-Mićanović makes it equally clear that ethnographies, regardless of the details of their production, are jointly constructed by the ethnographer and her research participants and that the inclusion of the self of the ethnographer in the field is, in many cases, a precondition of ethnography.

These realisations are clearly apparent in the 1990s which witnessed an increasing use of self-narrative as well as biography in ethnography, for example Okely and Callaway's *Anthropology and Autobiography* (eds, 1992) and Reed-Danahay's *Auto/Ethnography: Rewriting the Self and the Social* (1997). More importantly, feminist monographs such as Abu-Lughod's *Writing Women's Worlds* (1993) and Behar's *Translated Woman* (1993) showed how one could write experience-near ethnographies that reveal subjectivity without losing academic credibility.

A more recent example is Rapport's short essay, 'Hard-Sell or Mumbling "Right" Rudely' (1997). Here, Rapport places his self squarely at the centre of the action. He is drawn, after receiving an invitation and promise through the post, to a city centre hotel in the hope of receiving a substantial prize of some sort. Rapport describes his slow and steady humiliation at the hands of timeshare salesmen in a manner that is likely to cause his reader both amusement and discomfort. Unsurprisingly, he leaves the hotel after a gruelling and embarrassing two-hour 'hard-sell', with nothing more than the continued and now heavily tarnished promise of that prize – a prize that never materialises. Rapport offers an 'experience-near' auto-ethnography, an account that many of his readers will feel uncomfortably familiar with – the unfulfilled promise of free enterprise. Rapport's work, both in this essay and more generally (see especially Rapport 1994a), reflects and develops a more explicit connection with forms of writing that are traditionally thought of as 'fiction'.

Even these examples suggest, by their heterogeneity, that 'the literary turn', as it is often called, is hardly a coherent movement in anthropology. There are at least three separate, though admittedly overlapping, developments here. First, there is a movement towards experimentation in the style of ethnographic writing itself. Perhaps the most notable examples include Stephen Tylor's essay in *Writing Culture*, along with the biographical and dialogic examples cites above. If one accepts that ethnography is a 'form of writing' (this is impossible to deny, even if one refuses to countenance departures from the standard genre), then there is no reason not to experiment with non-standard forms. Such experimentation has been taken further in sociology than in anthropology under the label of 'auto-ethnography'. One might, for instance, look to the collections edited by Ellis and Bochner (1996; see also their extended meditation on experimental forms in Bochner and Ellis 2002). Their earlier collection include, for example, an account of the life of a mentally retarded woman by her (sociologist) daughter, a first-hand account of a bulimic, an extraordinary case study in child sexual abuse and a wistful piece on the author's father's journey across America in his Model T Ford in 1924. In each case, and despite the apparent idiosyncrasy of the topics, the author draws on the quotidian in order to illuminate more general themes.

In this collection, Dona and Dorothy Davis turn their attention to the experience, and in particular their experience, of being identical twins. This is as 'experience-near' as ethnography gets. They intimate, at one point, the possibility of existential unity, arguing, not that one individual may contain several selves, but that two individuals may share, at least for an instant, one self. In this case, and, indeed, in all cases here, experimental writing takes a back seat as the form and content of ethnography as a methodology are interrogated. Indeed, that case of the Davis twins' contribution is especially interesting and indicates not only the tenacity of the standard format of ethnographic writing but also its capacity to contain even the most unusual fieldwork: perhaps this is due to its flexibility – or, of course, to the ingenuity of the writer.

The second movement is the treatment of ethnographic texts *as* texts. During those years when the major paradigm in anthropology was characterised by its scientificity there seemed no point in bringing the ethnographic account itself under scrutiny. After all, texts in other scientific disciplines did not undergo the lit. crit. treatment. Perhaps it was the interpretive turn spurned by Clifford Geertz' work (1973) that prepared the ground for this possibility. Indeed, Geertz himself led the way with what turned out to be his most controversial book – *Works and Lives* (1988) – and Van Maanen published *Tales of the Field* (1988) in the same year, both books dealing with the rhetorical devices employed by influential anthropologists. Indeed the minor furore caused by *Works and Lives* indicates the suspicion with which some anthropologists viewed foregrounding anthropological writing (Spencer 1989). There have long been texts that are in a sense ambiguous with respect to genre (think of Bohannan 1954; Powdermaker 1966; Briggs 1970), which early on highlighted the inevitable subjective nature of ethnography as method and texts. If taken to its logical conclusion this realisation requires critical reading. More recently, there have been texts that at one level at least may well be seen to be fictional accounts, though each case needs to be treated as something *sui generis*. We are thinking particularly of Michael Jackson's *Barawa and the Ways Birds Fly in the Sky: An Ethnographic Novel* (1986) and Michael Taussig's *The Magic of the State* (1997). Indeed, here are two anthropologists, a New Zealander and an Australian, who most clearly exemplify a kind of experimentation that the editors of *Writing Culture* sought to encourage (though without providing specific direction). Michael Jackson has published not only non-standard ethnography (1989, 1995, 2002a, 2002b, 2005) but also novels and volumes of poetry (1986). And there is a continuity across genres in Jackson's work, facilitated by an existential perspective. Taussig, too, has been among the most adventurous ethnographers. In *Shamanism, Colonialism and the Wildman* (1987), he commends a certain ambiguity in ethnographic writing – at least in dealing with the kind of field in which he works:

Killing and torture and sorcery are real as death is real. But why people do these things, and how the answers to that question affect the question – that is not answerable outside of the effects of the real carried through time by people in action. That is why my subject is not the truth of being but the being of truth, not whether facts are real but what the politics of their interpretation and representation are. (1987: xiii)

It is evident from this passage that Taussig writes the way he does for a purpose and that purpose is critique. Taussig is not unconcerned with describing the everyday lives of Colombian people but he is considerably more interested in the political consequences of what he describes along with the moral and political standpoint adopted by the ethnographer. Indeed, critique is a purpose of the ethnographic genre that is flagged by several of those contributing to *Writing Culture.* Talal Asad had some time before edited a collection of articles interrogating the political implications of doing anthropology during what he called 'the colonial encounter' (1973). And, indeed, Marcus and Fischer's *Anthropology as Cultural Critique* was published in 1986 – the same year as *Writing Culture.* Marcus and Fischer complain (p. 111) that recent accounts of 'predicaments' in American culture 'fail to take account of the existing domestic cultural criticism'; indeed, 'they are careless precisely about that which would be sacred to anthropologists in considering other cultures – indigenous accounts'. The chapters in this collection do not make the same mistake. Rather, they consider their informants' voices as well as their own engagement with their informants as the core of ethnography. Nor do our authors wish to continue to dwell overlong on the predicament of ethnographic representation. In contrast, this volume seeks to take ethnography a further step forward, rather in the manner of Bruner: 'The problem is now two-fold: on the one hand we want to continue and deepen the critique, to correct its excesses, to explore and conceptualise new facets of our predicament as ethnographers in a postcolonial post-industrial era, on the other hand, we have to move ahead with the common ethnographic enterprise' (1993: 2).

Finally, a few anthropologists have begun to mine works of literature for ethnographic data – this is fieldwork in fiction as it were and the third movement in anthropology following the 'literary turn'. Mary Douglas has been carrying out such work for more than forty years, taking the Bible as her primary source. Some readers will be critical of our characterisation of the Bible as fiction; the case is clearer with regard to Rapport's work on/in E.M. Forster (Rapport 1994a), Paul Benson's edited collection (1993) and the work of Handler and Segal (1990). In relation to the latter it is worth quoting from Rapport's review of that text: 'Jane Austen's consistent attention to the subtleties of social life allow her fictions to be compared to anthropological studies, in regard both to what she represented and how it was narrated. Austen's texts can be treated as ethnographic data and so as analytic exemplars of intercultural defamiliarization and intercultural translation' (1994b: 216–217). Rapport avers that fiction (or at least some fiction) can stand as 'indigenous accounts'. Strathern, in *After Nature* (1992), draws similarly on a number of British writers, including Beatrix Potter, in order to illuminate national understandings of kinship.

These developments not only shaped the writing of culture by generating more experience-near accounts and cultural critique and by facilitating a more considered exploration of the connections between literature and anthropology, but clearly also had an impact on the doing of ethnography in the field. The increasing legitimacy of ethnography undertaken 'at home' constituted a further breach of the 'normal paradigm'.

Anthropology 'At Home'

We can use Strathern as a tie here, as we consider the growing tendency of anthropologists to carry out what is generally called 'anthropology at home'. As well as carrying out ethnographic research in Elmdon (Strathern et al 1981), a village in Essex, and on English kinship more generally, Strathern also posed some difficult questions for any who assumed that doing anthropology at home was a straightforward matter. Her typically subtle argument boils down to the claim that 'We cannot conclude that non-Western anthropologists will stand in the same relationship to their own society of culture as a Western anthropologist does to his/hers' (1987: 30). It is a question of there being different systems of self-knowledge from one to the other. According to Strathern, the kind of self-knowledge system existing among Mount Hageners, for example, prohibits one of their number carrying out native anthropology in the way that a British citizen might carry out anthropology at home among the British.[1] But this is in any case all too crude – in 2009, what can we possibly mean by 'British culture'? The important question here is the extent to which we can think of ourselves as 'native' to any particular group (see Narayan 1993). What kind of experience do we need to claim membership of a particular group, category or community – what markers are required to be considered a member by others? It is obviously not enough to be British to count oneself a 'native' in regard to Coventry Sikhs.

The unspoken rule in British and American anthropology was that one 'went away' to the field. Only by establishing significant physical distance between one's home and the field could sufficient objectivity be obtained.

Fieldwork at home was considered the province of sociology. This sentiment was further nurtured by an underpinning assumption that the country of one's birth represented a more or less homogeneous culture from which one must escape in order to find a legitimate and equally homogeneous 'other'. American anthropologists had long studied 'other cultures' on their doorstep – Native American Indians. British anthropologists, on the other hand, were not so fortunate, and were expected to follow Radcliffe-Brown and Malinowski to distant lands – in Oceania, Africa, Asia. From the late 1950s onward and for a variety of reasons – the increased cost of undertaking fieldwork far from home, difficulties in obtaining research permits and the growing awareness that in an increasingly multicultural Western society 'the other' is all around us – anthropologists were increasingly turning to geographically closer groups and places (Jackson 1987).

Max Gluckman, in Manchester, was an early proponent of 'anthropology at home' and influenced his students in their choice of field site, including Frankenberg (1957). Littlejohn's *Westrigg* (1963) was a further notable contribution to the anthropology of Britain, which dried up rather before a rebirth in Manchester during the 1980s (Cohen 1982, 1986, 1987; Rapport 1993, 1994a). Some Manchester scholars undertook fieldwork in factories and in public institutions, further breaking down what it was to 'do anthropological fieldwork'. It is worth noting, further, that those among Gluckman's students, including Turner, Van Velsen, Epstein, Mitchell and others, who continued to work 'away from home' in situations of very rapid social change experimented freely with both fieldwork methods and the construction of ethnographic texts. Messerschmidt (1981) and later Moffat (1992) broached the subject from an American point of view.

The tendency to stay 'at home' has presented anthropology with a number of challenges. For instance, the accountability of the anthropologist to those they have studied is more pressing – particularly when research participants speak the language in which the ethnography is written and may obtain copies (see Brettel 1993). Furthermore, at home the impact of one's research, because of its greater accessibility, might be very great indeed – in either a positive or negative way. As a result the administration of research ethics has grown apace.

Since the 1980s the conduct of ethnography in the country of one's upbringing is no longer especially contentious within the discipline. It is probably no coincidence that the majority of authors gathered here have carried out fieldwork 'at home'. The question of whether one 'should' carry out research away from home in the first instance, as claimed by Jackson (1987: 14), seems to us increasingly irrelevant. As Strathern points out (1987: 16), 'the preliminary question [is] of how one *knows* when one is at home'. Collins (2002) has written about this matter in relation to his fieldwork among British Quakers, arguing that one is never simply 'at home', and the assumption of the role of ethnography is enough to create a sense of difference if that is felt to be required for epistemological reasons. Obviously, there are also shades of 'at homeness'. Gallinat, in this volume, refers to that collective memory of times past – *Ostalgia* – the ambivalent feeling of Germans who were, until 1990, East Germans. Having grown up in East Germany, Gallinat experienced events and emotions, circumstances and situations much in the same way as many of her research participants. She is perfectly able to remember these experiences and presents them alongside the experiences of others. However, she is equally aware of the responsibility she has as an anthropologist to hold up her own as well as others' accounts for critical inspection. Whatever the degree one feels 'at home', however, there is always the possibility of drawing on significantly similar experiences to those one is working with in the field. As such, we would argue that a shared sense of a particular past as a means of drawing directly on one's own experiences is less a guarantor of than a stimulus for constructing worthwhile ethnography.

Interestingly, while Strathern acknowledges the likelihood of a greater reflexivity of those conducting fieldwork 'at home' (pp. 17–19), she omits consideration of the ethnographer's self as a resource that could further aid their investigation. However, she critically reflects on the possibility that those being studied 'at home' may feel that they are being exploited – why should they think so? We need at this point, then, to distinguish between the ethics of using oneself as a resource and carrying on our ethnographic research at home – they do not amount to the same thing, even though they are likely to overlap in practice.

Strathern refers to 'anthropology at home' as 'auto-anthropology' (1987). This usage of the terminology is not typical. More often, 'auto-ethnography', rather than 'auto-anthropology', is used in reference to fieldwork in which the ethnographic self is the *only* informant involved, as explained above. The growth of such autobiographical accounts has been exponential since 1990 (Ryang 2000), though such texts remain rare in anthropology. The pieces in this collection rely, without exception, on accounts drawn from both self and others. We do not seek to argue the benefits of auto-ethnography, though that is not to say, either, that we are dismissive of it.

Our point, put simply, is that those who may refer to themselves or are referred to by others as 'insiders' and are thus able to draw directly on personal experiences which may be more or less shared by research participants (see Shokeid 1997) are likely to have a different perspective on the field from those who can plausibly make no such claim. This sharing, we argue, as well as its lack can bring about important insights. Such processes of reflecting on experiences and of recall are about remembering.

Memory

Memory, is dealt with only briefly in *Writing Culture*. In this collection it looms large however. In a way this volume is a reflection on the facts that ethnographers come to the field with memories of their own, that their experiences there create more, and that they deploy these memories in field notes, and, over the years, in writing. In each of the chapters that follow, the author therefore feels it necessary to engage with the place of memory in relation to the ethnographic self.

Of the various kinds of memory, the contributors here are concerned almost entirely with autonoetic memory – or in Williams James's terms 'memory per se'. Auto-noetic or episodic memory involves the ability to recall personal experiences and is different from, for example semantic memory – the recall of 'facts' (often characterised as the difference between 'remembering' and 'knowing' (Tulving 1972). It is associated with other higher-order mental accomplishments such as introspection, reflexivity and anticipation. It is probably true to say that the contributors to this volume are concerned more with the auto-noetic facility more generally, even though several pay particular attention to memory. Collins argues that the self and memory are centrally and similarly involved in all human interaction, and so cannot be excluded from one small part of it, that is, ethnography (see Narayan 1993). Drawing on Schank (1990), he argues that the memory organises experience into retrievable units on which the self draws during social interaction. In this way, then, the self in consort with memory is implicated in ethnography, not only in the field but also in the study. Others, and in particular Coleman and Kohn (and Phipps, if to a lesser extent), argue that the idea of 'flashbulb memory', an idea originally introduced by Brown and Kulick (1977) and developed by Endel Tulving (1983, 1993; see also Bruner 1994), is especially relevant in this context. In this case, a present experience sparks a memory of an earlier experience, the connections between them generating further interpretation. There is a proto-analysis of current experience in the light of self-reflection: the self is the incubator of ethnography.

Furthermore, in both cases, however, memory is observed to be embodied, that is, felt directly, rather than understood cognitively (see Spry 2001). Of course, such embodied experiences are open to analysis in the same way as are those experiences felt by others. What is distinctive, unique even, is the experience itself – which gives the ethnographer a peculiar (and seldom discussed) purchase on one's field. Given that very little has been published on shared (not collective) memories, the Davis twins, in developing the idea of 'dualling', are in a position to contribute significantly to the discipline of memory studies. Their claim that their research contributes to the memory literature at three points (memory as material and embodied, memory as social action and interaction, and memory as shaped by social and cultural processes) accurately identifies the contribution that can be made by anthropology in general to studies of memory. Skinner's chapter is particularly illuminating in relation to embodied experience, indicating clearly the importance of 'shared experience' between ethnographer and informant. In this case, the perception of the other that the anthropologist has experienced dance as she has generates a palpable sense of rapport, the Holy Grail of the ethnographer. Phipps shows how deeply intertwined language learning and practice are with memory processes, and highlights the fact that ethnographers as language learners undergo these processes also. Indeed, the ethnographic experiences related in the chapters below suggest that rapport is likely to be more deeply felt when the embodied aspects of experiences are acknowledged and reflected upon.

Amit and Coleman remind us that forgetting is a key component of memory. Indeed, as Amit avers, given that memory is a process of selection (and of revelation?) then forgetting is a part of remembering. The question of intention arises once more in relation to memory. Neither Coleman nor Amit suggests that the anthropologist should attempt to dredge their memories for relevant experiences. And, indeed, Collins argues that the anthropologist as a competent member of society will always and already draw on their stock of experiences in making sense of the world: what is typical of quotidian life is typical of doing ethnography.

The Self

Whilst this collection does not intend to be a systematic interrogation of the nature of the self, it does seek to reveal certain aspects of the self and, more specifically, the ethnographic self, through its focus on the role of experience and memory in ethnography. The concept of the self in Western society is a relatively modern development. The self itself is a social construction and yet one that is persuasive within the societies where anthropology itself is 'at home'. Giddens (1991) locates the self as a highly reflexive endeavour within 'high modernity' contrasted with traditional societies which ascribed identities more readily through an individual's place within a community. Holstein and Gubrium situate the 'social self' (2000) within Western thought as it has developed during the past century.

Questions of the self and personhood have been of interest to anthropologists for some time, beginning perhaps with Marcel Mauss (1985 [1938]), taken further by Marilyn Strathern (1988) and the many anthropologists following her (Lutz 1988; Battaglia 1990; Jackson and Karp 1990; Myers 1991 [1986]), more recently explored by Anthony Cohen (1994) and Nigel Rapport (2003). This varied literature dwells mainly on cultural differences in personhood, certainly the main focus in Strathern's discussion of Melanesian 'dividuality' in *The Gender of the Gift* (1988), and to a degree ethnographies on personhood in Melanesia also acted as cultural critiques of individualism in the West. Lutz, working on emotions on the Micronesian atoll of Ifaluk (1988), makes this point apparent by what appears to be a direct comparison of the socio-centric self in Micronesia based on ethnographic research with the Western individual based in her knowledge (experience?) of US American discourses. These early works have long been criticised, partly for their focus on ideologies of personhood rather than everyday practices (LiPuma 1998), and partly for their superficial treatment of the Western self (Kusserow 1999). The individual, typically based in the US American context, has been seen as a single bounded entity that exerts agency and rational choice. On a continuum between socio-centric and egocentric concepts it is usually located on the most egocentric end. More recent work has aimed to address this imbalance, showing that individualist concepts can similarly entail socio-centric notions, and vice versa (LiPuma 1998; Kusserow 1999).

However, the issue of balancing ideologies of personhood with social practice remains a challenge, one that has been aptly taken up by scholars working on narrative. Holstein and Gubrium refer to this as 'discursive practice' and 'discourse in practice' (2000). The former is the focus of ethnomethodologists, they explain, the latter that of Foucauldian analysis. Yet both approaches have a parallel that the authors use to describe narrative self-construction: 'One source of convergence would surely be the recognition of the artful yet locally structured stories that comprise the contemporary self in practice' (p. 103). Holstein and Gubrium, like Giddens (1991) and others, remind us that in this time of high modernity the individual self is constructed across a much greater variety of contexts than at other times in history.

The literary or narrative turn that made this focus possible, also left its mark on anthropology with a growing number of ethnographers exploring self-construction through narratives. Kleinman firmly established narrative as a way of interrogating self-construction in illness (1988). Vieda Skultans's engaging ethnography *The Testimony of Lives: Memory in Post-Soviet Latvia* (1998) uses stories related to her in letters and interviews to explore questions of agency, suffering and culture, to name but a few. In a shorter article Skultans explores how her informants engage with their KGB files (2001). The interrogation protocols, she explains, are particular texts in that they are based on a highly restricted and repetitive lexicon, they take on a monological appearance – the language and choice of terminology of the interrogator is mirrored exactly in the responses of the interrogated; they are authorless – the protocols bear no signature or similar; and they lack representational value thus contradicting her informants' memories of the social realities of the narrated situations. In this situation Skultans observes how her informants re-establish agency and self-identity in their engagement with the files, and with her as dialogical partner. They do so through arguing with the protocols: they read passages, and respond, criticise and correct use of language, facts, they remember, add details on circumstances and persons involved. This harrowing example aptly shows that self-construction requires dialogue and relies on a perception of both the self and the other (see Bruner 2002).

The literature on the self in narrative highlights the social aspects of self-construction. To begin with it requires at least two persons, as Bruner points out: every story requires a teller and a told (2002). Secondly, in modern times contexts of self-construction are manifold. Just like memories, narratives are culturally and contextually bound. They must make sense as stories to the people around. Holstein and Gubrium (2000) go further in arguing that narratives are reactions not only to social contexts but simultaneously serve to shape these contexts. They do so not least because they are also grounded in the experiences of the narrator prior to this particular encounter.

This then means that the self is multiple, socially embedded and emergent, and thoroughly implicated in processes of learning, becoming, experiencing and remembering. This is also what the chapters in this volume reveal about the self in general, and the ethnographic self more specifically. It is indisputable that the self is central to all human interaction. At the very least, we all draw on our own memories in efforts to understand each other. Ethnography as the investigation of human interaction through observation and participation is hence dependent upon the ethnographer's self. Moreover, memory plays a significant part in fieldwork, and perhaps even more explicitly in the study. We do not write down every fieldwork experience – just imagine trying to do so – but rather carry much of that experience around with us as 'head-notes', that is, in our memory. If that is so, the self with its memory will provide a valuable resource in ethnography.

The Ethnographic Self as a Resource

The self can be brought into play intentionally, by holding fieldwork experiences, especially those from different fields, in juxtaposition in order to facilitate the illumination or complication of one by the other. We may choose to undertake projects, as in the case of Dyck and Amit, partly because of our previous experiences in a field and we might add that Collins chose to study British Quakers as a British Quaker; Skinner was an accomplished dancer before he commenced fieldwork on salsa; Nadel-Klein undertook her study as a fellow gardener, Phipps interrogates language learning as a former student of German, and, of course, the Davis twins have undertaken research on twins for the most obvious of reasons. In each case, they were consciously aware that their selection of field site would enable them to draw on their self-narratives, which would, in turn, enrich their ethnography.

At the heart of each of the chapters that follow is a consideration of what it means to be competent as an ethnographer. Social and cultural competence is developed during the lifecourse and, whilst related to memory, it goes further by relying on embodied knowledge that we are often unaware of. Competence can span vastly different phenomena, from riding a bicycle (or pony, in the Davises's case), knowledge about whether or not to judge somebody else's garden (Nadel-Klein), to being able to speak another language (Phipps). Some of our competences may therefore be required in the field, others will be developed during fieldwork, whilst our ethnographies may show whether we are competent authors and fieldworkers. Competence in culture, one's own or another, is closely related to, and yet a step forward from, cultural intimacy. Herzfeld argues that good fieldwork depends on a social intimacy with informants, which then may lead to cultural intimacy (2000). Yet a question arises. When arriving at the level of cultural intimacy and competence, have we closed the matter to analytic reflection? Or may it be that reflexive consideration of the acquiring of competences would serve to reveal processes of the production of culture and anthropological knowledge that we are looking for? This line of thought harmonises with Phipps's observation that important dynamics are at work at the interstices of expression between the interiorised remembered present and the exteriorised thick description of the field. Furthermore, Larsen, Rapport and Šikić-Mićanović show how situations where we are uncomfortable, feel at fault, struggle with ourselves and others are moments that bring us close to important anthropological insights as we straddle cultural conventions. Through the varied ethnographic examples provided here, we are arguing that such competence relies to an extent on drawing on the self as a resource grounded in either experience or memory or both.

There are hazards. We cannot avoid issues of ethics in admitting the self into the field. The first question we are required to face is the extent to which using the self as a resource is a ploy or conscious strategy. An existentialist might criticise the adoption of such a position as an example of bad faith – as representing ourselves publicly as something we are not. We can assume that there is a difference between experience (for instance of the unity two people achieve in dance) and the faking of that experience. This is a problem for anthropologists working at home in particular, because the possibility of 'faking it' is likely to be relatively easy. Secondly, we must be careful in implicating family and friends in our ethnography. We may assume that those very close to us 'will not mind' or even that we can speak for them in such matters – this seems to us a dangerous assumption. Do they not become informants the moment they enter our ethnography and therefore deserve the same respectful treatment as informants we met during our ethnographic investigations? Such an issue need not arise, but, when it does, it is incumbent on the anthropologist to face it squarely. Finally, we should ask ourselves *why* on any particular occasion we understand our own experiences to be relevant to the ethnography. If writing ourselves into our texts is a trope, we need to address the epistemological questions arising from this.

Not only serving as a resource for the ethnographer, the self might also be drawn upon by others. We can never wholly determine the way others see us. During interviews our research participants might, more or less explicitly, treat *us* as a resource in trying to establish our position as regards material or other resources; indeed, a certain symbolic capital might be accumulated merely by being seen as a confidante of the anthropologist. Alternatively, perhaps the ethnographer will be constructed as a conduit, receiving information which he or she will be expected to pass on in the interests of the research participant. There may be other gains, sought for and/or achieved – a greater sense of one's own importance for example, or the opportunity to unburden oneself to an insignificant stranger who can be relied upon to keep ones secrets. Larsen, conducting fieldwork in a small Norwegian village explores these aspects of ethnographic work.

Envoi: Towards an Integrated Ethnography

While Cohen (1994) argues persuasively for a self-conscious anthropology, we argue further that as anthropologists we should draw on our selves as a resource in doing ethnography. The chapters comprising this collection aspire to an approach to ethnography that seeks to achieve something other than reflexivity, though there is little doubt that without the 'reflexive turn' this book could never have appeared. Through this increasingly prevalent ethnographic self-awareness, we are provided with the possibility of a different kind or mode of ethnography. Ontologically, the new ethnography has the potential to be truly dialogical. This clearly has moral repercussions. However, the authors here are attempting to deal less with arising epistemological and ontological issues, and more with a set of methodological problems: given that anthropologists are far more likely in the twenty-first century to acknowledge a central role of the anthropologist's self in producing ethnography, how can we further shape this development in ways that produce more interesting ethnography?

We have attempted in this introductory chapter both to provide the disciplinary context for the key themes that are developed in the chapters that follow and, more importantly, to argue about the necessity of taking steps forward from self-reflexivity and what has been referred to as auto-ethnography. This volume explores a kind of ethnographic research and writing that utilises the anthropologist's experiences and memories in a systematic fashion. We aim to show how this creates greater transparency in the production of anthropological knowledge and how it serves to produce rich ethnographies. We have chosen to focus on the influential text *Writing Culture* but in doing so are well aware of the danger of glossing over most of the twists and turns of the story. To illustrate this point with a single example, here is a quote from Edmund Leach, one-time doyen of British anthropologists:

> The data which derive from fieldwork are subjective and not objective. I am saying that every anthropological observer, no matter how well he/she has been trained, will see something that no other such observer can recognize, namely a kind of harmonic projection of the observer's own personality. And when these observations are 'written up' in monograph or any other form, the observer's personality will again distort any purported 'objectivity'. (1984: 22)

The experiences of anthropologists are often highly relevant for their doing and writing ethnography. This is the case in particular for 'native anthropologists', for whom this may also mean memories from times before their professional training. Therefore, we argue that anthropologists should include personal experiences as data in their analysis. Not to do so seems to us (the authors of this chapter) at best to represent an opportunity lost and at worst a moral transgression. We would go further, however, in maintaining that no anthropologist can afford to omit consideration of the possibility that they may themselves be their own, intimate informants. Yet we acknowledge, reminded by Dyck in this volume, that this must also be a self-critical act. We therefore imagine an ethnography where the voice of the anthropologist, drawing on remembered experience, is one among others, and by this means we demonstrate a self-conscious methodology, which moves between the two poles of conservative self-reflexivity (as criticised by Salzman 2002) and poetic auto-ethnography (à la Ellis and Bochner 1996, 2002). We believe that this approach represents a substantive contribution to and expansion of ethnography.

The Book

The volume addresses the themes outlined above through its chapters. Each chapter addresses one or more of these issues. Some have a focus on memory, others on the self, some discuss anthropology at home explicitly, and others speak about varying fieldwork settings. Through the inclusion of chapters from a range of countries and settings the volume aims for the ethnographic richness and variety that have been the hallmark of the anthropological endeavour.

The book is envisioned to be used as a resource by readers, teachers and students. The chapters have been ordered into three – overlapping – sections. These are 'Being Self and Other: Anthropologists at Home', 'Working on/with/through Memory', and 'Ethnographic Selves through Time'. Within each section readers will find a number of contributions that present original ethnographic material from a wide variety of social contexts. The book can hence be read from start to finish following the line of argument we as editors imagined beginning here with the introduction and ending with Fernandez's thoughtful epilogue. However, chapters can also be read as distinct stand-alone essays, and the book may be dipped into depending on the reader's interests. Finally, we have attempted in this introduction to make apparent the implicit as well as the explicit connections between chapters though imagine that the reader will, typically, trace other continuities (and perhaps discontinuities) that we may well have missed.

Note

1. There is a subtle difference here, which we will not discuss further in this introduction.

References

Abu-Lughod, L. 1993. *Writing Women's Worlds: Bedouin Stories*. Berkeley and Oxford: University of California Press.

Asad, T. (ed.). 1973. *Anthropology and the Colonial Encounter*. London: Ithaca Press.

Battaglia, D. 1990. *On the Bones of the Serpent: Person, Memory and Mortality in Sabarl Island Community*. Chicago: University of Chicago.

Behar, R. 1993. *Translated Woman: Crossing the Border with Esperanza's Story*. Boston: Beacon.

Benson, P. (ed.) 1993. *Anthropology and Literature*. Urbana: University of Illinois Press.

Bochner, A.P. and C. Ellis. 2002. *Ethnographically Speaking: Autoethnography, Literature and Aesthetics*. Walnut Creek: Altamira Press.

Brettel, C.B. (ed.). 1993. *When They Read What We Write: The Politics of Ethnography*. Westport, Conn.: Bergin and Garvey.

Briggs, J. 1970. *Never in Anger*. Cambridge, Mass.: Harvard University Press.

Brown, R. and J. Kulick. 1977. 'Flashbulb Memories', *Cognition* 5: 73–99.

Bruner, J. 1993. Introduction: The Ethnographic Self and the Personal Self, in P. Benson (ed.), *Anthropology and Literature*. Urbana and Chicago: University of Illinois Press, pp. 1–26.

———. 1994. 'The "Remembered Self"', in U. Neisser and R. Fivush (eds), *The Remembering Self: Construction and Accuracy in the Self-Narrative*. New York: Cambridge University Press, pp. 41–54.

———. 2002. *Making Stories: Law, Literature and Life*. Cambridge, Mass.: Harvard University Press.

Clifford, J. and G.E. Marcus (eds). 1986. *Writing Culture: The Poetics and Politics of Ethnography*. Berkeley and Los Angeles: University of California Press.

Coffey, A. 1999. *The Ethnographic Self: Fieldwork and Representation of Identity*. London: Sage.

Cohen, A.P. (ed.). 1982. *Belonging: Identity and Social Organisation in British Rural Cultures*. Manchester: Manchester University Press.

———. (ed.) 1986. *Symbolising Boundaries: Identity and Diversity in British Cultures*. Manchester: Manchester University Press.

———. 1987. *Whalsay: Symbol, Segment and Boundary in a Shetland Island Community*. Manchester: Manchester University Press.

———. 1994. *Self-Consciousness: An Alternative Anthropology of Identity*. London: Routledge.

Collins, P. 2002. 'Connecting Anthropology and Quakerism: Transcending the Insider/Outsider Dichotomy', in E. Arweck and M.D. Stringer (eds), *Theorising Faith: The Insider/Outsider Problem in the Study of Ritual*. Birmingham: Birmingham University Press, pp. 77–95.

Crapanzano, V. 1980. *Tuhami: Portrait of Moroccan*. Chicago: University of Chicago Press.

Dumont, J.-P. 1978. *The Headman and I: Ambiguity and Ambivalence in Fieldworking Experience*. Austin: University of Texas Press.

Dwyer, K. 1982. *Moroccan Dialogues*. Baltimore: Johns Hopkins University Press.

Ellis, C. and A.P. Bochner. 1996. *Composing Ethnography: Alternative Forms of Qualitative Writing*. Walnut Creek, Ca.: AltaMira

Frankenberg, R. 1957. *Village on the Border*. London: Cohen and West.

Geertz, C. 1973 *The Interpretation of Cultures*. New York: Free Press.

———. 1988. *Works and Lives: The Anthropologist as Author*. Cambridge: Polity.

Giddens, A. 1991. *Modernity and Self-Identity: Self and Society in the Late Modern Age*. Cambridge: Polity.

Handler, R. and D. Segal. 1990. *Jane Austen and the Fiction of Culture: An Essay on the Narration of Social Realities*. Tucson: University of Arizona Press.

Herzfeld, M. 2000. 'Intimations From an Uncertain Place', in H.G. de Soto and N. Dudwick (eds), *Fieldwork Dilemmas: Anthropologists in Postsocialist States*. Madison and London: University of Wisconsin Press, pp. 219–35.

Holstein, J. A. and J.F. Gubrium. 2000. *The Self We Live by: Narrative Identity in a Post-Modern World*. Oxford: Oxford University Press.

Jackson, A. (ed.). 1987. *Anthropology at Home*. London: Tavistock.

Jackson, M. 1986. *Barawa and the Ways Birds Fly in the Sky: An Ethnographic Novel*. Washington: Smithsonian Institution Press.

———. 1989. *Paths towards a Clearing: Radical Empiricism and Ethnographic Enquiry*. Bloomington: Indiana University Press.

———. 1995. *At Home in the World*. Durham: Duke University Press.

———. 2002a. *The Politics of Storytelling: Violence, Transgression and Subjectivity*. Copenhagen: Museum Tusculanum Press.

———. 2002b. *In Sierra Leone*. Durham: Duke University Press.

———. 2005. *Existential Anthropology: Events, Exigencies and Effects*. New York: Bergahn Books.

Jackson, M. and I. Karp. 1990. *Personhood and Agency: The Experience of Self and Other in African Cultures*. Uppsala: Uppsala University.

Kleinman, A. 1988. *The Illness Narratives: Suffering, Healing, and the Human Condition*. New York: Basic Books.

Kusserow, A.S. 1999. 'Crossing the Great Divide: Anthropological Theories of the Western Self', *Journal of Anthropological Research* 55: 541–62.

Leach, E. 1984. 'Glimpses of the Unmentionable in the History of British Social Anthropology', *Annual Review of Anthropology* 13: 1–23.

Littlejohn, J. 1963. *Westrigg: The Sociology of a Cheviot Parish*. London: Routledge and Paul.

LiPuma, E. 1998. 'Modernity and Forms of Personhood in Melanesia', in M. Lambek and A. Strathern (eds), *Bodies and Persons*. Cambridge: Cambridge University Press, pp. 53–79.

Lutz, C. 1988. *Unnatural Emotions: Everyday Sentiments on a Micronesian Atoll and their Challenge to Western Theory*. Chicago: University of Chicago Press.

Malinowski, B. 1961 [1922]. *Argonauts of the Western Pacific*. London: Routledge and Kegan Paul.

Malinowski, B. 1967. *A Diary in the Strict Sense of the Term*. London: Routledge.

Marcus, G.E. and M.M.J. Fischer 1986. *Anthropology as Cultural Critique: An Experimental Moment in the Human Sciences*. Chicago: University of Chicago Press.

Mauss, M. 1985 [1938]. 'Category of the Human Mind: the Notion of the Person, the Notion of the Self', in M. Carrithers, S. Collins and S. Lukes (eds), *The Category of the Person*. London: Athlone, pp. 1–25.

Messerschmidt, D. (ed.). 1981. *Anthropologists at Home in North America: Methods and Issues in the Study of One's Own Society*. Cambridge: Cambridge University Press.

Mintz, S. 1960. *Worker in the Cane: A Puerto Rican Life History*. New Haven: Yale University Press.

Moffat, M. 1992. 'Ethnographic Writing about American Culture', *Annual Review of Anthropology* 21: 205–29.

Myers, F.R. 1991 [1986]. *Pintupi Country, Pintupi Self*. Berkeley: California University Press.

Narayan, K. 1993. 'How Native is a Native Anthropologist?' *American Anthropologist* 95(3): 671–86.

Okely, J. and H. Callaway (eds). 1992. *Anthropology and Autobiography*. London and New York: Routledge.

Powdermaker, H. 1966. *Stranger and Friend: The Way of an Anthropologist*. New York: W.W. Norton.

Pratt, M.L. 1986. 'Field Work in Common Places' in J. Clifford and G. Marcus (eds), *Writing Culture*. Berkeley: University of California Press, pp. 27–50.

Rabinow, P. 1975. *Symbolic Domination: Cultural Form and Historical Change in Morocco*. Chicago: University of Chicago Press.

———. 1977. *Reflections on Fieldwork in Morocco*. Berkeley: University of California Press.

Rapport, N. 1993. *Diverse World Views in an English Village*. Edinburgh: Edinburgh University Press.

———. 1994a. *The Prose and the Passion: Anthropology, Literature and the Writing of E.M. Forster*. Manchester: Manchester University Press.

———. 1994b. 'Review of Handler, R. and D. Segal (1990)', *American Ethnologist* 21(1): 216–17.

———. 1997. 'Hard-Sell or Mumbling "Right" Rudely', in N. Rapport, *Transcendent Individual: Towards and Literal and Liberal Anthropology*. London: Routledge, 141–63.

———. 2003. *I Am Dynamite: An Alternative Anthropology of Power*. London: Routledge.

Reed-Danahay, D. 1997. *Auto/Ethnography: Rewriting the Self and the Social*. Oxford: Berg.

Ruby, J. 1982. *A Crack in the Mirror: Reflexive Perspectives in Anthropology*. Philadephia: University of Pennsylvania Press.

Ryang, S. 2000. 'Ethnography or Self-Cultural Anthropology? Reflections on Writing about Ourselves', *Dialectical Anthropology* 25: 297–320.

Salzman, C.P. 2002. 'On Reflexivity', *American Anthropologist* 104(3): 805–13.

Schank, R.C. 1990. *Tell Me a Story: A New Look at Real and Artificial Memory*. New York: Scribner's.

Shokeid, M. 1997. 'Negotiating Multiple Viewpoints', *Current Anthropology* 38(4): 631–45.

Shostak, M. 1981. *Nisa: The Life and Words of a !Kung Woman*. Cambridge, Mass.: Harvard University Press.

Skultans, V. 1998. *The Testimony of Lives: Memory in Postsocialist Latvia*. London: Routledge.

———. 2001. 'Arguing with the KGB Archives: Archival and Narrative Memory in Post-Soviet Latvia', *Ethnos* 66: 320–43.

Spencer, J. 1989 'Anthropology as a kind of writing', *Man* 24: 145–64.

Spry, T. 2001. 'Performing Autoethnography: An Embodied Methodological Praxis', *Qualitative Inquiry* 7(6): 706–32.

Strathern, M. 1987. 'The Limits of Auto-Anthropology', in A. Jackson (ed.), *Anthropology at Home*. London: Tavistock, pp. 16–37.

———. 1988. *The Gender of the Gift: Problems with Women and Problems with Society in Melanesia*. Berkeley: University of California Press.

———. 1992. *After Nature: English Kinship in the late 20th Century*. Cambridge: Cambridge University Press.

Strathern, M., A. Richards and F. Oxford. 1981. *Kinship at the Core: An Anthropology of Elmdon a Village in North-west Essex in the Nineteen-sixties*. Cambridge: Cambridge University Press.

Taussig, M. 1987. *Shamanism, Colonialism, and the Wild Man*. Chicago: University of Chicago Press.

———. 1997. *The Magic of the State*. New York: Routledge.

Tulving, E. 1972. 'Episodic and Semantic Memory', in E. Tulving and W. Donaldson (eds), *Organisation of Memory*. New York: Academic Press, pp. 381–403.

———. 1983. *Elements of Episodic Memory*. Oxford: Oxford University Press.

———. 1993. 'What is Episodic Memory?', *Current Directions in Psychological Science* 3: 67–70.

Van Maanen, J. 1988. *Tales of the Field*. Chicago: The University of Chicago Press.

PART I

BEING SELF AND OTHER: ANTHROPOLOGISTS AT HOME

Chapter 2

PLAYING THE NATIVE CARD: THE ANTHROPOLOGIST AS INFORMANT IN EASTERN GERMANY

Anselma Gallinat

In this chapter I shall discuss the possibilities and implications of including personal memories as ethnographic data in 'ethnographies at home'. For many anthropologists who work at home their personal experiences preceding fieldwork and possibly even anthropological training can be expected to inform their fieldwork and writing. Kürti, an anthropologist from and working in Hungary, for example, writes: 'One of the first questions that should intrigue all anthropologists is: can I be my own informant? The answer to this almost banal question must be a resounding yes' (2000: 283). Memories will be invoked when reading other scholars' work. Descriptions of events and cultural practices in these works might be compared with one's own participation in similar occasions as well as one's lack of knowledge of such which may lead to a questioning of the analysis one reads. Based on prior experiences anthropologists at home may also choose their particular research interest, on which they may self-reflexively comment; on the basis of these experiences they may look for particular information, evaluate data as true, important or negligible, decide to take up some leads but not others and devise their writing up. Apart from self-reflexive comments on one's background, anthropologists at home and native anthropologists usually remain quiet about how their personal memories fit into their ethnographic data. This situation has a variety of reasons which relate to the history of anthropology and the still contentious status of such an ethnography of the familiar.[1] However, by including the self only self-reflexively we are omitting potentially important information. Moreover, we exclude information that is highly influential to our work from analytical scrutiny.

This chapter suggests that the anthropologist's memories are a resource and that their utilisation should be made more explicit. I will present two case examples that show how personal experience reaching beyond fieldwork can be included as ethnographic data. Here, the anthropologist moves between being ethnographer and informant while trying to maintain a double vision that combines both. The chapter begins with a self-reflexive positioning of the author with regard to this chapter. It then discusses some aspects of the debate surrounding anthropology 'at home'. I will focus on the question of whether ethnographers at home could, like their informants, claim authenticity. With reference to the case-examples, I will discuss the implications of an approach that includes the ethnographer as informant.

A Self-reflexive Starting Point

When joining the Department of Anthropology in Durham, UK, in 1999 to read for an M.Phil., I had seen myself as wanting to specialise in Native North America. I had fostered interests in religion, mythology and contemporary Native American literature during three years of previous study at the University of Göttingen, in Germany. My degree programme also included media studies and history. One of my specific interests concerned the education system of the East German socialist state in which I had grown up. I believed then, however, that I could only follow this up in history since social anthropology (*Ethnologie*) at Göttingen seemed focused on the study of indigenous, non-Western groups. After my arrival in Durham I heard that one of the professors there had an active research interest in the civil rights movement in East Germany. I therefore decided to make an anthropology of eastern Germany the topic of my postgraduate research. From this initial idea emerged my later Ph.D. thesis which explored cultural changes resulting from the fall of the Berlin Wall using the example of the *Jugendweihe* (youth consecration), a former socialist and now secular coming-of-age ritual, as its pivotal point.

Between leaving Göttingen and beginning fieldwork in Magdeburg, eastern Germany, I took two steps that reflected historical developments in anthropology. First, I consciously moved from the study of non-Western, non-industrialised (or worse 'traditional') groups to the study of a Western (or 'modern'), industrialised country. Therewith, I had moved on to the kind of 'anthropology at home' that Strathern terms auto-anthropology (1987: 16–37). With this term, she refers to 'anthropology that is carried out in the social context which produced it' (p. 17). With my choice of eastern Germany I reconfirmed this step also with regard to my own person since I was going to do research in the places of my childhood.

Anthropology at Home and Native Anthropology

Anthropology at home is still a fairly young practice in the discipline, Jackson's groundbreaking volume only dating back to the mid-1980s (1987). Until then, anthropology had been dominated by the idea that, for good ethnography, researchers needed to learn another culture like a child growing up. This would help one 'To grasp the native's point of view ... to realise *his* vision of *his* world', as Malinowski put it succinctly (1961 [1922]: 25). One's foreignness to a place and its culture was said to facilitate analytical distance – the maintenance of 'naiveté', according to Bernard (1994: 149). Furthermore, there were also notions of this prolonged stay in a foreign place as a test of, or even initiation ritual for, the apprentice anthropologist who had to cope with loneliness and culture shock. Since then, however, a good number of anthropologists have shown that working in a culture that one is familiar with does not necessarily grant insider status (Aguilar 1981; Messerschmidt 1981a: 9) nor does it preclude analytical distance since cultural knowledge is not all-encompassing (see also Abu-Lughod 1991; Narayan 1993).

However, there remain some problems with anthropology at home and native anthropology. The latter term refers, in particular, to anthropologists from the non-western world (see for example, Srivinas 1952; Abu-Lughod 1991, 1992; Narayan 1993; Kuwayam 2003). It stems from times when anthropologists trained an informant in ethnography, who then went on to study and write about their own groups (Narayan 1993: 672). In recent years the terminological boundaries between native anthropology and anthropology at home have, however, become increasingly blurred.[2]

Despite the past decade's flurry of 'ethnographies at home', this genre seems to remain contentious as a steady flow of reactive, critical articles suggests. Some authors, have focused on defending this kind of anthropology by criticising the assumptions underpinning the insider–outsider dichotomy arguing that one is never fully at home in one's culture (Abu-Lughood 1991; Narayan 1993; Collins 2002). Others have highlighted particular implications of native anthropology such as the question of rapport, and of accountability (Brettell 1993; Berger 2001; Jacobs-Huey 2002; Kuwayam 2003). Simultaneously, self-reflexivity, scholarly 'soul-searching' (Shokeid 1997: 631), has undergone some criticism (Salzman 2002). For the purpose of this chapter I want to highlight one issue in particular. This is the question of authority of voice, which potentially separates native and non-native anthropologists.

In an article from 1988 Appadurai discusses the relationship between the anthropological concepts of 'native' and 'hierarchy'. He remarks that nativity seems tied to our ideologies of authenticity: 'Proper natives are somehow assumed to represent their selves and history without distortion or residue' (1988: 37). Natives have a claim to authenticity, he argues, whilst 'we [anthropologists] exclude ourselves from this sort of claim ... because we are too enamoured of the complexities of our history, the diversity of our societies, and the ambiguities of our collective conscience' (p. 37). Presumably, 'our history' and 'our diverse societies' here refer to the self-reflexive complexity of the Western world. Appadurai's conservative reading of 'native', however, also excludes most native anthropologists since university education has shaped their awareness of complexity and postmodern relativity just the same. I would argue, though, that the boundaries between authentic/native and inauthentic/trained are often blurred to an extent that makes readings of claims to authenticity impossible.

Writing about his work in Armenia, Barsegian contends that 'native ethnographers can move between observation and participation' whilst 'the western anthropologists must settle for observation, his or her only accessible level of fieldwork' (2000: 123). Whilst I do not quite agree with Barsegian's terminology, his argument highlights the choice, available to native ethnographers, between being just native (participant) and being an ethnographer (participant observer). Barsegian's statement therefore also makes a claim to authenticity. The expression 'an anthropologist playing the native card' is taken from an article by Jacobs-Huey. She argues that a self-reflexive outing as native anthropologist might be understood as a 'non-critical privileging of their insider status' (2002: 791). The possibility of readers understanding native anthropology and/or anthropology at home in these terms is problematic. The fact that such issues are rarely made explicit exacerbates the problem.

If native anthropology is then considered authentic, it potentially precludes any debate about its ethnographic analysis, unless this debate is led by fellow native anthropologists. Such a prevention of debate is a problem for the discipline and we therefore need to ask how native anthropologists should conduct themselves to avoid a playing of the native card. In particular, how should native anthropologists write ethnography? The editors of this volume argue that all anthropologists rely on their personal memories and experiences, not only in order to establish rapport but both when writing down (their notes) and when writing up (their ethnography). The volume's central argument is that we should do this more openly, making our subjective ethnographic strategies explicit. This strategy takes us beyond self-reflexivity and opens the ethnographer's memories to analytical scrutiny. Self-reflexive revelations, in contrast, negate the possibility for analysis, according to Salzman (2002: 805–13). Salzman argues that these add little to published ethnographies since they often consist of brief and very general remarks concerning one's background, such as Young's contention 'because I was born in a city I found it boring to ask about … livestock deals' (Young 1996: 131, cited in Salzman 2002: 807). In fact, Salzman highlights their potential to mislead and, in the worst-case scenario, to deceive: 'So it is hard to see how such generalizations – by gender, religion, nationality, race and class – tell us much about the actual experience of any particular individual. It seems odd for anthropologists, of all people, to imagine that individuals, and particularly such peculiar folks as anthropologists, will mechanically conform to some generally held social stereotypes and cultural labels' (2002: 809). Reflecting on postmodern epistemology Salzman concludes that we ought to 'replace solitary research with collaborative team research, in which the perspectives and insights of each researcher can be challenged and tested by others' (2002: 812; see also Salzman 1994). The volume at hand highlights another possibility. It shows how the treatment of personal experience and memories as ethnographic data opens this information to readers' scrutiny. Srinivas observes that the social position of a native sociologist, which undoubtedly influences their work, can lead to insights. Those insights, however, 'have to be subject to rigorous testing' (Srinivas 1969: 154). This chapter therefore makes the case for a native anthropology that draws explicitly on relevant past personal experiences. Indeed, the native anthropologist used to serve as a key-informant to foreigner-anthropologists. Surely, the self continues to function as such in the doing and writing of ethnography today. By making the junctures at which our memories come into play explicit it is possible to subject these memories to our own and others' analytical inspection.

Possibilities for the deployment of memory have emerged for me on a number of occasions. As a child and especially as a teenager I collected evidence of passing times in the form of material items, documents and memories. As Coleman shows in this volume our past experience underpins very well our later professional choices. It is therefore not surprising to me, now, that both memories and material evidence accumulated during my past appear relevant to current fieldwork.

Case One: *Ostalgie* and 'East German' Identity

In recent years, anthropologists have described post-GDR eastern Germany with regard to a rising sense of identity and particularity, a privatisation of remembrance and a reaction to western German cultural and moral hegemony (Howard 1995; Berdahl 1999a/b; De Soto 2000: 96–113; Ten Dyke 2001a: 253–76). It seems clear that identity and change in eastern Germany are negotiated on the basis of significant personal and communal experiences made during GDR times, the *Wende* years of 1989 and 1990 and in the reunited present. Therefore, what people remember and which personal and social memories they talk about are crucial to the ethnographic enquiry (for example Berdahl 1999b; Glaeser, 2000; Ten Dyke 2000: 139–56; 2001b). My own field research reflects this tendency. Apart from participant observation I used life-story interviews to gain insights into how people made sense of both past and present after these great upheavals.

The phenomenon of *Ostalgie*, nostalgia for the East, has attracted attention among scholars and in the German public discourse alike. The former see it as the performance of an assertive 'East German' identity that glorifies the socialist past. The latter blames 'ostalgic' viewpoints for the failure of reunification, referring to 'the Wall in people's minds'. Being aware of the scholarly and German public debates, I had looked for *Ostalgie* during my field research period, albeit unsuccessfully. I could find no evidence of the *Ostalgie* parties that Berdahl describes: parties 'featuring East German rock music, party propaganda songs … and a double of the former Communist Party leader Erich Honecker' (Berdahl 1999b: 192). Neither did my informants seem to engage in *Ostalgie*; one exception to this rule will be discussed below. Most talked about this as something that other eastern Germans were practising and that was a bit too 'nostalgic', 'euphemistic', 'subversive' in the reunited present. Instead, there seemed to be a commercialisation of *Ostalgie* in the form of music compilations featuring socialist songs, board games drawing on knowledge of the GDR, books including recipe collections, jokes, anecdotes, books on interior design, and other goods. This suggested to me that since the mid-1990s *Ostalgie* had changed from a communal celebration of the once shared and now devalued past to commercialised objects, which were used selectively and carefully by people who were well aware of these objects' connection to the political identity claim of being 'East German' (Gallinat 2008). This interpretation seemed plausible since it reflected some of my personal experiences.

Whilst my informants would not talk much about *Ostalgie*, I could not escape the fact that I myself had come across it some years before undertaking this fieldwork. I had very nearly attended two *Ostalgie* parties similar to those described by Berdahl. The following is a written account of my personal memories of these two occasions. I shall then compare these with instances reminiscent of *Ostalgie* that I came across during fieldwork in 2001. This will highlight the differences between various kinds of memory practice and identity claims.

It must have been around 1994 and I was sixteen or seventeen years old. I had a number of older friends from the karate club where I was training. I was then living with my mother in a small town in the more western parts of Saxony-Anhalt, eastern Germany. Some of my friends from the club had heard about a local night club that regularly organised 'GDR discos'. Apparently these discos featured 1980s music, beer was sold for its GDR price and the place tried to recreate some atmosphere of the old times. We decided to try this disco out. It somehow sounded like an interesting thing to do, partly also because of its subversive connotation. Unification was only a few years ago and, although there were some voices of criticism and resentment by then, there was still a widespread expectation of having to appreciate the recent changes.

However, the four or five of us met somewhere in town to go to this disco together. Most of us had pulled a neckerchief from the Pioneer organisation we used to be members of out of the wardrobe.[3] I carried mine stuffed into my pocket feeling uncomfortable about wearing it in public. One of our friends had not brought any item of uniform at all; one or two others, in contrast, had put on their blue FDJ blouses but were wearing their coats over them.[4] For a little while we compared our manners of dress, commenting on individual choices. Then we made our way to this club. We never attended this disco and I am not sure why. I have a vague feeling that at least some of us did not enter because of my being under age and not allowed entrance to the party. This was the first encounter with *Ostalgie* that I can remember.

Some years later, in 1997 or 1998, I went to another *Ostalgie* party. This happened in the small village where my boyfriend's family lived. The party was an annual event in the village pub and had a firm place in people's social calendar. I agreed to go even though I had some qualms about attending. I had become very conscious of my own family's history with the GDR state, which was a critical and difficult one. I had taken this criticism on board and rejected nostalgia for the GDR. However, not wanting to spoil the weekend, I agreed to go. This was also a social occasion for me, a chance to meet many of my boyfriend's friends, which I was looking forward to. However, I refused to wear any piece of socialist uniform. I remember that we arrived at the door to the pub where we ran into a few others of our age most of whom were wearing FDJ blouses. It was immediately noted that I had not dressed up.

The event started with a dinner, for which we had a choice between two popular East German dishes; neither of them were favourites of mine. Later on the disco opened and we danced and sang along to socialist propaganda songs as well as pop hits from the 1980s. In another part of the house someone had prepared a small bazaar. We had a look at it and I seem to remember some technical appliances (an orange hair dryer?) and an NVA

(East German army) uniform. I am not sure whether these items were for sale or just exhibited or on auction. When we saw the uniform I seem to recall that my boyfriend exchanged some jokes with another villager about whose attic this piece had come from.

The atmosphere throughout the event was jovial. The purpose was to have fun together whilst remembering and also celebrating the past. During the evening we young people – there were maybe five or six of us – also received a certificate. In GDR-style language it congratulated us for having 'participated in this event in true socialist spirit'.

These two events exemplify the character of 'ostalgic' practices. The parties were inherently communal activities that provided space for new shared experiences on the basis of an active re-evaluation of the past. In this way the practices also served to reconnect past and present in a situation of great upheaval. Such a connection is paramount to identity whether personal or social.[5] In all this, 'ostalgic' practices were also about contesting the new hegemonic order, which was perceived to be primarily West German. The practices described above could therefore be called a wave of re-evaluation of the communal past, which is undeniably the socialist past, and an affirmation of this new nostalgic view of life in the GDR as a shared interpretation. This movement appeared at a particular historical point in eastern German history (see Berdahl 1999a: 205), some years after reunification when the harsh realities of the new situation began to be acknowledged and mixed with the experience of western German hegemony which included a devaluation of the East German past as a totalitarian period.

During my fieldwork in 2000 and 2001, I found no such social practices. However, I observed two instances that were reminiscent of *Ostalgie* and yet of a different character. For this research I stayed in a small town in Saxony-Anhalt. In order to make contact with people living in this urban setting I joined a number of clubs and groups, one of which was a choir. It was at the choir's *Fasching* party (German carnival) that the following incident took place.

The evening had been spent in a good-humoured and lively spirit, eating, drinking and talking and, later on, also dancing. This mood only changed when the DJ announced at 1.00 a.m. that he was leaving. Even though most of the older members had departed by that time, our group of about ten younger people, most being in their early thirties, did not feel like breaking up the party. Instead we stayed on and soon enough a friend got a guitar out and we were singing along to popular oldies. After a few numbers he intoned an FDJ song. The only person who was somewhat puzzled was myself, but when I announced that maybe I should take notes, I was told to 'drop it'. The recital of 'socialist propaganda songs' (Berdahl 1999a: 192) continued for some more time until we ran out of tunes.

The second incident occurred during an interview. I had visited a middle-aged woman to do a life-story interview with her. The interviews had been planned as open interviews followed by a semi-structured part that included questions about interviewees' memories of the Fall of the Wall and their thoughts about Germany/ eastern Germany today. During this particular interview the woman's husband had walked through the room and every now and then commented on the matter of our conversation. He had particularly strong feelings about my question asking whether they thought there were any differences between eastern and western Germans. His wife had before voiced a fairly stereotypical view of West Germans as 'insidious'. This seemed motivated by adverse experiences her husband was having at work. He explained that his colleagues, all of whom were from western Germany, seemed to expect him to leave his thirty years of GDR experience behind. He felt that any criticism he voiced about procedures, about any aspect of work, was rejected as invalid because of his lack of experience with this, the West German, system. However, he felt that his experience of two different systems gave him more expertise, rather than less. Most certainly, he felt the need to be taken seriously as a professional. Talking about these difficulties, he suddenly got up to fetch a CD from the shelf. He showed it to me explaining that he had greatly enjoyed the CD's success and agreed with its song. This CD features just one song by an eastern German singer called Kai Niemann. It was produced in 2000 and was an overnight success in the eastern parts of Germany. The song is called 'In the East' and highlights some of the attributes and quirks that make eastern Germany distinctive. This song does not, however, embrace past socialism. Rather, it is a cautious and self-critical parody of the hailed East German identity.[6]

These latter two examples are distinct and quite different from the *Ostalgie* parties mentioned above. Whilst the *Ostalgie* parties were intended and arranged celebrations of the communal past utilising socialist symbols, the incident at the *Fasching* party was inadvertent. A number of people had come together to celebrate *Fasching*, as is customary. They thereby also drew on a shared past but one that was not, as yet, politically tinted. When the DJ had left a small group of friends decided to make music themselves. For this purpose they utilised a stock of shared songs which somewhat unwittingly came to include socialist propaganda songs. These were, however, not sung because they symbolised socialism. Rather, they came in handy because everyone knew their text. They also have a simple tune and a catchy rhythm. Everybody had sung these songs during their childhood and as teenagers, and these times of their lives happened to have taken place in East Germany. Whilst it is plausible that these songs were also attractive because of their ambiguity in the postsocialist present, they had not been selected as signifiers of East German identity in the same way in which the parties had been orchestrated.

The second case of the song by Nieman is again different. This example shows very well how in a moment where the individual past is under attack the person reaches for an oppositional identity, which he expects to be shared by others. This incident distinguishes itself from the *Ostalgie* parties in that it is not a social practice but rather the rhetorical strategy of a single person that utilises more widely shared symbols. As explained above, the song itself contains a good portion of self-critical humour. Whilst it calls on some socialist symbols, it uses a wider range of references than just these (see note 6).

Comparing the incidences that occurred during fieldwork and the commercialisation of GDR attributes (also noted during fieldwork) with my personal experiences in the mid-1990s, I suggest that *Ostalgie* itself is a thing of the past. It was a communal practice that occurred during the mid-1990s when eastern Germans were awakening to the harsh post-socialist realities and exploring the need for connecting this present to their past and developing a shared criticism of reunification. These needs, which were not experienced by all eastern Germans in the same way, were, with time, satisfied and 'ostalgic' practices transformed. Feelings and assertions of East German identity have remained but occur on a more individual plane, where they mix with an acknowledgement that East–West German stereotypes do not always mirror social reality (Gallinat 2008). The material expressions of the *Ostalgie* movement have been customised by the commercial world.

Returning to the subject of this chapter, the example above shows how my personal memories play an integral part in my reading and doing ethnography in eastern Germany. This goes beyond the establishment of rapport with informants on the basis of our shared upbringing, as Berger, for example, highlights (2001: 504–18), but concerns instead the importance of my personal memories as ethnographic data. Maintaining an ethnographic double vision of my informants and of myself as informant, my own voice adds crucial information to the analysis. I have therefore included my voice explicitly here, marking the section in the same way in which I would mark excerpts drawn from interviews and other textual sources.

The second example of ethnographic double vision consolidates my argument and raises some further questions. It is concerned with notions of the person in eastern Germany.

Case Two: Personhood in Eastern Germany

During socialism East German authorities had promoted the development of so-called 'socialist personalities'. This was a notion of the person that was informed by the East German version of Marxism–Leninism and contemporary psychology and applied, in particular, in the education of children and young people. As Kürti states, 'In European societies, ideas about controlling and monitoring children and youth are rooted in Christian beliefs and values. Beginning with the modernist period, however, regimes on both the right and left took it upon themselves to control and monitor young people' (2002: 113). This was due to a 'belief that youth had been corrupted by the previous regime and thus must be brought under control and re-educated according to the needs and wishes of the new state' (ibid.).

In East Germany the aim of creating a 'new human being' in socialism had been included in the programme of the ruling party in the late 1950s.[7] The exact expectations of socialist personalities were changed and reformulated various times but constituted a coherent argument in the 1980s. This was presented to fourteen-year-old teenagers during the *Jugendweihe* (youth consecration), for example, a socialist coming-of-age ritual (see Gallinat 2005) that included a vow of loyalty to the socialist state. During the ceremonies the young people also received a book published specifically for these ceremonies. The latest *Jugendweihe* book from 1983 includes an entire chapter on personhood: 'You and Socialism' (pp. 209–61). The socialist personality is here described as follows: 'We understand thoroughly developed socialist personalities to be educated, politically aware, to be human beings strengthened in morals and character, who are able and willing to fulfil the manifold demands that are asked for in social life, in work, in learning, and in political activities, as well as in spare time and family life' (Zentraler Ausschuß 1983: 214). Unsurprisingly, the socialist personality is introduced as one that complies with the social rules and norms that are deemed valuable by the ruling elite. The text nevertheless recognises and encourages the individual constitution of persons: 'Personalities are people who distinguish themselves by individual attributes and creative abilities' (Zentraler Ausschuß 1983: 211). However, it links these individual developments closely to the communal purpose of societal progress: 'To develop a socialistic personality includes the firm conviction to be capable in a certain field ... All this for the good of the whole society and the own good' (Zentraler Ausschuß 1983: 219). This notion of the person is also inherently relational, which is best expressed by the concept of *Kollektiv* (collective).[8] These were organisational groups that existed almost anywhere in the social environment, whether at work, in the classroom or even in the block of houses one lived in. The *Jugendweihe* book explains that *Kollektive* are important decision-making bodies, which should seek unanimity. In cases of disagreement the collective should have primacy: 'the solution of upcoming contradictions requires subordination under a collective aim' (Zentraler Ausschuß 1983: 247–48). Relationships formed the basis of the social organisation in *Kollektiven*, and finally society. In a logical conclusion, the ability to sustain these is emphasised by the text: 'The ability to establish relationships with friends and colleagues, to shape them in such a way that they become productive for everyone … also belong to it [character traits of socialist personalities]' (Zentraler Ausschuß 1983: 213).

This is an ideal view of personhood that is presented to young people with the intention of shaping and moulding their development into good and faithful citizens of the socialist GDR. Whether teenagers ever read this chapter in their *Jugendweihe* book is doubtful. These ideas, however, also related to practice in various arenas of GDR society. For example, *Kollektive* were real existing social groups at school, in the workplace and in the mass organisations (see Kharkhordin 1999; Anderson 2000: 18–19, 43–55). The Pioneer and FDJ organisation emphasised socialist values and engaged their members in suitable activities. Sights of, or at least propaganda about, groups of pioneers cleaning parks, collecting waste for recycling and helping elderly citizens were not uncommon.

The unofficial structures created by the socialist economy of scarcity, where people had to develop skills of accessing and storing scarce goods that was strongly reliant on connections (see Verdery 1999: 27), further underpinned ideas about relationships and communal values although the closeness of social networks thus developed stretched the official notion of *Kollektiv*.[9]

When doing field research in 2001, I was interested in whether the Fall of the Wall had had an effect on notions of the person and, if so, how this was perceived by my informants. As I was also interested in their perception of unification, I asked in my interviews whether interviewees saw any differences between eastern and western Germans. This was often responded to in the affirmative, although with varying degrees of dichotomisation and relativity. The main contrasts that were discussed related to stronger individualistic attitudes among western Germans and more socially oriented character traits among eastern Germans. In the former case this was often expressed in terms of 'careerism' and 'elbow mentality'. These terms describe an orientation towards one's individual success at the expense of social relationships. The elbow mentality refers literally to the use of elbows to push others out of the way whilst climbing the career ladder. In this regard many interviewees also said that 'western

Germans can sell themselves better'. With regard to eastern Germans there was acknowledgement that they often lacked such marketing skills. Additionally, ideas about modesty and humbleness with regard to individual aims were expressed. Nadine put it like this: 'We here ... Not everyone but many, are still a bit more ponderous. ... Or we have less need to present ourselves ... that you rather let yourself be guided. Rather [that] than to guide yourself.'

It was also acknowledged that dispositions in the eastern parts were changing or under threat of change. In a later part of her interview Nadine explored the different strategies of two county administrators she has worked under, one from the western parts, the other from the eastern parts of Germany. She explained that the western administrator, being happier to make decisions and to take leadership achieved more in the new united Germany: 'So that in the first four years with our *Westler* we did more than in the six or seven years with our East [administrator].' Other interviewees explained that they were expecting the more communally oriented values in eastern Germany to change because stronger individualist dispositions seem facilitated by the current political and economic context.

The evidence presented so far suggests that a crucial change in emphasis regarding personhood from pre- to post-Fall of the Wall eastern Germany is seen to be coming about, which is reflected in my interviewees' commiserations about potential differences between eastern and western Germans. The change is due to the new economic structure but also different political and philosophical values that come with processes of westernisation. Various authors have highlighted the relation between economic, political and cultural factors and personhood in 'high modernity' (Giddens 1991; see also Rose 1989) and/or Euro-America (Lutz 1988: 81).

This change concerns a move from a notion of personhood that was oriented towards social relationships and community to a personhood that is oriented towards individual agency and self-actualisation. The latter term is used by Junghans in a description of the discourse of civil society initiatives in Hungary (2001: 383–400). Such initiatives are usually based on training courses in the United States or western Europe. The therewith imported discourse of self-actualisation and techniques of spontaneity and improvisation based on individual choice and agency jar with some Hungarians' ideas of mastery as depending upon actual knowledge and practice (Junghans 2001: 393).

The evidence presented with regard to changes in values and personhood in eastern Germany has been far from ideal, however, being patchy and inconsistent. My argument is indeed exemplified best in East German pupils' school records. At the end of every school year the head teacher wrote a report for every pupil, which was presented together with the final grades. In this report he/she would praise or criticise certain skills, character traits or mannerisms of the pupil in question. Set within the educational system this discourse stands in direct relation to the language used and favoured by the current government. In the following I shall present excerpts from my own school records, which remain the only ones I have unlimited access to. The reports quoted here stem from the years 1988 to 1990, during which I was eleven to thirteen years old.

Under the socialist system, in 1988 precisely, the certificates described me as 'possessing a sense of duty, which positively influences the class', as being 'helpful and reliable', thereby highlighting social abilities and a sense of community (Zeugnis 1988). A year later my teacher wrote that I was 'friendly and polite' and 'ready to participate in class actively' (Zeugnis 1989). This wording is slightly less oriented towards a moral purposefulness but still appreciates skills in social interaction. The report from 1989 reads in detail: 'Anselma is a friendly and polite student. She works purposefully and industriously. This also shows in her willingness to participate actively in class. Because of her exemplary behaviour towards her fellow pupils and the teachers she is respected and accepted.'

In 1990, however, only the term 'purposeful' connected my self to my previous incarnations. Now I was commended for possessing a 'broad general knowledge' and 'an ability to think logically' (Zeugnis 1990). Moreover, the report states that 'she thinks critically about problems and develops her own standpoint' (Zeugnis 1990). Individual abilities such as logical thinking had, at times, been mentioned before 1990, for example in 1986. Now, however, they became skills that supported a pupil's success and were worthy of praise. Critical thinking had never been included in the reports before being a trait that is underpinned by self-actualisation – 'she develops her own standpoint' – and by the individual as 'the *source* of morality' (Lukes 1973: 101), in contrast to moral values set externally and followed by individuals, as the socialist personality suggests. Simultaneously, communality moved from the centre of the character evaluation to its periphery. Communal values used to be the first listed. By 1990, however, skills centred on individual talent took the first place while socially relevant abilities had moved to the back (Zeugnis 1990). The report from 1991 says: 'Anselma's work has been characterised by purposefulness and continuity for many years. She has a variety of interests and strives to expand her knowledge. Her ability to think logically is well developed. She thinks critically about the problems of our times. Her helpfulness and comradeliness are praiseworthy.' It seems that by 1990 and 1991 (Zeugnis 1991), within the space of just twenty-four months, individual traits had become more significant than the relationships between pupils in the class. Whilst social skills were still being evaluated they had moved from the top of the educational agenda to its bottom.

The changes in the school's discourse about personhood, which are expressed in the school reports, show clearly the move from a communally oriented to an individually oriented notion of the self in the education discourse. The former is associated with character traits that concern social skills, helpfulness and a concern for the group. The latter, in contrast, centres on notions of individual choice, morality and self-actualisation. However, how this tendency was realised in social practice leading to cultural change is a more complex question that concerns ongoing longer-term developments. The interviews nevertheless suggest that, whilst there remains an emphasis on communal values, which is perceived as different from western German values, this is likely to change.

Playing the 'Native Card'?

Various authors have defended the practice of anthropology at home against critics who argue that geographical distance from the field also supports analytical distance from the observed. These authors usually argue that one is never truly at home in a culture. In this chapter I have taken a further step by using my memories and documents from my childhood as ethnographic data. Is my writing in this fashion a playing of the native card that hinders critical reading because of my claim to authenticity?

Appadurai seems to argue that this is not so because my own anthropological training has made me too aware of social and cultural complexities. Yet the observed instances of *Ostalgie* occurred before this training. This, however, raises yet another problem, that of memory. These observations differ from fieldwork observations firstly because they were made prior to anthropological training. They are therefore not the ethnographer's observations but rather the memories of a native participant, a young girl/woman from eastern Germany.

They differ from fieldwork observations secondly because they were not noted down in field notes, to which I could now refer. Instead, these recollections are memory accounts that are given in the present of a particular research agenda. Could it therefore be that I only recall instances that suit my intended argument, or that I frame my memories in a preordained fashion?

Although this is an important point to consider, I believe it should not hinder this type of auto-ethnography. Part of my research was the collection of memory accounts from all my informants. Just as for me, it can be argued for each one of them that they presented their memories in a way that suited their personal agenda in relation to this interview with me. This personal agenda will have been influenced by their interpretations of my research project and my personality. This is particularly so in the politically charged climate in Germany, where most people are highly aware of identity claims and stereotypes that may challenge German unification. My own power of recollection seems no more fraught here than that of my informants. Anthropologists always deploy memories from fieldwork: why not memories from before fieldwork as well, as long as these do not become the only voice to be heard? Additionally, there is the problem of bias and subjectivity. Although my informants pursued their agenda, I had the final say in selecting certain interpretations and certain interviews to substantiate my arguments. This is a problem of all types of interpretive approaches that use highly qualitative methods. The detailed representation of my own experiences, however, renders these subjective aspects more explicit and allows the reader to critically engage with them.

These issues also emerge in case two but in a less problematic fashion. Because written records were used, the question of framed recollection is of less relevance, the question of honesty in the presentation remains. Other issues include the extent of self-revealing that was part of this case example. Might it be embarrassing to readers that I, the author, out myself as someone who did well in school, and, more importantly, someone who did well in socialist school? According to theorists such as Jowitt, I was then a subject and performer prone to dissimulation (1974), in contrast to the western autonomous individual I should be now. Generally, I would argue that, considering this academic chapter, readers could guess that I did well at school, maybe was even 'a bit of a nerd'. Indeed, my relationship to the GDR state should always be part of any self-reflexive introduction to any ethnography. If it remained there, however, it would be a piece of information that has little further value. Last but not least, this section may have conveyed ability to 'see the absurd' and 'laugh at myself', as Srinivas would encourage me to do (1969: 163).

In this chapter, I have shown that the anthropologist can usefully draw on her own experiences and memories of that experience. Furthermore, I have made clear that including personal memories as data in the text contextualises them and opens them to analytical scrutiny. I have provided two case examples of how this can be meaningfully achieved. As one voice amongst many from the field the recollections of anthropologists at home have an important role to play in making the doing and writing of ethnographic research more transparent, honest and illuminating about the nature of humanity.

Notes

1. Described as 'the study of one's own society' by Srinivas (1969: 147–63).
2. Eastern European scholars for example, who are university-educated anthropologists, consider themselves and are referred to by anthropologists from abroad as 'native anthropologists' (Balzer 1995; Kürti 1996: 11–15; Barsegian 2000: 119–29).
3. The Pioneers (*Jungpioniere* and *Thälmannpioniere*) were socialist children's organisations for pupils of six to fourteen years of age. Children then advanced to the Free German Youth organisation, the FDJ.
4. See above.
5. The literature on memory, for example, highlights its importance to both social and individual identity (Jedlowski 2001: 29–44; Climo and Catell 2002: 1–36; Berliner 2005: 197–211). Linde discusses the role of coherence in the individual telling of life stories (1993).
6. An excerpt from the song, translated by the author:

   > The real experts know that the men in the East are the better kissers, ...
   > That the walls in the East are more durable,
   > That most people here get it quicker,
   > That nearly everything is somewhat better than in the West.
   > ...
   > Everybody knows that we here always did our best and that the *Ossis* [East Germans] also invented the *Golf* [a VW model],
   > That time does not pass quite as fast,
   > ...
   > That the butter here tastes more of butter and the *Sekt* a little more like *Sekt* [sparkling wine].
   > (Niemann 2001)

7. The Soviet Union had also developed ideas about personhood. Throughout its history these took various forms including the notion of *lichnost*, the heroic figure, and the later *Homo Sovieticus*, which also became a literary character. See, for example, Kharkhordin (1999).
8. The term collective is most often connected with agriculture and the collective farm (for example Humphrey 1983; Verdery 1996: 146–52. On personhood and collectivity in the Soviet Union see Kharkhordin (1999), on the Czech Republic see Holy (1996: 20 n. 3).
9. Kharkhordin (1999), for example, shows well the tensions and contradictions inherent in the authorities' views of personhood, which, in the later SU, encouraged individuality but not too much individuality. Similarly the official discourse in the GDR encouraged the establishment and maintenance of social relationships as long as these were purposeful and geared towards socialist ideas and goals.

References

Abu-Lughod, L. 1991. 'Writing against Culture', in R.G. Fox (ed.), *Recapturing Anthropology*. Santa Fe: School of American Research Press, pp. 137–62.
———. 1992. *Writing Women's Worlds: Bedouin Stories*. Berkeley: University of California Press.
Aguilar, J. 1981. 'Insider Research: an Ethnography of a Debate', in D. Messerschmidt (ed.), *Anthropologists at Home in North America*. Cambridge: Cambridge University Press, pp. 15–26.
Anderson, D.G. 2000. *Identity and Ecology in Arctic Siberia: The Number One Reindeer Brigade*. Oxford: Oxford University Press
Appadurai, A. 1988. 'Putting Hierarchy in Its Place', *Cultural Anthropology* 3(1): 36–49.
Balzer, M.M. (ed.). 1995. *Culture Incarnate: Native Anthropology from Russia*. Armonk: M.E.Sharp.
Barsegian, I. 2000. 'When Text Becomes Field: Fieldwork in "Transitional" Societies', in H.G. De Soto and N. Dudwick (eds), *Fieldwork Dilemmas: Anthropologists in Postsocialist States*. Madison: University of Wisconsin Press, pp. 119–29.
Berdahl, D. 1999a. '"(N)ostalgie" for the Present: Memory, Longing and East German Things', *Ethnos* 64(2): 192–211.
———. 1999b. *Where the World Ended: Re-Unification and Identity in the German Borderland*. Berkeley: University of California Press.
Berger, L. 2001. 'Inside Out: Narrative Autoethnography as a Path towards Rapport', *Qualitative Inquiry* 7(4): 504–18.
Berliner, D. 2005. 'The Abuses of Memory: Reflections on the Memory Boom in Anthropology', *Anthropological Quarterly* 78(1): 197–211.
Bernard, H.R. 1994. *Research Methods in Anthropology: Qualitative and Quantitative Approaches*. London: Sage.
Brettell, C.R. 1993. *When They Read What We Write*. Westport: Bergen and Garvey.
Climo, J.J. and M.G. Catell. 2002. *Social Memory and History*. Walnut Creek, California: AltaMira Press.
Collins, P. 2002. 'Connecting Anthropology and Quakerism: Transcending the Insider/Outsider Dichotomy', in E. Arweck and M.D. Stringer (eds), *Theorising Faith: the Insider/Outsider Problem in the Study of Ritual*. Birmingham University Press, pp. 77–95.
De Soto, H. G. 2000. 'Contested Landscapes: Reconstructing Environment and Memory in Postsocialist Saxony-Anhalt', in D. Berdahl, M. Bunzl and M. Lampland (eds), *Altering States: Ethnographies of Transition in Eastern Europe and the Former Soviet Union*. Ann Arbour, Michigan: University of Michigan Press, pp. 96–113.
Gallinat, A. 2005. 'The Ritual Middle Ground? Personhood, Ideology and Resistance in East Germany', *Social Anthropology* 13(3), 291–305.
———. 2008. 'Being "East German" or Being "At home in eastern Germany"? Identity as Experience and as Rhetoric. *Identities: Global Studies in Culture and Power* 15(6): 665–86.

Giddens, A. 1991. *Modernity and Self-Identity: Self and Society in the Late Modern Age*. Stanford: Stanford University Press.

Glaeser, A. 2000. *Divided in Unity: Identity, Germany and the Berlin Police*. Chicago: University of Chicago Press.

Holy, L. 1996. *The Little Czech and the Great Czech Nation: National Identity and the Post-Communist Transformation*. Cambridge: Cambridge University Press.

Howard, M.A. 1995. 'Die Deutschen als Ethnische Gruppe? Zum Verständnis der neuen Teilung des geeinten Deutschlands', *Berliner Debatte INITIAL* 4/5: 119–31.

Humphrey, C. 1983. *Karl Marx Collective: Economy, Society and Religion in a Siberian Collective Farm*. Cambridge: Cambridge University Press.

Jackson, A. 1987. *Anthropology at Home*. London: Tavistock.

Jacobs-Huey, L. 2002. 'The Natives are Gazing and Talking Back: Reviewing the Problematics of Positionality, Voice and Accountability among "Native" Anthropologists', *American Anthropologist* 104(3): 791–804.

Jedlowski, P. 2001. 'Memory and Sociology: Themes and Issues', *Time and Society* 10(1): 29–44.

Jowitt, K. 1974. 'An Organizational Approach to the Study of Political Culture in Marxist-Leninist Systems', *American Political Science Review* 68(3): 1171–91.

Junghans, T. 2001. 'Marketing Selves: Constructing Civil Society and Selfhood in Post-Socialist Hungary', *Critique of Anthropology* 21(4): 383–400.

Kharkhordin, O. 1999. *The Collective and the Individual in Russia: A Study of Practices*. Berkeley: University of California Press.

Kürti, L. 1996. 'Homecoming: Affairs of Anthropologists of and in Eastern Europe', *Anthropology Today* 12(3): 11–15.

———. 2000. 'The Socialist Circus: Secrets, Lies and Autobiographical Family Narratives', in R. Breckner, D. Khalekin-Fishman and I. Miethe (eds), *Biographies and the Division of Europe: Experience, Action and Change on the "Eastern Side"*. Opladen: Leske+Budrich, pp. 283–302.

———. 2002. *Youth and the State in Hungary: Capitalism, Communism and Class*. London: Pluto Press.

Kuwayam, T. 2003. '"Natives" as Dialogic Partners: Some Thoughts on Native Anthropology, *Anthropology Today* 19(1): 8–13.

Linde, C. 1993. *Life-Stories: the Creation of Coherence*. Oxford: Oxford University Press.

Lukes, S. 1973. *Individualism*. Oxford: Basil and Blackwell.

Lutz, C. 1988. *Unnatural Emotions: Everyday Sentiments on a Micronesian Atoll and Their Challenge to Western Theory*. Chicago: University of Chicago Press.

Malinowski, B. 1961 [1922]. *Argonauts of the Western Pacific*. New York: E.P.Dutton.

Messerschmidt, D. 1981a. 'On Anthropology "at Home"', in D. Messerschmidt (ed.), *Anthropologists at Home in North America*. Cambridge: Cambridge University Press, pp. 1–14.

Narayan, K. 1993. 'How Native is the Native Anthropologist?' *American Anthropologist* 95(3): 671–86.

Niemann, K. 2001. *Im Osten*. Berlin: Sony Music Entertainment (Germany).

Rose, N. 1989. *Governing the Soul: The Shaping of the Private Self*. London: Free Association books.

Salzman, C.P. 2002. 'On Reflexivity', *American Anthropologist* 104(3): 805–13.

———. 1994The Lone Stranger in the Heart of Darkness. In R. Borofsky (ed.), *Assessing Cultural Anthropology*. New York: McGraw-Hill, pp. 29–39.

Shokeid, M. 1997. 'Negotiating Multiple Viewpoints: the Cook, the Native, the Publisher, and the Ethnographic Text', *Current Anthropology* 38(4): 631–45.

Srinivas, M.N. 1952. *Religion and Society among the Coorgs of Southern India*. New Delhi: Oxford University Press.

———. 1969. 'Some Thoughts on the Study of One's Own Society', in M.N. Srinivas (ed.) *Social Change in modern India*. Berkeley: University of California Press, pp. 147–63.

Strathern, M. 1987. 'The Limits of Auto-Anthropology', in A. Jackson (ed.) *Anthropology at Home*. London: Tavistock, pp. 16–37.

Ten Dyke, E.A. 2000. 'Memory, History and Remembrance Work in Dresden', in D. Berdahl, M. Bunzl and M. Lampland (eds), *Altering States: Ethnographies of Transition in Eastern Europe and the Former Soviet Union*. Ann Arbour Michegan: University of Michigan Press, pp. 139–57.

———. 2001a. 'Tulips in December: Space, Time and Consumption Before and After the End of German Socialism', *German History* 19(2): 253–76.

———. 2001b. *Dresden: Paradoxes of Memory in History*. New York: Routledge.

Verdery, K. 1996. *What Was Socialism and What Comes Next?* Princeton: Princeton University Press.

———. 1999. *The Political Lives of Dead Bodies: Reburial and Postsocialist Change*. New York: Columbia University Press.

Zentraler Ausschuß für Jugendweihe (ed.) 1983. *Vom Sinn unseres Lebens*. Berlin: Verlag Neues Leben.

Zeugnis. 1988. School report of Anselma Gallinat, Barby, 1 July 1988.

———. 1989. School report of Anselma Gallinat, Welbsleben, 30 June 1989.

———. 1990. School report of Anselma Gallinat, Welbsleben, 6 July 1990.

———. 1991. School report of Anselma Gallinat, Welbsleben, 12 July 1991.

Chapter 3

FOREGROUNDING THE SELF IN FIELDWORK AMONG RURAL WOMEN IN CROATIA

Lynette Šikić-Mićanović

Introduction

Self-awareness and attention to one's thoughts, feelings and experiences or 'narrative of self' have been contested in the social sciences. Criticisms include claims of narcissism, self-absorption, exaggeration, exhibitionism and self-indulgence on the part of the researcher that uses personal experience as a central focus of their research (Okely 1992; Bochner and Ellis 1996; Ellis 1998; Coffey 1999). However, the researcher's experience is crucial as it is not the unmediated world of others but the world between ourselves and others that adds reality to the field (Okely and Callaway 1992). Postmodernist critiques of ethnographic writings (see Clifford and Marcus 1986; Denzin 1986; Clifford 1988) have moved many ethnographers to become increasingly reflexive about their own roles in the social worlds they study. Scholars now acknowledge the construction of research material that is to a large extent shaped and influenced by the personal background and experiences of the researcher (see Abu-Lughod 1991; Tedlock 1991; Behar 1996). As anthropologists, we are reminded that long-term immersion through fieldwork is generally a total experience (demanding all of the anthropologist's resources – intellectual, physical, emotional, political and intuitive) and that this experience involves so much of the self that it is impossible to reflect upon it fully by extracting that self (Okely 1992: 8). In order to manage this total experience, anthropologists have been concerned about the 'problem of reflexivity' and the ways in which 'our subjectivity becomes entangled in the lives of others' (Clifford and Marcus 1986; Geertz 1988; Rosaldo 1989). Narayan (1993) elaborates that every anthropologist carries both a personal and ethnographic self – simultaneously belonging to both personal and professional worlds – and that these worlds should not be seen as distinct entities. Contrastingly, it has been argued that no matter how aware and reflexive we try to be 'the author's intentions, emotions, psyche and interiority are not only inaccessible to readers, they are likely to be inaccessible to the author herself' (Grosz 1995: 13). In an attempt to challenge this suggestion, I argue that my personal experiences in the field are an important and accessible source of ethnographic data. Hence, the researcher should not be rendered invisible but rather foregrounded as an embodied, situated and subjective self. This is because interpretations are always filtered through our own cultural lens, as Scheper-Hughes (1992: 28) points out: 'we cannot rid ourselves of the cultural self we bring with us into the field any more than we can disown the eyes, ears and skin through which we take in our interactive perceptions about the new and strange world we have entered'. Clearly, what researchers observe, do and record in the field depends on their own lived experience and changing self, which will either facilitate or hinder their observations and interpretations.

The Researcher's Role in Shaping the Data

Focus on and analysis of the anthropologist's identities and lived experiences are important because the researcher as the research instrument (Punch 1994) will influence the course of research in many ways. To foreground lived experiences and a changing cultural self we need to examine our 'positionality', which refers to aspects of identity in terms of race, age, class, gender, religion, ethnicity, nationality, sexuality, personality and other attributes that are markers of relational positions in society. Aptly, Naples (2003) warns that if we fail to explore our personal, professional and structural locations as researchers, we inevitably reiterate race, class and gender biases in our work. Spivak (1988) writes that those researchers/writers that self-consciously carry no voice, body, race, class or gender and no interests into their texts seek to shelter themselves in the text, as if they were transparent. In addition, reflexive processes need to be documented, not just in general terms such as class, gender and ethnic background but in a more concrete and nitty-gritty way in terms of where, how and why particular decisions are made at particular stages (Mauthner and Doucet 1997: 138). Specifically, Luttrell (2000) claims that the research questions, theoretical approaches, study design, researcher's temperament, personality and intended audience all influence how a researcher shapes research. For this reason, there is a need to reflect on the bearing of the researcher's identity on both the fieldwork and the data since the 'self' of the ethnographer has an effect on every aspect of the research process, especially the gendered aspect of the self (Coffey 1999: 6).

Thus, 'our understanding of other can "only" proceed from within our own experience, and this experience involves our personalities and histories as much as our field research' (Jackson 1989: 17). Further, Chacko (2004: 61) reminds us that acknowledging positionality as a critical element in formulating, conducting and reporting fieldwork can make the researcher more vigilant about power relations and their impacts on the exchange and production of information and knowledge. Hence, our obligation is to come clean 'at the hyphen', as Fine and Weis (1996: 263–64) explain: 'we have a responsibility to talk about our own identities – why we interrogate what we do, what we choose not to report, on whom we train our scholarly gaze, who is protected and not protected as we do our work.' Clearly, the researcher has a pivotal role in determining both how the fieldwork develops and the outcome. At the same time, there is a limit to how reflexive we can be and how far we can know and understand what shapes our research at the time of conducting it. Some researchers (Doucet 1998; Mauthner et al. 1998) claim that these influences may only become apparent once we have left the research behind and moved on in our personal and academic lives.

My Positionality

Acknowledging that research is produced by situated and embodied researchers, there is an imperative need to take into account the impact of the researcher's identity on fieldwork and the data. Beyond doubt, the position and context from which the researcher speaks (Haraway 1991: 5), what he or she looks like and what social groups they are perceived as belonging to matter in the production of ethnographic accounts. Moreover, positionality usually refers to both who a researcher is in the eyes of the community and who community members are in the eyes of the researcher (Caplan 1993). My positionality has been shaped by a combination of identifiers. These include: female, feminist, white, Croatian/Australian citizenship, married, mother, Catholic upbringing, with relatively high levels of access to different forms of capital – economic, cultural, social and symbolic.[1] The ordering of these identifiers does not correspond to a perceived higher value. Some identifiers, such as my whiteness, Croatian heritage/nationality and *snaha* (daughter-in-law) status, eased initial acceptance and helped me fit into village life. They provided the basis for increasing trust and openness in interactions especially since fieldwork (between 2002 and 2003) took place in a post-war zone where hostilities and fears are still common. Most of my participants were Catholic Croatians because I thought they would be more forthright with me about issues of ethnicity/nationality/religion and how this intersected with gender. Although I have never lived in these rural communities, I have visited as a *snaha* since 1989, so my research was informed and enriched by my long-term knowledge of the setting and the prevailing norms. As a married women (i.e. married to someone from one of the villages) with two sons (in a sociocultural system where the social value of women depends on whether they have sons or not), I fell into traditional societal norms more fully. The conventional image presented by my background and familial situation indeed served to open many doors.

My Research Orientations

The topics and populations researchers choose to study or not to study are influenced by a wide range of personal, aesthetic, theoretical and ideological factors (Lee 1995). Researchers are motivated by their own interests, their political and intellectual commitments, demands of their careers, the need to publish, peer approval, as well as a sense of self-worth and promotion (Bosworth et al. 2005). In a 'more concrete and nitty-gritty way', my choice to study aspects of gender relations was influenced by my own personal experiences or positionings. I particularly wanted to focus on how femininity is performed and understood in a rural context because, after migrating to Croatia, I found that in certain contexts I had to change: that *different* audiences required *different* performance and that I could not always be the *same* woman. To counter any suggestion that this is a self-indulgent project, I was convinced that this would be a worthwhile study as anthropological research with rural women in Croatia is scarce. I set out to analyse critically and articulate my experience of my shifting identities as an important part of the research process, while investigating how rural women attempt to negotiate the meaning of their roles and statuses. Thus, this study draws on my personal experiences and memories as an anthropologist exploring constructions of femininity among rural women in Croatia.

Specifically, I wanted to research what it means 'to be a woman' in these rural communities (i.e. the values, experiences and meanings that are culturally interpreted as feminine and typically feel 'natural' for or are ascribed to women). In addition, I had a particular interest in doing femininity or 'doing being a woman' to 'fit in' as a researcher in these rural spaces. Contrary to my expectations this posed considerable challenges. In this chapter I shall therefore explore how my own femininity was critiqued and scrutinised and how in turn I closely monitored and reflected on my behaviour and appearance. I attempt to show how experiences of misfitting or fitting differently and the resulting embarrassment/awkwardness can sway researcher focus and empathy and, produce important anthropological insights whilst also threatening one's personal and professional confidence.

In the following I adapt a social constructionist perspective. Such a perspective is useful in addressing concepts of the 'self' as well as the 'other' and argues that meaning is 'constructed' by those engaged in interaction – i.e. meaning is shaped by the frames participants bring to their encounters (Goffman 1959). In other words, both the researcher and the researched engage in a symbiotic process during which the data and relationships are 'co-constructed' (although these are not the only two influencing factors). I wish to explore the ways in which this process impacts on the research context and shapes the data and the researcher's interpretations.

Field Research

Fieldwork for this study was among both women and men in six rural villages in Slavonia,[2] in the county of Vukovar-Sirmium, one of the twenty-one counties in the Republic of Croatia that was established in 1993, following Croatia's independence. The county is situated in the very north-east of Croatia. Research for this study involved structured questionnaires for demographic details and open in-depth interviews designed to explore a variety of gender issues (their family life, socialisation practices, education and work experiences, personal life choices, perceptions of womanhood in rural spaces, ideal femininities, household division of labour, gender roles, women's rights and aspirations, etc.). Selected questionnaires followed by interviews were completed by sixty seven rural (farm) women (single, married and widowed mostly in their thirties and fourties) as well as some of their husbands (fourteen) in their homes. This was most frequently the kitchen/family room, where the most important domestic or 'inside' functions of the household take place – where women cook, members of the household gather, eat, sleep, etc., as well as backyards or workplaces. This research also included time that I spent with village women and girls in less structured settings, which helped me understand more about their experiences and lives, for example helping women with their household chores or preparation for and participation in community events such as feasts and holy days, as well as rites of passage. I also kept a field diary in which I addressed issues related to the research as it was necessary to reflect on my presence in the field and to account for the ways in which my assumptions, feelings, biases and anticipated outcomes might influence my interpretation and representation of the women's experiences (Harding 1987; DeVault 1990).

Access and Rapport

Initially, I was introduced to participants through personal contacts – affinal relatives and friends– who were very important for not only gaining access but rapport to remove any suspicion or reason for distrust. Researchers have shown that establishing rapport is an essential element in ethnographic studies (see Dewalt et al. 1998: 267). One particular person was instrumental in facilitating entry into households as well as institutions (e.g., the local primary school and council) in the initial stages of my fieldwork. Owing to his good reputation and high levels of social capital, it was relatively easy for him to set up meetings for me. He often liked to walk 'arm in arm' with me along village streets, where 'nothing' goes unnoticed. Undoubtedly, a gesture such as this eased access but also communicated mutual friendship, closeness and trust to potential participants as well as onlookers. Nonetheless, since the process of gaining access to participants does influence the data that are collected, I often wondered about the following issues during my fieldwork. How many would have voluntarily participated or how many felt trapped into participating in the research as a favour to this highly respected and influential person? Were these quality data reflecting 'truths' in view of his presence? Could they really believe my assurances of anonymity and confidentiality when he was absent?[3] After some first interviews it became easier to set up further ones as interviewees relayed positive reports about my work to other villagers. Since the research relationship is a social relation that has some effect on the results obtained, active and methodical listening as well as signs of attention, interest, encouragement and recognition have been recommended (Bourdieu 1996). I attempted to appear relaxed, pleasant and friendly while not being overly inquisitive, anxious or threatening. I also found that non-verbal behaviour such as watching and listening intently as well as looking engaged and interested had an impact on relations and responses. In addition, 'being open' with participants was another requirement as participants always wanted some degree of information about me. In an attempt to reduce power differentials, I was prepared to invest my own personal identity in the relationship to connect with research participants and to obtain valid accounts of what their lives are like. I consequently also invited them to share any thoughts or questions about the study. Oakley (1981) reminds us that the process of meaning-making is often illuminated by 'questions asked back' (see Jordan 2006: 174). She adds that, when those being studied have a sense that they are understood by someone who faces the same life challenges, a certain reciprocity and trust can emerge.

Research Dilemmas and Challenges

Dilemmas faced by researchers using both qualitative research methods and a feminist approach have been well documented (Golde 1970; Fonow and Cook 1991; Reinharz 1992; Bell, Caplan and Karim 1993; Wolf 1996; Coffey 1999). Relevant to this study is the affirmation by Fluehr-Lobban (1998: 178) that 'everyday dilemmas' are part of ethnography and are contingent on the identity of the researcher. Although the researcher can circumvent some, there are dilemmas and tensions that develop unexpectedly and spontaneously (perhaps in situations where the researcher has little control over events). In the following I will share some of the personal dilemmas and challenges I encountered while being and becoming feminine in these rural spaces for the purpose of research.

There is an almost unanimous and consistent belief among the women in this study that employment has to fit in with childcare arrangements rather than the other way around whereas men's employment is more fixed and non-negotiable. Researchers have claimed that 'work for a wage is less important to a woman's social identity than her domestic duties' in a patriarchal society (Massey, et al. 1995: 360). Women in this study claimed that wage work/careers outside the home are not compatible with being a good mother, wife and homemaker. In a gatekeeping way, they do not consider that their husbands could feasibly share domestic roles or childcare responsibilities. Predictably then, considering their traditional upbringing and perspectives, levels of education and the restricted paid-work opportunities in rural areas in this county, as well as the paucity of childcare provision, more than three quarters of the women in this sample are not formally employed.[4] Similarly, other researchers have found that respondents raised in rural settings in Croatia tend to hold more negative attitudes towards women becoming involved in wage labour (Brajdić-Vuković et al. 2006).

Women frequently told me that one of the advantages of village life is that mothers have more time for their children and that they 'never' leave them.[5] Nothing in their accounts of motherhood directly challenged the idea of women as caring nurturing beings, for whom having children is the ultimate and central experience of their lives. Inevitably, questions related to the care and upbringing of my own primary-school-aged children surfaced throughout fieldwork and admittedly created uncomfortable feelings and undermined my confidence considerably. I constantly felt 'judged' as a mother who did not devote adequate time to her children; who was not always home for them or for her husband. The way many women perceived me was undoubtedly far from ideal since I carried out most of my fieldwork while my children were at school in Zagreb, approximately 300 kilometres away. Although they accompanied me on field trips during school holidays (and this may have resulted in more egalitarian power relations as accompanied researchers become 'observers observed' (Cupples and Kiddon 2003)) I do not think that these short intervals with my children[6] changed their opinion of me. In their eyes, considering the amount of time that I spend away from home and the importance that I give my professional work I did not match what is considered to be an 'ideal' woman in these villages. Not only are the women there expected to be 'at home' and largely responsible for the well-being of their families but they also carry the responsibility of being the moral guardians of society. Especially in the post-transition/post-war period, women have been expected to make every effort to preserve and protect all that is good and right in society. This great responsibility also means that the woman is to be blamed if things go wrong. Succinctly, a woman summed up their general attitude about career women and why women do not aspire to be any more than 'housewives' in rural areas: 'They seem ideal until we look at their children and their families' (Marica, 51).

Inevitably, this experience of responding or sharing information about the upbringing and care of my children generated more research focus (although awkward at times) on rural women's perception of motherhood and career women. On the other hand, regardless of my uneasy feelings, the positive aspects of my status as a mother in facilitating access to research participants and enhanced rapport were evident, as 'talking about our children' seemed to collapse barriers and diminish suspicions. Simultaneously, this raised the question of how I should most appropriately describe myself in gender terms (Reinharz 1997). Which dimension of self – researcher, mother, career woman, wife – should be most appropriately foregrounded to present myself? Walsh (2004) reminds us that the ethnographer should create different self-presentations for different settings and that this requires constant attention and monitoring of oneself and others' responses, although Nayaran (1993) notes that 'we cannot focus on one world and then on the other as our personal and professional selves become entangled'. In retrospect, as noted by other anthropologists (see Lofland and Lofland 1995; Bloustein 1999) a great deal of my fieldwork was conducted in a sort of psychological 'schizophrenic' divide, where the language and content of the discussions differed according to whether I was talking to a single woman, a daughter-in-law, a mother-in-law, a farm woman, an employed/educated woman, a housewife, etc. and whether I was engaged or disengaged in fieldwork.

Despite my dubious status as a 'working woman', I always found that my marital status earned me respect. This status is favoured because marriage for a woman is a legitimate strategy for accessing resources when she leaves her natal household and power as she gets older (especially if she has sons). It also imparts a sense of belonging and facilitates acceptance in the community because single women over thirty are pitied and stigmatised. Women who are unmarried and 'old' have disrupted the intended and wished-for life cycle. More importantly for me personally, I felt it absolutely necessary to preserve and maintain this 'respectability' through marriage while I was conducting research, since my partner was absent for most of the time.

In giving accounts of their lives it was not uncommon for my research participants to construct me in particular ways, assuming that my experiences of gendered socialisation, familial and religious practices were similar to theirs. My very different memories and lack of knowledge on these themes would often expose the fact that my 'self-presentation' was not quite genuine since girls learn early about 'doing femininity' properly. From an early age, girls are encouraged to participate in highly regarded 'traditional women's tasks' such as cooking, cleaning, ironing, sibling care, needlework and similar craftwork to prepare them appropriately for adult life. This is knowledge 'that *all* girls should and need to know.' Having assumed that I had been taught in the same way, the women were surprised by my detailed questions (consistent with the work of a social scientist conducting research) about gendered socialisation, familial and religious practices. Indeed, my lack of handicraft skills was exposed very quickly. During the winter, when there is less farm work or gardening to do outdoors, many women engage in crafts at home generating an additional income for the family. However, I failed to participate or indeed show any knowledge of domestic handicrafts. Here, then, was another instance where I failed to 'fit in' because 'women that just sit around while their hands are idle even while socialising are not highly regarded in these village communities', as one villager remarked. In many ways, in their eyes, I was not a 'proper/authentic' woman because otherwise I would know this from home, not have to ask so many questions and be more apt at doing 'women's work'.

Inevitably, domestic space and the labour within it are closely tied to a woman's identity in these rural communities. Besides all of her other jobs, a 'good' housewife makes sure that her husband and children are well-kept (clean, ironed underwear and clothes). Creased trousers and soiled garments reflect her lack of competency and laziness more than anything else: she is not doing 'respectable' femininity properly. This presented another dilemma for myself, as I do not iron. This practice of our household placed me immediately in a very problematic, almost embarrassing, position. Once word had got out about this in the villages not only what I wore but anything that my family wore was surveyed scrupulously by both women and men. This made it more than clear to me that washed and ironed clothing is one of the most effective and visible ways of 'doing gender', and more importantly, of doing 'respectable femininity'.

Yet, in other instances, my and my family's different lifestyle created opportunities for dialogue. For example, when I told a husband and wife couple what my husband does at home (dish-washing, laundry, vacuuming, cooking, etc.) he asked me several times if this was not 'woman's work'. As we discussed this issue, the wife voiced her opinion about the unfairness of this division in their own home so the outcome provided a space during which differing perspectives were exchanged. Apart from providing interesting data about the contestation of gender roles as well as processes of negotiation and mediation, this unfolded as one of the advantages of interviewing respondents in couples and groups, rather than individually as planned. It also revealed the biased nature of my own frames of reference since I sought to identify men as the primary benefactors of women's household labour. As I had no prior experience of life in extended households, I was not aware that older women were often the ones who appropriate and control women's labour. In light of these new insights, I had to reformulate my research questions and refocus my 'ethnographic eye'.

Strikingly, in Slavonia, women and men are not only seen to be different but this male–female difference is superimposed on many aspects of their social world. Most of the women that were a part of this study spend much of their time with other women in accordance with the customary spatial and temporal arrangements of the village. It is not common for married couples (with the exception of just a few)[7] to do things together (e.g., childcare, preparing meals together, walking together, going out together, sitting together at church, etc.) in the village spaces. In this study, I took advantage of my own positionality as a *snaha* and this identity helped me to an extent to downplay 'a sense of difference' and earned me a degree of acceptance. Doing the same types of work in the household as well as my engagement in social events with women that were a part of this study confirmed that 'anthropologists learn not only through the verbal, the transcript, but through all the senses, through movement, through their bodies and whole being in a total practice' (Okely 1992: 16). An example of this embodied knowledge is my physical labour which became a large part of fieldwork as an act of reciprocity. I helped other women prepare for rites of passage, e.g. christenings, weddings, funerals, as well as annual events such as *rakija* (brandy) production in late summer and pig slaughters in late autumn. Embodied knowledge of ritual as well as daily practices became part of my informal data collection which is fundamental to any research. I learned through participation, which consequently created a sense of mutually shared womanhood that facilitated more 'natural' dialogue and conversation. Although the traditional segregation of sexes and mutually exclusive scripts for being male and female provided me with an opportunity to have first-hand experiences of 'being a village woman' (and not a man), they were also a real source of frustration for myself. I found it particularly difficult to be a part of this segregated social world whenever my partner visited. His being there evoked a real sense of being caught between entirely different worlds and identities: the one of the village ethnographer/proper woman and that other of wife/mother in my family which resonates older memories and experiences. These experiences of misfitting led me to think about women's reluctance to traverse boundaries in these villages. Clearly, women conform to the expected behaviours and practise 'proper' femininity to avoid being gossiped about in the community. If they spend a lot of time away from home 'unjustifiably', they also run the risk of being gossiped about. These are just some of the ways in which women can be labelled incompetent mothers and homemakers. Their sexual morality may also be questioned. Thus, in a gender system that demands compliance, women are careful to adopt behaviours that are associated with being a 'good' woman, and at the same time they keep an eye on their kinswomen and neighbours as well as the anthropologist who asks them questions they have not been asked before.

'Being a woman' in these spaces is also underpinned by all aspects of bodily praxis – e.g. their clothing, style, appearance and consumption. Specifically, dress simultaneously communicates and constitutes gender and ethnic identities (Eicher and Roach-Higgins 1992; Kaiser 2001). 'It tells us who we are, what we have been and what we are becoming' (Keenan 2001: 13). Clothes, beautification procedures (make up, jewellery, skincare, depilation, perfume) and deportment (posture, carriage, demeanour) are all cultural symbols that are manipulated to express the self – to indicate to others that this person belongs to a certain group and is a certain type of person. In the villages, 'appropriate' clothes and appearance are important for group membership and acceptance and for knowing that one's body can be portrayed with confidence. As dress and body adornments serve as a discursive daily practice of gender, 'what to wear' in light of 'you are what you wear!' was a constant dilemma throughout my fieldwork. I knew, for example, that I could not wear the same clothes at home, out 'in the field' and at church (which I normally do). Moreover, I was often encouraged to wear particular items of clothing (aprons or full-length, floral pinafores) that are traditionally worn by women even when 'work' is over.[8] These garments resemble domesticity and mirror women's function as domestic labourers and mothers. Even though I disliked wearing them, I realised that by doing this I could 'pass', i.e. look like someone who had the usual reasons for being there, and this would be more productive for data collection. In effect, following the clothing conventions made me feel much less conspicuous and created feelings of solidarity and shared identity with the other women. Interestingly, with these gender values inscribed on my body I was also led to thinking more about femininity/domesticity and female sexuality.

As clothing style is the first identifiable way in which women indicate allegiance to a particular social grouping there was a high degree of consensus among both women and men as to what the dress codes are in these rural spaces. Participants cited examples of devalued signifiers of excessive femininity, such as short skirts, bare backs, see-through blouses, too much make-up, tight-fitting clothes, shorts, tank tops, exposed and emphasised parts of the anatomy – cleavages, legs, etc. Overall, clothes that accentuate female body parts or make them more visible are inappropriate since the women's concern with appearance is about conveying respectability which in turn secures cultural and symbolic capital. 'Excessive' or 'sexually alluring' femininity even for younger women is coded as vulgarity and extremely unbefitting. Since appearance is the means by which women are labelled, identified and positioned by others, too much attention (sexuality in excess) to one's appearance is also a sign of sexual deviance and denotes low moral value. Circulating religious discourses in rural spaces (in the absence of glossy magazines and billboards) provide constant reminders of what is appropriately worn when women leave their private spaces. For example, while I was doing my fieldwork, female churchgoers regardless of age were asked by the priest to cover their arms and not to wear revealing clothes when the days started to get hotter. This shows that the prevailing rules about dress code were very clear-cut and I was certainly careful not to arouse attention through unbefitting clothing, especially so during the summer as difficult as this was at times in the searing heat. Despite my efforts, I failed on several occasions and would be reminded that my choice of dress was inappropriate with regard to decency and formality.

Such situations often led to humiliating experiences for me personally. However, and as noted by Okely (1992: 17), key crises brought about by ignorance and unfamiliarity with the group's rules or rhythms are also informative. First, these situations opened up a whole new area of discussion exploring how women's bodies and the ways they are dressed often come to represent the larger community. Since women are, then, the bearers of traditional culture in these rural villages, I realised that if I was 'too daring' or 'too casual' in self-presentation, especially in public spaces I would run the risk of being gossiped about and, secondly, unavoidably influence all aspects of the research process. Thirdly, being gossiped about would also compromise me personally and I wished to avoid the accompanying embarrassments. Thus, my attempts to conform to prevalent gender norms paved the way for shared relations with women as well as access, fuller understanding and sociality.

Concluding Remarks

Undoubtedly, this fieldwork experience among rural women in Croatia revealed a great deal about myself as well as my cultural background and differences. All these 'new' ways of being gendered in rural villages were vastly different from anything I knew or had learned. However, since qualitative ethnographic research needs to be more than a continual process of self-discovery I wanted to do more than covertly contrast my own gendered experiences with theirs to come up with research results. As it is crucial to examine the lived world between ourselves and others in anthropological research, I have attempted to show that a researcher's personal experiences and background are an important and accessible source of data in ethnography. Their importance and relevance are apparent because ethnographic fieldwork is constituted within a discourse of immersion, reflexivity and rapport where the self cannot be easily extracted. Since the researcher inescapably shapes research, it is important to foreground the ethnographic self as embodied, situated and subjective rather than invisible or transparent. Our personal experiences and memories as well as our temperaments and personalities inevitably influence our choice of research sites, themes, design and theoretical approaches. Further, all that constitutes the self has a further impact on research relations and interactions (access) in the field where new knowledge is created, shaped and negotiated. Thus, besides being an important ethnographic resource, personal experiences can be an accessible source of data only if the researcher is willing to explain their own identities and interests that determine the course and outcome of ethnographic research. Although researchers may be reluctant to disclose details, dilemmas during fieldwork can also sway research focus and empathy, as they are contingent on the identities and experiences of the researcher. Admittedly, I was most comfortable with and had most empathy for those women that were more educated, more mobile and less overtly religious – who attempt to challenge (although with little success) traditional gendered values and attitudes in these rural communities. In comparison, I found it relatively difficult to relate to women whose personal development and achievement are through their husbands, children and social activities with other women in this study. Unfairly, I felt disappointed with these women who seemingly lacked any gender consciousness only because I was trying to unjustly position them into my narrative of gender, which lays emphasis on individualism, achievement and self-analysis. Besides effectively showing the biased nature of my own frames of reference, difficulties during fieldwork provided opportunities for revising research plans, creating space for dialogues, exploring unanticipated research themes and refocusing for wider meanings. For these reasons, there is a compelling need to constantly interrogate one's own positionality and to scrutinise the cultural baggage that weighs us down and causes dilemmas. Through interrogation of our own beliefs and feelings rather than just the questioning of others, we can become open to new forms of situated knowledge.

Inevitably, anthropological fieldwork is wrought by tensions between 'fitting in' for research purposes, conformity to unshared values and attitudes, social stigmatisation when failing to 'fit in' and the opportunities for research insights provided by such crises. Based on my fieldwork experience, I found that by conforming to gendered expectations (whenever possible), that is, the successful enactment, or performance, of conventional femininities I received more response and cooperation from my participants which ensured more success in the field. Nevertheless, even though my gendered performance, as well as whiteness, Croatian heritage/nationality, *snaha* and marital status facilitated access and was more productive for data collection, these performances and identities were 'not enough' in some cases. Experiences of misfitting or fitting differently caused awkwardness and embarrassment, undermining both my personal and professional confidence. On the other hand, they also generated anthropological knowledge, insights and understanding, because I learned that doing fieldwork in these rural communities was about learning to do one's gender in accordance with certain sanctions and proscriptions and although it was at times frustrating and uncomfortable with consequences for the research itself, it can also be described as a wonderful experience in which I collected a unique body of data. For this reason, it is important to consider how our selves and our experiences influence research processes. In addition, this experience shows that we need to write more of these kinds of experiences and memories into research accounts, because the invisibility of the researcher only limits our understanding and upholds researchers' power over their participants.

Author's Note

This chapter is a modified version of an earlier paper presented at the Ninth EASA Biennial Conference, 'Europe and the World', 18–21 September 2006 in Bristol, UK. I am indebted to the editors of this volume for their encouragement and support. I am also grateful to the Wenner-Gren Foundation, which kindly provided a grant to cover costs at the conference. Due to potential breaches of confidentiality and anonymity, I have omitted certain data where the identity of a person can be worked out or is obvious even if a pseudonym is used. I thank Vered Amit for this recommendation and for drawing my attention to the ways we unknowingly make people vulnerable in our work.

Notes

1. My background is fundamentally different compared with most of the female participants in this study, since rural (farm) women in Slavonia have limited access to different forms of capital as a result of gendered expectations, values, attitudes and practices, which in turn determines their marginal position.
2. Research for this study was conducted in rural villages that are very close to the border of neighbouring Bosnia-Herzegovina. They included Gunja (pop. 5,033), Bošnjaci (pop. 4,653), Drenovci (pop. 3,049), Posavski Podgajci (pop. 1,568), Rajevo Selo (pop. 1,407) and Račinovci (pop. 982) (Census 2001). The villages in this county are relatively large with a satisfactory level of infrastructure compared with other rural spaces in Croatia.
3. This also shows that the community being researched is not a passive component; it also has a bearing on what the researcher is included in and excluded from, which is most likely determined by the researcher's positionality. As agents, according to Goodwin et al. (2003: 576), participants shape the data, the data-collecting opportunities and the course of the fieldwork as well as what and when they choose to tell or not to tell.
4. The rate of employment among women in the county of Vukovar-Sirmium is the second to lowest out of twenty-one counties in Croatia (26.3%) while the unemployment rate for women in this county is second to highest at 31.0% (Census 2001).
5. As pillars of emotional support, many women told me that they stayed at home while their sons were fighting on nearby front lines during the recent war, in which 64% of this county's population was exiled (Buljan 2000).
6. My research participants' observations of and responses to my interactions with my children, partner, in-laws and other relatives provided me with more detailed understandings of gender, sexuality, marriage, family, motherhood, nationality and religion.
7. The few couples who told me that they 'live and do things differently' compared with others in the villages explained that they were different because they had the financial means, experiences abroad and urban aspirations.
8. Wearing a protective garment for most of the day is very common among women in these rural communities and some do not leave home without it, even when away on holidays.

References

Abu-Lughod, L. 1991. 'Writing against Culture', in R. Fox (ed.), *Recapturing Anthropology: Working in the Present*. Santa Fe, N.Mex: School of American Research Press, pp. 137–62.

Behar, R. 1996. *The Vulnerable Observer: Anthropology that Breaks Your Heart*. Boston: Beacon.

Bell, D., P. Caplan, and W.J. Karim (eds). 1993. *Gendered Fields: Women, Men and Ethnography*. London and New York: Routledge.

Bloustein, G. 1999. 'Striking Poses: an Investigation into the Constitution of Gendered Identity as Process in the Worlds of Australian Teenage Girls'. Ph.D. diss., University of Adelaide.

Bochner, A.P. and C. Ellis. 1996. 'Talking over Ethnography', in C. Ellis and A.P. Bochner (eds.), *Composing Ethnography: Alternative Forms of Qualitative Writing*, eds, Walnut Creek: AltaMira, vol. 1, pp. 13–45.

Bosworth, M., D. Campbell, B. Demby, S.M. Ferranti and M. Santos, 2005. 'Doing Prison Research: Views from Inside', *Qualitative Inquiry* 11(2): 249–64.

Bourdieu, P. 1996. 'Understanding', *Theory Culture and Society: Explorations in Critical Social Science* 13(2): 17–37.

Brajdić-Vuković, M., G. Birkelund and A. Štulhofer. 2006. *Between Tradition and Modernization: Attitudes to Women's Employment and Gender Roles in Croatia*, Memorandum no. 3, http://www.iss.uio.no/forskning/memoranda/memorandum03.pdf.

Buljan, Z. (ed.) 2000. *Vukovarsko-srijemska županija* (The County of Vukovar-Sirmium). Vinkovci: Privlacica.

Caplan, P. 1993. 'Learning Gender: Fieldwork in a Tanzanian Coastal Village, 1965–85', in D. Bell, P. Caplan and W.J. Karim (eds.), *Gendered Fields: Women, Men and Ethnography*. London and New York: Routledge, pp. 168–81.

Census of Population, Households and Dwellings. 2001. Zagreb, Republic of Croatia: Central Bureau of Statistics.

Chacko, E. 2004. 'Positionality and Praxis: Fieldwork Experiences in Rural India', *Singapore Journal of Tropical Geography* 25(1): 51–63.

Clifford, J. 1988. *The Predicament of Culture: Twentieth-century Ethnography, Literature and Art*. Cambridge, Mass.: Harvard University Press.

Clifford J. and G.E. Marcus (eds). 1986. *Writing Culture. The Poetics and Politics of Ethnography*. Berkeley: University of California Press.

Coffey, A. 1999. *The Ethnographic Self: Fieldwork and the Representation of Identity*. London: Sage.

Cupples, J. and S. Kiddon. 2003. 'Far from Being "Home Alone": the Dynamics of Accompanied Fieldwork', *Singapore Journal of Tropical Geography* 24(2): 211–28.

Denzin, N.K. 1986. 'A Postmodern Social Theory', *Sociological Theory* 4: 194–204.

DeVault, M.L. 1990. 'Talking and Listening from Women's Standpoint: Feminist Strategies for Interviewing and Analysis', *Social Problems* 37: 96–116.

Dewalt, K.M. and B.R. Dewalt, with C.B. Wayland, 1998. 'Participant Observation', in H.R. Bernard (ed.), *Handbook of Methods in Cultural Anthropology*. Walnut Creek, Calif.: AltaMira, pp. 259–99.

Doucet, A. 1998. 'Interpreting Mother-work: Linking Methodology, Ontology, Theory and Personal Biography', *Canadian Women's Studies* 18: 52–58.

Eicher, J.B. and M.E. Roach-Higgins. 1992. 'Definitions and Classification of Dress: Implications for the Analysis of Gender Roles', in R. Barnes and J.B. Eicher (eds.), *Dress and Gender: Making and Meaning*. New York: Berg, pp. 8–28.

Ellis, C. 1998. 'What Counts as Scholarship in Communication? An Autoethnographic Response', *American Communication Journal* 1: 1–5.

Fine, M. and L. Weis. 1996. 'Writing the "Wrongs" of Fieldwork: Confronting our Own Research/Writing Dilemmas in Urban Ethnographies', *Qualitative Inquiry* 2(3): 251–274.

Fluehr-Lobban, C. 1998. 'Ethics', in H.R. Bernard (ed.), *Handbook of Methods in Cultural Anthropology*. Walnut Creek, Calif.: AltaMira, pp. 173–202.

Fonow M. and J. Cook (eds). 1991. *Beyond Methodology: Feminist Scholarship as Lived Research*. Bloomington, IN: Indiana University Press.

Geertz, C. 1988. *Works and Lives: The Anthropologist as Author*. Stanford, Calif.: Stanford University Press.

Goffman, E. 1959. *The Presentation of Self in Everyday Life*. Garden City, NY: Anchor Books.

Golde, P. 1970. *Women in the Field: Anthropological Experiences*. Berkeley: University of California Press.

Goodwin, D., C. Pope, M. Mort and A. Smith. 2003. 'Ethics and Ethnography: An Experiential Account', *Qualitative Health Research* 13(4): 567–77.

Grosz, E. 1995. *Space, Time and Perversion*. London: Routledge and Kegan Paul.

Haraway, D.J. 1991. *Simians, Cyborgs and Women: the Reinvention of Nature*, London: Free Association Books.

Harding, S. 1987. *Feminism and Methodology*. Bloomington, Ind.: Indiana University Press.

Jackson, M. 1989. *Paths Toward a Clearing: Radical Empiricism and the Ethnographic Inquiry*. Bloomington, Ind.: Indiana University Press.

Jordan, A.B. 2006. 'Make Yourself at Home: the Social Construction of Research Roles in Family Studies', *Qualitative Research* 6(2): 169–85.

Kaiser, S. 2001. 'Minding Appearances: Style, Truth and Subjectivity', in J. Entwhistle and E. Wilson (eds.), *Body Dressing*. New York: Berg, pp. 79–102.

Keenan, W.J.F. (ed). 2001. 'Introduction: "Sartor Resartus" Restored: Dress Studies in Carlylean Perspective', in *Dressed to Impress: Looking the Part*, New York: Berg, pp. 1–49.

Lee, R.M. 1995. *Dangerous Fieldwork*. Thousand Oaks, Calif.: Sage.

Lofland J. and L.H. Lofland. 1995. *Analysing Social Settings: A Guide to Qualitative Observation and Analysis*, 3rd edn. Belmont, Calif.: Wadsworth.

Luttrell, W. 2000. '"Good enough" Methods for Ethnographic Research', *Harvard Educational Review* 70(4): 499–523.

Massey, G., K. Hahn, and D. Sekuliç. 1995. 'Women, Men, and the "Second Shift" in Socialist Yugoslavia', *Gender and Society* 9: 359–79.

Mauthner, N. and A. Doucet. 1997. 'Reflections on a Voice-centred Relational Method: Analysing Maternal and Domestic Voices', in J. Ribbens and R. Edwards (eds.), *Feminist Dilemmas in Qualitative Research: Public Knowledge and Private Lives*. London: Sage, pp. 119–46.

Mauthner, N.S., O. Parry and K. Backett-Milburn. 1998. 'The Data are Out There or Are They? Implications for Archiving and Revising Qualitative Data', *Sociology* 32: 733–45.

Naples, N. 2003. *Feminism and Method*. New York: Routledge.

Narayan, K. 1993. 'How Native is a "Native" Anthropologist?', *American Ethnologist* 95(3): 671–86.

Oakley, A. 1981. Interviewing Women: A Contradiction, in Terms, in H. Roberts (ed.), *Doing Feminist Research*. London: Routledge, pp. 30–61.

Okely, J. 1992. 'Anthropology and Autobiography: Participatory Experience and Embodied Knowledge', in J. Okely and H. Callaway (eds.), *Anthropology and Autobiography*. London and New York: Routledge, pp. 1–28.

Okely J. and H. Callaway (eds). 1992. *Anthropology and Autobiography*. London and New York: Routledge.

Punch, M. 1994. 'Politics and Ethics in Qualitative Research', in N.K. Denzin and Y.S. Lincoln (eds.), *Handbook of Qualitative Research*. Thousand Oaks, Calif.: Sage, pp. 83–97.

Reinharz, S. 1992. *Feminist Methods in Social Research*. New York: Oxford University Press.

———. 1997. 'Who am I? The Need for a Variety of Selves in the Field', in R. Hertz (ed.), *Reflexivity and Voice*. Thousand Oaks, Calif.: Sage, pp. 3–20.

Rosaldo, R. 1989. *Culture and Truth: The Remaking of Social Analysis*. Boston: Beacon Press.

Scheper-Hughes, N. 1992. *Death without Weeping: The Violence of Everyday Life in Brazil*. Berkeley: University of California Press.

Spivak, G.C. 1988. 'Can the Subaltern Speak?' in C. Nelson and L. Grossberg (eds.), *Marxism and the Interpretation of Culture*. Urban: University of Illinois Press, pp. 280–316.

Tedlock, B. 1991. 'From Participant Observation to the Observation of Participation: the Emergence of Narrative Ethnography', *Journal of Anthropological Research* 41: 69–94.

Walsh, D. 2004. 'Doing Ethnography', in C. Seale (ed.), *Researching Society and Culture*. London: Sage, pp. 225–38.

Wolf, D. 1996. *Feminist Dilemmas in Fieldwork*. Boulder, Colo.: Westview.

Chapter 4

SOME REFLECTIONS ON THE 'ENCHANTMENTS' OF VILLAGE LIFE, OR WHOSE STORY IS THIS?

Anne Kathrine Larsen

As we grow older we tend to focus and reflect more and more on our past. This is also the case for anthropologists reviewing their private as well as professional lives. While our early fieldwork will in most cases be interpreted by a young novice, later fieldwork is experienced by an older person who has accumulated not only more fieldwork proficiency but also greater life experience. The mature fieldworker is also in a position to contemplate her previous fieldwork. The anthropologist in the course of fieldwork is sometimes compared with a child learning to speak the language and to handle the cultural codes in general. While this may represent an ideal aim, the analogy with socialisation is of course inexact in several points; for example, the anthropologist is an adult who arrives in the field with baggage of her own. This provides her with a preset personality and cultural outlook as initial tools for interaction and interpretation. Moreover, she normally spends only a limited time in the field, probably for one extended period or possibly also for consecutive, generally briefer, follow-ups. The consequence is that she can only encounter some few cross-sections of the field from which she extracts data, and these may be used to make generalisations on behalf of the whole group or category studied.

This chapter will focus on my very first fieldwork and on how my own experiences in the community gave me hunches that led to theoretical understanding. In the words of Kirsten Hastrup, I became my own informant (Hastrup 2005 [1995]: 51). But I will also take a critical view of this work in retrospect and discuss some crucial aspects of the position and characteristics of the fieldworker for the process of collecting and interpreting data. While this aspect of reflexivity has been a popular theme in anthropology for several decades (see for instance Rosaldo 1984; Okely and Callaway 1992; Hastrup 2005 [1995]), there are still new viewpoints that can be brought into the discussion.

Entering the Field

It was in the late 1970s. One afternoon, in the midst of winter, I arrived at the rural hamlet in Norway where I intended to do fieldwork as part of my postgraduate studies in social anthropology. I was born and brought up in Norway, albeit in an urban area. So this was not fully 'anthropology at home'. My plan was to spend the next twelve months there in order to follow life in the valley through all seasons. Partly inspired by the Green Wave of that time, I was drawn towards the countryside, with the intention of studying changing values and ideologies among the rural population. As this hamlet had long been known to me as the cradle of my patrilineal kin and moreover had interested me due to the unusual clustering of the houses, it was a suitable locus for my research. Maybe the idea of the bounded 'village', as a surveyable unit for an anthropological study, also attracted me.[1] The hamlet consisted of about a dozen farms and fifty people. The close proximity of the houses, as well as the system of ownership and usage of the land, created an interesting social framework for social interaction. The hamlet was situated in a valley with other farms and hamlets, and seven kilometres away a service centre was located by the fjord of that district. Although the hamlet became the immediate focus of my research, much information was also gathered from the wider village area.

Through previous contacts with one of the men in the hamlet, I was invited to stay with him and his family on their farm. My host was a widower, and apart from him and his elder brother – both middle-aged – the family included the widower's under-aged son. I was received in a hospitable manner, and felt that I was quickly integrated into the household through our long chats during the winter days. I told them about the anthropological idea of participant observation, which they found interesting, and they assumed the responsibility for exposing me to a farmer's way of life seriously.[2] In fact, various people in the hamlet expressed their approval and told me they were impressed that an urban girl wanted to participate in and learn various work tasks related to farming and country life in general.[3] However, while my manual labour was applauded, I was occasionally quizzed about the objectives of my study and what I intended to write about the hamlet.

While farm life is very busy from early morning until late at night throughout the summer months, life in winter is more dormant. Apart from milking and tending to the animals for some few hours morning and evening, people kept inside their homes through much of the day. During the first few weeks I went for daily walks in the alleys between the houses hoping to meet villagers, but never saw anybody. Apart from the occasional lights from a car leaving or returning to the hamlet, the only sign of life was the row of lights from the windows of the barns and the nearby sound of the milking machines twice a day. The alleys and the surrounding fields were covered by snow, and daylight lasted only a few hours every day.

Through the members of my host household, however, I did get acquainted with a few other persons in the hamlet during the first weeks. Upon our first meetings, some of the farmers told me that in this hamlet, with its dense settlement, people lived as if they were 'one big family', an expression I heard repeated on other occasions also. One of the persons to whom I had been introduced was an elderly farmer, who was considered to be knowledgeable on various matters pertaining to the hamlet. I soon realised that this man was a very good informant who would enlighten me systematically about the past and present in the valley. He had spent nearly all his life here and could talk for hours on the various activities on the farm as well as on the background of the other local families. He would sometimes tell me that the explanation for what had happened or decisions made could be found in the less flattering traits or conduct of some persons (like alcohol and/or physical abuse). This also pertained to stories told about himself and his family. Once, he was in the course of telling me about something slightly sensitive and said, in his careful manner, that he would like me to know both the good and the bad sides of the story. Another person from the village, who had shown a special interest in my research, was listening in the background. Now he interrupted and said that my informant should not say such things about the village. Their task was to draw attention to the positive qualities of the farmers and not to spread slander. He later added he would point out those whom I should interview and socialise with. He could in fact take me around and introduce me to those I should talk to, as he knew many of those who would be interesting for me. Others would best be avoided.

This event, of course, does not reflect anything unique for a fieldworker: on the contrary. It was, however, the first step in my understanding the basics of village dynamics. The emerging problem for me as a fieldworker was how to handle such attitudes from people who had become important actors in my fieldwork so far, both through their role as 'key' informants and as people I spent time with. On the one hand, I felt there were expectations as to whom I should mingle with and what I could and should discuss. On the other hand, there was the need for the anthropologist to socialise as widely as possible and gather all types of information. I became to a certain degree associated with my initial networks but, again, this did not entirely prevent access to other parts of the village community. Indeed, I found that people I came to know later on were interested in what had been going on among those I had mingled with previously. This became another lesson on village life for me.

One of the villagers I came to know during these first months was a bachelor. During my year in the village, he initiated several relationships, and naturally some of the other villagers were curious about them. As they knew I had done fieldwork there, they would question me more or less directly about these women – who they were and what was going on between them and the bachelor. I found this truly awkward, as I felt this to be a private matter between him and his female friends. Thus, I adopted a strategy of telling as little as possible, and politely but clearly conveyed the message that as a researcher my ethical duty was not to transmit private information from one household to the other. But the result of this consciously aloof attitude was simply that people lost interest in me. I was perceived as secretive and unresponsive. Moreover, my reluctance to participate in this exchange of gossip seemed to turn me into a sort of asocial non-person. So I understood that something more substantial had to be conveyed, but struggled with the decision of what to tell and how much to say. I felt that villagers saw me both too close-mouthed and too lax with information and I was painfully aware that I was not very good at achieving the right balance.[4]

The next challenge became my relationship to this bachelor's girlfriends. Sexual relationships are everywhere fraught with difficulties, and this was not less so in the valley. As I was available and willing to listen to whoever approached me, I was sought out as a confidant not only by the bachelor, but – as another female – also by the women, before a final decision was made to give up the relationship. A lot of interesting data could potentially be distilled from what I observed and overheard and, not least, from what I was told by each of the unhappy parties. But, even so, this double position of attempting to befriend both parties in this affairs was not received well by the suitor, and I was accused of meddling negatively in the relationships.

Moving into Another Position

As the months went by, my interaction with people in the hamlet intensified. I spent time participating in farm work, especially giving a helping hand with the cows and other animals in the barn. My host family was very forthcoming in introducing me to all kinds of activities, which made fieldwork pleasant. I still recall the satisfying feeling of having performed something truly meaningful after milking and feeding the cows, as well as cleaning their stalls in the early morning. This was a feeling I seldom achieved during my normal life as a student.

Apart from hours of interesting conversation with members of my host family and others, much time was also spent throughout the winter and early spring writing down so-called 'hard fact information' on village life. In between these activities I went for long walks with my host family's sheepdog along the strips of the fields, and also further into the outland in the surrounding hills. This gave me time to restructure my thoughts, but also to bump into villagers tending the forest or doing some repair work on a road or a bridge. These encounters could spur small talk and questions. Sometimes however, the closeness of village life became too much for me. Although people were forthcoming, it was difficult staying for so long in the same environment and I started to miss the long talks with my fellow students and friends from town. When I found the situation becoming unbearable, I would take my small car and drive not only to the village centre some kilometres away, but continue further across the mountain roads to some other villages. Although much of this area was bustling with activities during summer and the tourist season, wintertime is quite the contrary. But these long drives on my own made things easier, and on my way back – as I drove up the valley towards the hamlet – I almost literally came to see both rural life and my own behaviour and position there in a new and refreshed perspective.

After spending the winter and spring in the hamlet, I had nevertheless developed a compelling urge to be more on my own and, to a greater degree, be able to regulate more of my daily interaction with people. Simultaneously my host family was expecting various visiting relatives during the summer season and was therefore possibly in need of more space to house their visitors. I found this to be a good opportunity to change my abode, and found a small cottage which I moved into, located on a farm slightly outside the hamlet. In this area, the farms were more scattered and with their surrounding fields gathered in one piece. So I took leave of my host family, who had generously taken me into their house, and – I would say – confidence.

My new residence had its own challenges. While my former household consisted of males only, I now came to interact daily with the farmer's wife on the farm where my cottage was situated. Actually, she was a middle-aged widow, but although the farm had been handed over to her son who lived in another house on the farm, she continued to involve herself in farm activities like milking and taking care of the animals. Apart from assisting her occasionally in odd jobs on the farm, I spent many an evening together with her in her house, doing needlework while we chatted about life in the valley and life in general. Perhaps she appreciated a companion with whom she could discuss matters, which was not always available in the vicinity. For me, she became both a companion and indirectly a mentor on village culture.

A recurrent theme among many of the farmers was the condition and management of the various farms in the valley. But households that were rumoured to be experiencing family troubles also sometimes became a topic for discussion. During my stay in the valley, there were some families that were rumoured to have experienced problems for some time, and where separation could be a possible result. This was in the 1970s, and to my knowledge matrimonial break-ups were not so common in the area. In terms of inheritance, it was generally accepted that one of the sons would eventually succeed his father on the farm and should therefore be brought up and trained there. In the case of divorce, however, the children would most likely follow their mother whilst their father would remain on the farm. These matters preoccupied people in the village, and became the topic of several conversations I heard and participated in, not least since I had occasionally been in contact with one such family and some relatives. First and foremost villagers speculated on the possibility that this couple would actually split up. Perhaps because I was an outsider, I was asked directly for information that could shed light on this. And opinions were expressed as to which party in the marriage was at fault and what measures ought to be taken.

The relatives of the family were, of course, worried about the situation. They felt uncertain about the future and the position of the farm, and were curious as to whether I had heard any rumours about what was going on in the marriage, about the intentions of the couple, what people in the village felt about the situation, and so forth. As I rambled around the valley chatting with people, it was expected that I would pick up rumours. And lastly, members of the affected household themselves might bring up the subject when we met, and expressed everything from pain and anger to confusion about their own situation. As I attempted to have an open attitude in order to obtain an insight into the different viewpoints, I experienced the fact that the anthropologist – through her feedbacks – not only used her own self as a resource in understanding other people, but also became a possible resource to them. Again, I found the circumstances challenging as to what information I could and should hand on to others.

This time I felt a greater freedom to move around in the village without feeling that I had to give explanations. I could simply leave my cottage and venture venture along the fields without being observed by others. Living in the midst of the hamlet had meant that any venture out of the house was potentially spotted. And moving to a place outside the hamlet meant there was even less chance of me being associated with any of the families. While I had been identified with particular groups of people in the hamlet people had sometimes found it difficult to talk freely with me about one another's activities. After moving out of the hamlet, I was given more information about some of those I had spent time with when living in the hamlet. This new information helped enormously in illuminating the nature of social relationships in the village. Furthermore, I found that this new information altered, or at least supplemented, the picture that was conveyed both by themselves and others during the previous period of my stay in the hamlet. This information related primarily to events that had taken place before my arrival and which set the history of some of these families and farms in a somewhat different light. At the same time they could be praised for the way they had coped with past problems, and favourable qualities referring to the same people were also accentuated. Although gossip was readily transmitted, it could quickly be balanced by other mitigating information.

The fact that after moving out of the village I stayed on my own prompted more visitors to come and see me, and especially single persons. Some saw my new place as somewhere they might consume liquor, an activity not always appreciated by other villagers. Perhaps the anthropologist's position as an insider/outsider opened up a liminal space. I had to strike a balance here as to the signals I communicated; moderate drinking was accepted though it had to be within the bounds of social acceptability. It was important for me to establish a certain reputation, not only vis-à-vis my visitors but also towards other villagers. My new position, living on my own and partly secluded from the view of other villagers, necessitated this in a different manner from before. A balance was sought between appearing liberal, but not seeming excessively compliant. It was now easier to establish an intimate conversation as this was often a setting without other listeners, and some confidential words were uttered during these visits. For some of my guests, the visits may have functioned as a place where they could let off some steam from the everyday pressure of social life.

Emerging Theory

I have chosen to focus on two slightly different positions that I experienced when moving from one homestead to another during my fieldwork, and how they created conflicting demands upon my social and ethical behaviour. I have also presented two sensitive situations pertaining to sexual relationships in the village which created some concerns among people and which demanded that I could not be indifferent to those involved. That is, my 'neutral position' as a researcher (if there is such a thing) was challenged. These situations stand as epitomes of the challenges I felt throughout the year of my fieldwork in the valley.

Going through my diary afterwards brought back memories stored as pictures or snapshots, sounds and smells. Reading about the first preparations of the fields in spring, I could smell the melting snow and ice as well as the dung spread out on the plots. The cold in the air and the fragrance from the falling leaves of the trees in autumn would also come back as I read about my experiences later that year. I would actually 'hear' the echo of the occasional shot from hunters in the valley preparing for the deer hunt. And as I read about the statements of the people I quoted, I could hear each of their voices speaking in their characteristic dialect. But, more interestingly, my various moods and emotions would come back when I read. As I approached delicate situations in my diary, I would experience feelings of anxiety and frustration. On the other hand, through slacker passages in my daily records, reflecting what I perceived as a lack of interesting data, feelings of helplessness and desolation could emerge. Of course, there were other situations that brought back happy memories of walks in the forest and the mountains with their spectacular views, warm feelings related to intimate conversations in the late evenings, and laughter pertaining to funny events during an occasional drinking spree. My diary was written in a fairly 'matter-of-fact' manner. Although I aimed at rich descriptions of what occurred as interesting situations, there was little or no mention of my own feelings and reactions to the event. Reading these 'factual' notes nevertheless triggered a whole range of emotions. And, as memories descended upon me and I relived my year in the countryside, I came to realise that I had possibly touched upon some of the same experiences and challenges that villagers themselves have faced.[5]

Such perceived cross-pressures as described above are something anthropologists experience every now and then in their diffuse roles as researchers, outsiders, visitors, household members and friends. But I felt this challenge so persistently and ubiquitously that I started paying special attention to how the villagers themselves had handled comparable situations. How much did they mix with each other, and what characterised their interaction? My conclusion was that there were some 'instrumental' occasions when people in the hamlet met, albeit less often than in the past. They would meet to decide on various matters regarding property and labour, and to execute some tasks jointly. Their houses and courtyards were situated close to each other, which called for cooperation and a certain understanding between them in order to facilitate social life. At that time, their fields were still scattered, which necessitated different arrangements to coordinate the maintenance and use of roads. And some of the farmers held joint ownership of machines, which demanded regulations on usage. Now and then, a member of one family would make a short visit to their neighbour to borrow or sort out something. Neighbours would also participate in ritual occasions such as funerals, but again this was much more pronounced in earlier decades, when such arrangements demanded the assistance of others. But some of the families in the hamlet were also related and this would naturally imply more social involvement with their kin even today.

Social gatherings followed certain patterns of procedure, which included, for instance, legitimate topics and careful manners of speech. They enabled people to communicate their acknowledgement of each other and, to a certain degree, re-establish or, within limits, contest common values, moral norms and views of the world. Their status as fellow villagers was re-established, and secured the continuation of social life in the valley. The most interesting part, however, could be observed when they stumbled into each other informally or paid each other the occasional visit for some demanding purpose. Their behaviour would then be characterised by a certain demeanour; they would never ignore each other, but (perhaps after some silence) take time to address each other following certain set rules. There would be a lot of seemingly neutral small talk, but during these conversations careful questions about each other and other villagers were indirectly asked, and information was given in the same way. Hints were made, but not one-sided judgements or opinions that could later be used against them. Through the response to these hints the other party could then carefully signal whether or not they understood and 'knew', and if they 'accepted' the contents of this rumour. At the same time, nothing had been explicitly stated. When witnessing these encounters, I was often left with a vague feeling that I had not perceived what was actually going on. Much of the talk was indexical: as an outsider I often did not know the people, events or circumstances that were mentioned, and would therefore not grasp the whole context in comparison with those who shared the same background and only needed a few cues in order to understand. But still I grasped this feeling of something meaningful being communicated purposely. Only during drinking sessions, which mainly involved some of the male villagers, would controversial opinions be voiced explicitly. But these would be presented more as a series of partly unrelated and uncontested monologues.

As I started to review my fieldwork from an analytical distance, I drew the conclusion that the villagers had developed special manners of interaction as a direct way of tackling the difficult social demands made upon them. These demands were found to arise from a structural situation where the need of each farm unit to take care of its own interests had to be balanced against the need to cooperate and cohabit with their neighbours in the hamlet. I came in fact to see much of the culture as permeated by ways of coping with these cross-pressures. And I came to reject the idiom of the hamlet as one big family, at least if a major criterion for a family is a certain degree of intimacy and common interest. I came to the conclusion that adult villagers simply found it awkward to befriend their neighbours.

The notion of friendship needs elaboration. Following Eric Wolf we can distinguish between expressive or emotional friendship and instrumental friendship (Wolf 1969 [1966]: 10); my use is closest to the first category.[6] What I found somewhat lacking, was the rather regular and continuous interaction between two (unrelated) persons in the neighbourhood that involved confidential statements of private information, followed by discretion and support by the other party. On the other hand I sometimes heard villagers introduce people that we bumped into as 'their best friend'. This I would take to be an amiable or strategic gesture to please the other party. Symptomatically these people did not currently live in the village, although they may have been attached to it previously.

In some ways the hamlet did resemble the image of a family; people were always present in the vicinity, they interacted and would certainly lend a helping hand if needed. Although villagers would talk about each other using critical and funny remarks, they could on the next occasion speak of the same person in an empathetic way. This balanced and multifaceted picture is perhaps a trait that is characteristic for those who have cohabited and known each other for generations. What I found fairly restrained among villager people was – in a liberal usage of Goffman's terminology –the confidential 'backstage' behaviour that could be found predominantly within households. In these private places, sensitive information was exchanged and discussed rather freely, leaving the 'front region' behaviour for neighbours and others in the surrounding world (Goffman 1972 [1959]: 109ff.). As I observed the villagers moving into the immediate world outside the family, the carefully balanced mode of interaction became noticeable.

At the time of my fieldwork there were many children and youths in the hamlet, as the majority of farmers were in their forties and fifties. Coming back a few years later and meeting some of them who in the meantime had taken up farm work, strengthened this view of village behaviour. It turned out that they had adopted many of the same mannerisms as their parents, which had not been so noticeable before. These young men were preparing themselves for taking over their parents' farm, and were representing its interest. Their cautious behaviour became a fitting strategy towards this end.

Whose Story is This?

Thus it was that I found village life to be a perpetual struggle both to maximise the economic interest of the farm and at the same time to balance this against one's own reputation as competent farmer and good neighbour. This middle course could be hard to strike: one should be industrious, but not stingy; forthcoming, but not gossipy; and sociable, but not work-shy or lazy.[7] Some of the villagers managed to do this rather well, while others fell somewhat short of living up to these expectations. This understanding of village life came to permeate both my thesis and related publications (Larsen 1981, 1984). Years later, however, I started to question the premises of my model. Although I still support the main contentions, I asked myself whether people in this *Gemeinschaft* really experienced their social life as a 'razor's edge'.

Although much of the cultural context in this rural setting was something that was also found in the urban life that was familiar to me, I had come to focus on the differences that struck me. Social life in town was characterised by more diversity of subcultures, thus allowing for a greater array from which to choose whom you mingled with. Intimate information could be shared within certain confident relations disconnected from more compelling relations. This situation allowed for a cherished freedom, I thought – but had I come to exaggerate its importance? Perhaps the family idiom was not the myth I perceived it to be; perhaps the interaction among people in the hamlet did, after all, counteract feelings of loneliness, providing them with a common identity, assurance and some sympathy towards each other – though in a muted and seemingly distanced manner.

Reviewing some of my later studies, I further came to see that I often use models that carry the notions of conflict, as for instance the cognitive dissonance model (see Larsen 1996), and started wondering whether this was an idiosyncrasy of my own way of thinking and my own ways of experiencing social environments. Could it be that my own frustrations with ambiguous and contradictory values, ideologies, expectations, etc. were projected unduly into the field situation? That the embarrassment I felt when confronted with such matters in the field basically reflected my own personality, reinforced by the insecurity of youth and my unclear position in the community? In spite of being an outsider, I ventured to ask fairly personal questions; I was (initially) a household member, who nevertheless visited all the other households; I was a scholar and a writer, but at the same time a young, unmarried girl – and so on and so forth. Interestingly enough, the majority of my interactions were not with people in my own generation, but with the middle-aged and older people in the community. This was partly a reflection of the fact that older people were seen as those being able to provide me with interesting data of the past and present, which gave us some cause to interact, especially in the first months of my stay. But I also think that those my own age, who in other context would constitute my natural comrades, could find my presence awkward and did not know how to relate to someone who, in spite of age similarities, seemed so different.

Later in life, I came to think that my own role during this apprentice fieldwork could have been handled differently. Instead of seeking ways to oblige everyone and to avoid conflict, which I abhorred, I could gradually have signalled a clearer stand and dared to voice my opinion more strongly. Perhaps I should have been more choosy regarding whom I befriended or became close to, not least since friendship was a difficult type of relation to handle among grown-ups in the valley. I could furthermore also have adopted a careful, diplomatic manner, which might have resulted in a different quality of interaction. To use Goffman's term, giving off signals that I was less associated with particular persons and households might have paved the way for a greater interaction with the villagers (Goffman 1972 [1959]: 14). In short, I could have presented a more conciliatory and yet assertive stand. Margaret E. Kenna maintains that the anthropologist is very likely to make a fool of herself and become humiliated during her first fieldwork, but will later acquire more experience and a greater self-assertiveness which leads to a more adequate comportment (Kenna 2004 [1992]: 150). I would add that the anthropologist later in life has gained not only more professional experience, but also life experience and a certain social standing that may be of pertinence for her fieldwork interpretations. But, again, will such experiences carry other biases, and, with reference to my own study, which theoretical paradigm might then have evolved?

It is useful to be reminded that there are two sides of our fieldwork position that need to be considered. We have come to recognise that anthropological data are something collected in the course of interaction *between* the anthropologist and the 'informant' (Rabinow 1977: 38–39, 119; Hastrup 2005 [1995]: 16). Not only do our different stances furnish us with different pairs of spectacles through which social life can be viewed and interpreted, but our very positions and dispositions also elicit certain reactions and behaviours from our surroundings. Many anthropologists have emphasised how they tried to take on and even internalise the appropriate forms of conduct in the society they study (see for instance Kondo 1990: 11ff.; Coffey 1999: 65–66). This may bring about a greater acceptance by their hosts and make the anthropologist blend in among the informants so that life can go on as normal. On the other hand, abnormal or less acceptable behaviour may also bring about interesting reactions from the people you study, and may actually make evident cultural norms and values that are otherwise hidden or obscure.[8]

So, just as there may be numerous variations of the relationship between the anthropologist and those she studies, this only reflects the numerous facets of the cultures we intend to describe. This was certainly the case in my interaction with Norwegian farmers. Since my initial fieldwork, undertaken in my mid-twenties, I have kept more or less regularly in touch with some of the people in the valley. If possible, I visit the place for a couple of days every year. But since I arrived there as a novice, my life as an anthropologist has also evolved. I have since come to do fieldwork in South-East Asia as well as in the Middle East. And I believe that my involvement with Eastern cultures has resulted in a more Asian and 'refined' comportment, which I carry back into my Norwegian field and which is sometimes exposed. Moreover, coming back to the village, my old informants are eager to hear about and discuss the places I have visited and the ways of life there. The world has grown smaller, and they are interested in the Muslim question and hearing about the poorer parts of the world.[9] Growing diversity of experience, both in and out of the field, brings new dimensions into my interactions, and adds new angles to my perception of village life. Some of my previous findings have been substantiated, while other understandings are being elaborated or modified. And the experience of both the young and the middle-aged anthropologist contributes to this picture. But it must also be remembered that this is not quite the same hamlet as it was almost thirty years ago.

Conclusion

I have tried to show that information on village life was not simply something 'out there' that could be reaped as a bounded and integrated entity. The position and disposition of the anthropologist, including her age and sex as well as personality traits, may bring about different responses from different people, and the contents and frequency of the interaction between her and her research participants will vary. What is more, as time goes by, the initial self-righteousness and spirit of adventure of the young anthropologist may gradually be replaced by an accumulated experience that allows for a greater insight and tolerance, but which perhaps is also charged with a more rigid outlook. This may then bring forth new types of engagements and also relationships with old informants. The hamlet can be compared with a diamond; as light reflects upon it, it shines back. But its colour, intensity and brightness will change according to the type and angle of the ray that hits it. The ideal research tool would have been something equating 'sunlight', then, which contains the whole range of visible wavelengths, revealing all aspects of village life. That, however, cannot be accomplished by a solitary fieldworker. She may, however, through various approaches, be able to grasp some of the important dimensions that constitute the composite character of the community. The alternative is to turn off the light altogether in order to avoid these often subtle and complex, everchanging appearances. Although we can still feel and measure the hard facts of the stone, the shine and beauty of the gem will be lost.

Notes

I would like to thank the editors of this volume and Solrun Williksen for their comments and suggestions.

1. The present-day Norwegian countryside is characterised by its scattered location of farms.
2. The term 'farmer' may include all family members on a farm.
3. Judith Okely has described how her participation in manual farm activities during fieldwork in Normandy softened up the farmers' stereotypical view of her and facilitated the communication between them as they now had some shared experiences (Okely 1992: 17).
4. Max Gluckman has brought attention to the difficult position of the anthropologist in relation to gossip during fieldwork (Gluckman 1963: 307–16).
5. This brings to mind Unni Wikan's notion of how resonance between people enables us to understand others (Wikan 1992).
6. Robert Paine later pointed out that it is hard to imagine the existence of either one of these friendships without including qualities of the other, and is therefore sceptical of a clear dichotomy between them (Paine 1969: 506).
7. This is reminiscent of Nigel Rapport's experience of a farmer's wife in the English village where he conducted fieldwork. The anthropologist felt victimised by her frequent disapproval of his actions, and found himself trapped in a series of double-binds that condemned his behaviour whatever he did (Rapport 1992).
8. Alfred Gell has described how he by chance got on the trail of a cultural norm among the Umeda of New Guinea. During fieldwork he once accidentally cut himself in the finger and automatically put the bleeding limb to his lips. The shocked and disgusted expressions of the onlookers made him realise that he had broken a food taboo (Gell 1996: 116).
9. During my second period of fieldwork, carried out in Malaysia during 1988–92, people were interested in conversing about the ways of life in my native country. When I returned to this field twelve years later, people were also eager to discuss my new experiences among the Bedouin during ongoing fieldwork in the United Arab Emirates.

References

Coffey, A. 1999. *The Ethnographic Self: Fieldwork and the Representation of Identity.* London: Sage.

Gell, A. 1996. 'Reflections on a Cut Finger: Taboo in the Umeda Conception of the Self', in M. Jackson (ed.), *Things as They Are.* Bloomington and Indianapolis: Indiana University Press, pp. 115–27.

Gluckman, M. 1963. 'Papers in Honor of Melville J. Herskovits: Gossip and Scandal', *Current Anthropology* 4(3): 307–16.

Goffman, E. 1972 [1959]. *The Presentation of Self in Everyday Life.* London: Penguin Books.

Hastrup, K. 2005 [1995]. *A Passage to Anthropology: Between Experience and Theory.* London: Routledge.

Kenna, M.E. 2004 [1992]. 'Changing Places and Altered Perspectives: Research on a Greek Island in the 1960s and in the 1980s', in J. Okely and H. Callaway (eds), *Anthropology and Autobiography* (ASA Monograph 29). London and New York: Routledge, pp. 147–62.

Kondo, D.K. 1990. *Crafting Selves: Power, Gender, and Discourses of Identity in a Japanese Workplace.* Chicago: University of Chicago Press.

Larsen, A.K. 1981. *Frøysa i Sunnylven: naboskap på et vestnorsk mangbølt klyngetun i historisk og komparativt perspektiv.* Master's thesis, Oslo: University of Oslo.

———. 1984 '"Elska din granne, men lat grinda stande" – sosialt samvær i en vestnorsk bygd', in A.M. Klausen (ed.), *Den norske væremåten. Antropologisk søkelys på norsk kultur.* Oslo: J. W. Cappelens forlag AS, pp. 164–77.

———. 1996. 'The impact of the Islamic Resurgence on the Belief System of the Rural Malays', *Temenos: Studies in Comparative Religion* 32: 137–54.

Okely, J. and Callaway, H. (eds). 1992. *Anthropology and Autobiography* (ASA Monographs 29). London and New York: Routledge.

Okely, J. 1992. 'Participatory Experience and Embodied Knowledge', in J. Okely and H. Callaway (eds.), *Anthropology and Autobiography* (ASA Monographs 29). London and New York: Routledge, pp. 1–28.

Paine, R. 1969. 'In Search of Friendship: An Exploratory Analysis in "Middle-Class" Culture', *Man* (NS) 4(4): 505–24.

Rabinow, P. 1977. *Reflections on Fieldwork in Morocco.* Berkeley: University of California Press.

Rapport, N. 1992. 'From Affect to Analysis: the Biography of an Interaction in an English Village', in J. Okely and H. Callaway (eds), *Anthropology and Autobiography* (ASA Monographs 29). London and New York: Routledge, pp. 193–204.

Rosaldo, R. 1984. 'Grief and Headhunter's Rage', in E. M. Bruner (ed.), *Text, Play and Story.* Washington, DC: American Ethnological Society, pp. 178–95.

Wikan, U. 1992. 'Beyond the Words: the Power of Resonance', *American Ethnologist*, 19(3), 460–82.

Wolf, Eric R. 1969 [1966]. 'Kinship, Friendships and Patron-client Relations in Complex Societies', in M. Banton (ed.), *The Social Anthropology of Complex Societies* (ASA Monographs 4). London: Tavistock Publications, pp. 1–22.

Chapter 5

THE ETHICS OF PARTICIPANT OBSERVATION: PERSONAL REFLECTIONS ON FIELDWORK IN ENGLAND

Nigel Rapport

Introduction

In his acclaimed *Reflections on Fieldwork in Morocco* (1977), Paul Rabinow argued that the strength of an interpretive social science lay in experiential, reflective and critical activity; certainly, to sociocultural anthropology, a positivistic stance was not appropriate. For anthropologists and the informants they met 'in the field' lived in different ongoing life-worlds: the point of fieldwork and its recounting was to set up a third world of partial meeting and translation (Rabinow 1977: 5, 151).

In the years since Rabinow's reflections, such ideas have been developed into their own sub-genre, amounting to a template for a new type of activity and a new type of product to be called anthropological research (Rapport 1994). George Marcus describes anthropology's primary data as deriving from the anthropologist's personal relations in the field; to turn these into the epistemological basis of further interpretation and objectivation then calls for self-reflection (1980: 508). There are no real things there – 'cultures', 'societies' – to serve as the absolute objects of an anthropological description: there are only the constitutive discourses in which fieldworkers have partaken while engaging in the activity of research.

As a product, then, anthropological research should convey a sense of its own locatedness: of its political, historical, philosophical precedents and implications. More nearly, it should express a sense of the emergence of its data through particular personal relations and particular discourses.

Like a modernist novel, research should be presented so as to highlight the discourse between the writer and his subjects, not having them as the passive mouthpieces of the writer's omniscient views. In this way, the substance of the research account emerges as if through dialogue, a 'dialogic imagination' (Collins 2002), through an interweaving and a juxtaposition of views from different life-worlds which thus come to be connected. The ultimate product is characterised neither by an authorial transcendence nor by a final authorial synthesis. The text that emerges, it must be accepted, has ambiguities that are ineradicable, and meanings that are infinite and ineffable. Finally, it is through this unresolved juxtaposition of interwoven voices that cultural critique is to be effected; through a reciprocal probing into two or more life-worlds, questions can be framed from whose challenge neither side can hope to escape.

This kind of anthropological self-reflection has become well-known and widely rehearsed, not to say canonised. What I undertake here is a personal reflection on two aspects of this template for 'writing culture': *first, an admittance of self-criticism into the product of research and, second, an emphasis on emergence in the activity of research.* Emergence is the keynote: it is an *emergent* world of social relations that is to be represented, in a textual form that will *emerge* from an interweaving of perspectives on the social world, and which is intended to eventuate in an *emergent* sense of social reality in the text's reader (including its writer). Here is ethnography – the activity and the product – as a becoming: not only a record of experience but a making of experience by a writer and a means of experience for a reader. To write, in Stephen Tyler's pithy phrasing, is to 'bring something into presence', something not there before (1986: 131). Ethnography is writing social reality.

And because of this, it seems to me, ethnography can also 'right' social reality. An emergent ethnography can set itself up in a critical position to the living that preceded it. If new social relations are being described, in a new way, so as to evoke a new sense of social reality, then the juxtaposition between this and the existing, the old, is tantamount to ethnography taking up an ethical position.

It is the notion of an emergent moral text that I elaborate upon in what follows, in the context of an account of the first fieldwork that I undertook in the rural, upland village and dale of Wanet, in north-west England. In particular, by centring my account on social relations in which I played a significant part, on the personae 'Nigel Rapport' adopted in the field, and by juxtaposing these relations and personae with those I was party to previously – relations and personae I consciously kept distant, kept secret, from Wanet – I hope to exhibit the emergence of a moral ethnography: a coming to terms with the moral precedents and implications of my work, and the discerning of a personal-moral position from which to engage with an audience.

Through recollections of a first fieldwork, this chapter works towards prescription of both a methodological and a social-political kind. Here is an attempt by 'Nigel Rapport' at once to write and right social reality.

An Emergence of Routine Relations in the Field

Wanet is a narrow rural dale, situated in a very scenic area of upland, northern England. Traditionally, Wanet's economy centred around pastoral hill farming with a full accompaniment of artisans and traders. This was not a peasant economy, however, for the community was wholly party to the cash nexus, individual farmers and their farm-labourers producing cash crops (wool, beef and milk, primarily) for a commodity market that included ready sales of land and labour. The economy was nonetheless based on large numbers of people labouring on the land; nowadays, farming remains the single most frequent occupation but it is mechanised farming, on a larger scale, catering for far fewer family units and fewer paid labourers.

Wanet's comparative remoteness and distance from urban centres of population have entailed no isolation from city folk. The railways began bringing in large numbers of visitors to sample the scenery in the latter years of the nineteenth century and, since then, the building of the motorways and the popularisation of the private car have brought more. In recent years Wanet has seen an influx of residential newcomers, buying up property in the dale, raising prices and making housing scarce. Some of this purchasing is for holiday homes. Most, however, is for houses to retire to, or houses to escape the urban rat race in while still following one's profession as artist, architect or teacher, or even still commuting to the high-tech job in the city. Of the 650 residents of the dale, then, some 190 are now relative newcomers – or 'offcomers': come from 'off-aways'. A National Park encompassing Wanet (and much else) was set up in the 1950s to regulate the traffic of visitors to an area of 'outstanding natural beauty' but it also served to preserve the heritage and 'settled village harmony' of the place. Standing between residents and tourists, the Park wardens and officers ensure littering laws are abided by, footpaths are kept open and kept to, and alterations to local land use and buildings do not go against local traditions – drystone walls, stone farmhouses, divisions of land into treeless high allotments, pastures and valley bottom meadows beside the tree-lined beck.

The largest gathering of houses in the dale is known as Wanet village – or, more affectionately (and harking back to a history of more prominence), Wanet Town. Around 180 people live here. But there are also smaller if less nucleated gatherings and hamlets in the dale such as Thurn, Robbgill and

Riggdale. It is in these gatherings of houses that the offcomers tend to live – especially Wanet Town – while the farmhouses that dot the fell-sides at various heights tend to remain in the hands of the locals. And the tourists tend to gather in these centres too – again especially Wanet Town – when not walking the lanes and the fells or caving in the dale's potholes. Most of the shops in the dale are now geared to the tourist trade (cafes, souvenir, knick-knack and craft shops) and they are to be found in the centres of settlement, as are the guest houses and the dale's three pubs – the Eagle and the Mitre (Wanet Town) and the Spade and Becket (Thurn). However, the distinction is not a hard-and-fast one, and, while Wanet Town might be swamped on a fine summer weekend with hundreds of sightseers, and while many local people now drive out of the dale to do their shopping at supermarkets, many locals live in the main gatherings of houses too (and compete with offcomer money when a cottage goes on sale at auction), and local farms and their land and buildings abut directly onto them too. Above all, the main gatherings – especially Wanet Town and Thurn – still feel like the centres of the dale, moreover still attached to their historical hinterlands. Not just the pubs, then, but the churches and most chapels are here, and the primary schools and the doctors' surgeries and the post office. This is where the dale's Parish Council meets, and the Parochial Church Council, and the Charities' Committee and the Sports Committee and the Reading Room Association and the Women's Institute and the Mothers' Union, as well as newer organisations such as the Wanet Commerce Corporation, the Badminton Club, the Choral Society, the Thurn Thespians and so on.

Moreover, the distinction between locals and offcomers is not hard and fast either. While pervasive for some people at some moments, it is irrelevant for and at others, when any number of very different distinctions can come to the fore: updale (Wanet Town) versus downdale (Thurn); Methodists versus Church of England; those who work the land versus those who do not; those highly capitalised farmers in the 'big league' versus those just getting by on crowded, rented plots; those in business, who profit from the tourists, versus those who do not; the young drinkers of the Mitre versus the old hands of the Eagle; domino players versus darts throwers; Tetley beer drinkers versus Courage beer drinkers; beer drinkers versus lager drinkers; weekend drinkers versus regular drinkers. And so on.

I was twenty three when I moved into Wanet in 1980: an anthropology doctoral student undertaking a year's field research on changes in English rural life. The gradual process by which I became part of habitual 'talking relationships' and acquired a number of local 'talking partners', as well as my feelings about the experience, cannot be the specific subject of this essay (see Rapport 1993). Suffice it to say that in my attempts to fit in with the life and practice I found in Wanet, to accommodate myself to what I understood of the people I met, I offered myself for work most days as a casual farm labourer (on a farm run by Fred and Doris Harvey), before visiting people in their houses, shops and cafes, and drinking in the local pubs at night, and playing darts and dominoes, and on whist drives, and singing carols and acting in plays, and organising youth clubs and Sunday School parties, and attending meetings of various committees and the Parish Council. My interest lay in participating locally in as much as I was able and in taking note of what I heard and saw. I could not be too naive about this – people were too suspicious of outsiders, nervy about offcomers and foreign spies and terrorists and tax inspectors and dole scroungers, to countenance snoopers – but as discreetly as possible I adapted myself to local expectations, learned what and how to say and act. Being a farm lad, a darts partner and so on helped me escape the suspect category of 'student', of being too 'academic' and 'bookish' – words of foreignness and no little disparagement. Indeed, overtly to ask questions of local people and their lives was, by definition, a 'foreign' pursuit, for British people would know the same things anyway without asking. To ask questions was not merely nosy but a challenge to local identities. Who was the real Briton? Who had the right to be living in Wanet? And whose information on Britain and Wanet and even themselves was better, more intelligent, more extensive, more traditional and more useful and relevant today? Learning to belong meant knowing without asking.

To complete this brief introduction to Wanet, let me convey something of the sense I had of two of the people I was most close to: Doris Harvey and Sid Askrig. Doris ran a farm with her husband Fred, on which I worked most days as an apprentice farmhand, and Sid was a builder employed by Doris and Fred to put up a new farm shed, to whom I was assigned for a number of months as a builder's mate. Both Doris and Sid were born and bred in Wanet, both are now in their thirties. Let me try to bring to life my sense of the two of them and of the relations that we shared by recounting and juxtaposing a few snippets of our conversation as I recorded it in my field journal – as Doris and I milked and mucked out the cows on Cedar High Farm or 'haytimed', or as Sid and I mixed cement and laid blocks. At least, as I was the young and more or less quiescent and acquiescent partner in the exchange, below are some of the habitual things *they* would say to me.

Doris and Me

You learn something new in the country every day, you know, Nigel. Being out on the farm is the best life ... And they say farming is more intelligent than other jobs too, 'cause when you learn them it's in. But on the farm there's a hundred and one things that can go wrong, like on a cow, and you gotta look after them all ... But city people have no idea. Most of the public are so stupid and short-sighted ... People are too soft now. They're just eager to finish work and sit down and watch telly or go out driving. I hate how soft everyone's got, and they're getting softer and softer.

I worked for every stick on this farm, you know, Nigel. But you want to do all of a job properly, without anyone's help, don't you? And get your own benefits. It's every man for himself and I'm working for the farm. I could never work for 'the nation' or for other people.

I've just realised how much more government control there is over us in the past few years. Before, we were separate but now we're ordered about by the National Park people and the District Council, and there's the Milk Marketing Board and the government at every turn. We're controlled now, Nigel ... And the real shame is how the government stops you working. They should give business and money interests priority.

I pity town-dwellers. I do, Nigel; I'd go mad there. It's a different mentality ... But why do they have to trail? I never have – more than a few hundred yards from one part of the dale to another. And they don't understand a village way of life but they always still try and change it. They say you gotta change with the times, but we're losing our character. Even the church has gone up the shit now – all pompous and fur coats 'cause of all these foreigners here.

Trouble is all the interbreeding we've *got here now, Nigel, of course. Invasions from* all over. Chinese, and lots of Arabs about. And Hebrews. And the curry-eaters that smell. And Blacks too ... I've nowt against these tribes mind, but it can't be natural for them here, can it? And they breed too fast, too. Like rats. And living twelve to a room: it's disgusting! Why do they let them? They should all go home and breed with their own kind ... I mean no animal likes breeding with another kind, does it? And they aren't really born to cities, are they? Nor clothes. I mean they're more used to running round jungles naked.

These rioters in Liverpool are disgusting, aren't they, Nigel! And now it's London and Manchester too. Why do they let them behave like that? They should lock them up with rats ... And I can't understand why the government is being so weak and soft. They just talk about an illness, and finding causes. There's no 'illness'. These rioters just need their wilfulness braying out of them.

Your kids should give you all you need in life, see Nigel. They should make you happy and I s'pose annoyed and make you cry sometimes too. But they still need pulling up on small matters 'cause little things grow to big ones. It's logical. And that reflects on the whole family. Cos there's still a right and a wrong way to be learnt ... And they say we just don't know all we'll have to answer for in the end ... I don't know: I'd happen murder mine if they stole.

I always vote Tory and I'd not vote at all before I voted Labour. It's been brayed into me. 'Cause only the Tories can give the country the harsh medicine it needs. It's too easy under Labour. Right, Nigel? Trouble is, so many people are uneducated and uninformed and naive to vote. Happen they shouldn't be allowed to ... Fred and me have sort of halfway tastes at the moment, anyway. But I did see a nice posh bank manager at Lloyds last week about a loan.

Folk prefer to pity you than envy you. They dislike it if you try and get ahead and make a little money and improve yourself. And be a bit bigger and better than you were. They soon change their opinions ... Aren't people horrible, Nigel? I hate Wanet sometimes.

Fred! I really think you should call Sid about that awful walling. Tell him to do it again on his own time. Or get Keith – or Nigel here – to redo it. That'd cap him. 'Cause we can't have the farm wall like that. People will come and think you did it!

Sid and Me

Walling's yet another of my skills, thou knows, lad. And I'm looking forward to starting here. I like this work. It either gets you fit or fucked. And you'll need a pair of gloves, lad, if you're gonna keep up with me. 'Cause you'll be lifting a few! I'm certainly gonna learn you something: you'll be seeing stones in front of your eyes before we're finished.

Kids today are just too cute by half, eh, Nigel? They'll argue with you that black is white and yellow's no colour at all. They're spoilt and always think you can get something for nothing. They don't respect you. They're just bread-grabbing buggers ... I mean, I was a bit mischievous as a lad but not hard to handle like kids today. Everything's a hassle to them. They know bugger all, but they think they're so intelligent that they won't be told. All they want is some aggro ... Like these soccer hooligans trying to look tough, with their boots on and jeans rolled up: if I found them on my plate I'd think they were a meal of spare ribs! ... No, what they need is discipline. Or else just shooting with sawn-off shotguns and burying in shit heaps.

When Doris and the wife and me were kids by Millwood Farm, we used to have great fun, Nigel. Even the weather was better in them days. And we lacked nowt ... People were different and all. Thoughtful, not spiteful and gossiping and laughing at each other.

It's these outsiders who are to blame. Everything worked better before they stuck their stumps in everywhere ... Us locals should get rid of them all. We shouldn't mix with them or cooperate or tell 'em what we think even. 'Cause these people can argue anything. And get you saying anything. And they always answer your question with another. Eh Nigel?

We should send the troops into Brixton and send all the Blacks home, right Nigel? I mean Amin threw out all those Whites from Uganda, didn't he? And English people should come home ... And in Ireland the same. They should give the army more of a free hand to sort them out. Either kill the lot of them or pull the troops out and let them sort themselves out ... Trouble is, the English must be the least violent race around. If this was America, that SAS lot would've got busy and shot up everything by now and it'd all be done with.

I know what I'll appreciate: when there's a civil war in this country between the police and all these agitators and demonstrators and half-caste types and Blacks. That's what this country needs and I know which side I'll be on. I just hope the police will call on me to help restore law and order ... Aye! That'll be the day, lad.

God, I'd like to do old Robby Baines. I would that, lad. I wish he'd cross me in public, then I'd have an excuse to drop him. If I was as ugly as him, I reckon I'd cut off my own head ... And Eddy Milden's another: narrow-backed, snout-nosed bastard. He just won't be told. Mean and arrogant and stupid. And if you say owt to him he goes crazy and opens his great gob and shouts hisself hoarse. Great twined bugger. Well, he's got a surprise coming next time I pass him on a public road `cause I'm gonna fill his gob with a bunch of fives. For free!

Nay but you're an idle lad, Nigel. Now just stop y' chittering or you'll get a slap round the lug and a gob-full of this calf shit ... I wish your tongue'd get *rigor mortis*! I do that. Now no more of your impudence. You don't even know enough not to argue, do you?

Well, I better get back and see what the wife's got for my tea tonight. Two mouldy crusts and a worm most likely, if the old bat's the wrong side out again like yesterday ... But, if she's not too twined, we'll see you for a jar at the Eagle later, Nige.

An Ethical Account of Relations in the Field

From positions of strangerhood and anomaly, from being just another offcomer in Wanet, what I achieved with Doris and with Sid were routine ways of behaving together which we regarded as legitimate, and which we regularly repeated. Our intercourse became habitual, something to be expected. And yet it was based on a deliberate act of separation and disguise, of my separating feelings and beliefs from outside Wanet from those I exhibited in relation to Doris and Sid within the dale. In particular, I had stopped using 'anthropology' as the explanatory label for my interests and activities, and settled for something that seemed locally suited: 'local social history'. Let me explain this decision, or at least place it in its disciplinary, circumstantial and biographical contexts.

Anthropologist Jean-Paul Dumont, considering, with the security and satisfaction of hindsight, his stock response to the (Venezuelan) Panare, while engaged in his fieldwork, that he had come to 'learn their language', reflects that at the time this half-truth satisfied him completely; the objects of his doctoral thesis, he treated his Panare with 'a paradoxical blend of absolute good and bad faith' (Dumont 1978: 43–44). He tried to make himself understandable in their terms, told himself he was not in the business of doing them harm and thus justified his presence to himself. The stakes, he recalls, were high after all: mistakes by him, rejection by them, and he could be out of anthropology and an academic career. That neither of these things happened is evidenced by his book; but then having been introduced by the Venezuelan gendarmes, and a Westerner to boot, the odds in the power game, he admits, were stacked rather in his favour from the start.

As I prepared myself for my first field trip, I remember being similarly buoyed up by paradox, not to mention chauvinism. I was a scientist about to gain 'his' people, his fund of private data with which to address academic debate; after long years of what felt like impotent, neophytic reading of other anthropologists' empires – Firth's (Polynesian) Tikopia, Fortes's (African) Tallensi, Leach's (Burmese) Kachin – in which, ultimately, they were not to be gainsaid, I was at last to lay claim to an academic personality of my own. Mine, moreover, would be a British empire: an ethnographical fortress in England, not in some remote and backward area of Africa or South-East Asia. Studying the natives of Cumbria, I felt, was not the perpetration of a harmful act so much as a pilgrimage: a chance for me to partake in a joint celebration of our Britishness; after three generations and a hundred years on British soil, a representative of the Jewish Rapport family would definitely have arrived. It was true I was going to Cumbria to gather information on them, but my feelings were of friendship, modesty, respect, even longing: I had come through Clifton and Cambridge but now, in my early twenties, it was they who were going to complete my education, complete me as a Briton. They were going to show me that my Anglophilic leanings and yearnings and my dislike of ethnic (Jewish) isolationism were justified. In Wanet I was going to learn that Englishmen of the soil were different from their Continental counterparts, as from their counterparts in the ethnographies of more distant tribesmen and peasants. For these were people of rampant individualism, who had long enjoyed that legal and political liberty which had freed them from an overbearing and overdetermining society or social structure, long demanded that freedom of conscience which had unshackled them from the irrationalities of custom and religion, and long fostered those notions of solidarity, alongside eccentricity, that had culminated recently in the welfare state.

Mine, then, was to be a lucky sojourn, not in conditions of rudeness and superstition but at the heart of civilisation, among the descendants and peers of Britons I could thus better learn to appreciate, emulate and know: John Stuart Mill, Emily Bronte, Charles Darwin, Christina Rossetti, Edward Elgar, E.M. Forster and so on. In short, my preparations were a pleasant time for I was readying myself for the fulfilment of a long process if not two of them: by fieldworking in England I would be becoming more completely British and more fully an anthropologist at the same time.

From these jingoistic heights, however, my doctoral supervisor soon brought me down. Having decided upon the research location and gained accommodation, Anthony Cohen counselled discretion and caution. It was a tourist area and yet I should tell few friends where I was going; his experience in Shetland was that sudden visitors from another life could be most unsettling, particularly in terms of how local people had come to see you. Moreover, when I had moved in, I should be extremely careful about how I explained myself, and give little away before I had an idea about how the information was likely to be received. It was possible, for example, that my youth and apparent unemployment would count against me, as might the taint of the newcomer: I should dissociate myself from the tourist, the visitor, the second-home owner, as far as possible. As stranger and academic, in short, I would receive little licence for naivety or idiosyncrasy. Fitting in was the important thing, and, at least initially, avoiding the formal accoutrements of research: camera, notebooks, tape recorder. For these smacked of the outsider – the tourist, the official, the bureaucrat, the busybody – and an intrusive one to boot.

When I did move into Wanet, I realised the appositeness of this advice. It was a very anxious time, and I felt that all my efforts had to go into staying *in situ*: to remaining in Wanet, to not being seen as a tourist or townie and to getting close enough to local people to gather data on their behaviour. As Judith Okely has observed, even if longing for another life and identity is often the unconscious compulsion to undergo an anthropological quest, the fantasies and romance are soon transformed by the act of fieldwork, by the concrete knowledge of another lived-in reality (1983: 46). It was very hard work; people did not seem so enlightened, so liberal, so happy, and nor were they particularly welcoming: indeed, their eccentricities often seemed turned against me. The pettiness of local lives, the mundanity, depressed me; and how would I have felt, I reflected, if one of them had suddenly turned up on my doorstep and expected to be found a place in my life? In fact, the academy seemed very far away, other ethnographic accounts of natives' lives pale, simplistic and unreal, and what I was up to felt rather like snooping. But I soon banished the latter thought: it was the only way to keep on. Besides, this was what was expected of me as an anthropologist after all; it was what all those eminent names had done before me; it was for the advance of understanding and the betterment of science; it was for my Ph.D. And when Doris began interrogating me, and Sid threatened to silence anybody who reported on his mates to anyone in the outside world, it became a battle of stubbornness and wits which I wanted to win: my relations, my world, my class, my vision, my project, me, against them.

And here I was, I reflected, back on familiar ground after all: for defining myself in opposition and dabbling with contradictions were what I was most wont to do. That is, before fieldwork, I had been a Welshman, not an Englishman; but Jewish and not Welsh; and yet an atheistic Briton and not a Jew. I had been a public schoolboy and not a state school inmate; but someone who kept to his Cardiff vowels and eschewed a Home Counties' poshness; and yet someone for whom Cardiff schools were not considered good enough. I had been middle-class not lower-class, but from Jewish immigrant origins; and yet I was now finally escaping the taint of commerce and trade. I had had a comfortable upbringing and had looked out over a large back lawn onto the housing estates beyond; but I espoused an empathy with the have-nots who had to achieve by struggling and did not inherit with grace; and yet I did not want to give up the security of my material well-being. I had believed in social justice, been moved by 'to each according to his needs'; but I feared the tyranny of the majority that might ensue outside a benevolent despotism; and yet I did not want any bounds put upon the free development of individual personalities. I wanted to keep on improving myself: to be stronger, more well read, more well known; but I also wanted to lose myself in the anonymity of a group; and yet I did not want to belong to any one social identity, category, situation, group and be robbed of my specialness, individuality and potential.

What these habitual feelings reveal, I suggest, is a character at once seeking the security of social stereotypes as a means of defining himself and others, and yet, once reached, fearful of how these definitions might encompass and 'explain' him completely; someone hovering between achievement and belonging, constantly wavering between 'arriving' and achieving another identity that expresses him more completely, while not feeling that any one set or type defines him, or that he lives up to it adequately. For to feel complete rapport – or completely a Rapport, for that matter – was to admit that I could achieve no better and be no happier; and surely I was destined for greater things, and my climb of improvement would continue. If I fitted any one social category or sat content in any one social situation, then what was left of me which was visible and unique, which gave purpose and meaning to my individual life, and made a special biography calling for particular explanation? I would merely be an assimilating Jew, or a middle-class Briton, or an ex-public-schoolboy, or one of the Cardiff Rapports, or part of the professionalising nouveaux riches, and so on. So, here I was in Wanet, and the experience was to be seen as another learning one, its relations to be gained and then sloughed off so that another me might emerge onto the social stage: a stage more suited to an appreciation of my array of gradually fashioned but now commendable accomplishments, a stage where I might not have to pretend to fit other people's expectations and adapt myself to their alien agendas.

This, then, was the persona whom the shock of fieldwork in Wanet brought to the fore: self-conscious, insecure, but determined to do whatever it took to survive the year and retrieve from it what was needed in order to pass the test to my doctorate, climb the next rung. It became another experience in the construction of a better self, once I realised that here was somewhere else I did not want to stop. Besides, I had my real 'colleague' in my own old persona; faced by the fieldwork situation it was a comfort: like an old team or a stratagem that had won through before, getting me from exam to exam, prep school to public school, undergraduate to postgraduate – and now would do so again. No doubt, my abiding anxiety and consciousness of hostility were in part of my own making and the result of my expectations (of how they would feel about a nosy outsider) fulfilling themselves. No doubt, secreting notes about my person and writing up my journal at night made me imagine threatening innuendos in Sid's account of his shotgun, in Fred's monosyllables, in Doris's talk of castrated tups, but I was alone, a fifth columnist, and felt deserving of their dislike and rebuke. I was like one of those 'trailing Hebrews' they kept complaining about, drag-rats who wandered in from nowhere and disturbed local life before wandering away into the desert again. *Settling into Wanet, in short, entailed trading my fairy-tale hopes for more customary expectations: not feeling at home with consociates because my real place was in opposition and contrast.*

The self-centredness, the selfishness, of this fieldwork persona seems very bald now, but I do not believe it is unique. Jean-Paul Dumont, remember, only felt it necessary to justify his behaviour when once again safely ensconced in academia. As far as I was concerned, if I was to remain in the field, a debilitating conscience was a luxury I could not afford. I felt uneasy that I could not explain my project in its own terms, but then by the hours of free labour I was providing my main informants with I was repaying something at least. (And the gift of £100 which Fred and Doris gave me as a going–away present – not before, they said, because they reckoned I would just drink it away down the pub – went some way to assuring me that I had not been a burden.) I was aware of the basic non-mutuality inherent in the whole exercise – I had not asked to study them and they had not invited me – but, by accepting their aggression, granting them daily superiority, adopting uncomplainingly whatever lowly statuses they chose to accord me, I tried to salve the sore of my 'writing them up' later. Indeed, after I had been in Wanet a number of months, felt more confident that I would pass the test (almost imagine the feeling of its end) and had got to know my informants better, I even allowed myself moments of thinking that perhaps they were right: their values and skills *were* superior to mine; here *were* the true descendants of Renaissance Man wholly practical, able in so many ways and self-sufficient; and, as a few people were saying, maybe I should find a nice local girl and a small farm for rent and settle down.

Since leaving the field and returning to the academy, I have not kept up ties. It is now some thirty years later. My informants and their valley homes appear in my accounting in disguised forms, and I feel that my constructions of the people they were and the relations we shared one year quite a while ago do not harm them now. In general, I would echo the sentiments of John Barnes (cited in Akeroyd 1984: 154) that there is no immaculate praxis for fieldwork: ethical and intellectual compromise are intrinsic characteristics of social research and whichever choice is made is unlikely to bring complete satisfaction. The competent fieldworker is he or she who learns to live with an uneasy conscience but continues to be worried by it. Indeed, if ethics come to be understood as situational 'work rules', as Vidich and Bensman prescribe (1964: 347) – local norms of proper practice by which specific relationships are structured and maintained, and expressed – then I believe I am able to lay claim to ethical relations with Doris and Sid and others.

An Acount of Ethics in (British) Complex Society

What I have said thus far could be dismissed still as a rationalisation for my bringing of Doris and Sid into print. Whether or not I claim to have preserved the integrity of our local relations and working practices, using Wanet locals as anthropological informants can still appear as an unfair advantage. So let me offer a more constructive suggestion of how the ethical dilemma can be brought to good effect (if not closure).

A little before I left the field, I remember phoning a confidante in Cardiff and telling her how fed up I was with fieldworking and the roles I had adopted in Wanet. 'Look on the bright side,' she said. 'Soon you'll be leaving all those country bumpkins behind, and what they think won't matter any more.' This had the effect, however, of increasing my melancholy: I had a sudden sense of the plurality and relativity of values and versions in contemporary society. I felt, in effect, that there was now no way that I could escape from Doris and Sid and the rest onto some 'higher plane' of objective knowledge. Even when I left Wanet, we would still all be living in Britain and I would merely be exchanging one set of talking relationships and working practices for another. I might claim superiority (my versions were more scientific, more artistic, more liberal, etc.) but in those versions and my faith in them would I not be precisely equivalent to Doris and Sid? Their prejudices, strategies and insecurities were clear counterparts of my own. British complex society was a world without agreed notions of truth and right and with an inexhaustible supply of them. The notion that came to mind was that there were as many claims to knowledge and ways of knowing as there were individuals, all jostling, rewriting, subverting, comparing, translating and parodying one another without consensus and without end. I was living Nietzsche's prophesied 'age of comparison'.

This also extends, it seems to me, to systems of ethics. In a pluralistic world, ethical truths are multiple and contradictory. If ethics are seen as situational work rules, then each holds to account a different set of routine practices, each pertains to a particular individual or group of interactants, each is exclusive and constituted in opposition, without there being any necessary overarching totalism – so that what is ethical to one party and in one situation may be heretical in the next. The 'pragmatic morality' is to establish the propriety and normativity of individuals moving between these situational 'ethical' routines as they need and will. Here are individuals as Nietzsche's 'wandering encyclopedias' of social forms.

Moreover, this is something to which people in Britain can claim to have long experienced. By all accounts, British society has long exhibited this complexity, composed as it is of individuals in movement between a plurality of distinct caste-like groupings, bounded against outsiders by working camaraderie, by shared knowledge of eccentricities, proclivities and skills, by common pride in distinct histories. A maximisation of group distinctions and memberships may be said to be a British fetish, with one's social life spent, in large measure, exploring and maintaining discriminatory practices and evaluations, and wending ways through social landscapes chock-a-block with the diversions of classificatory division. The English language, far from being an instrument of easy communication in Britain, may be seen to serve as a vehicle of social exclusion: an emblem of exclusiveness in accent, terminology and subject matter; a means of sifting that information which members of other groups may gain access to from that which should be restricted to one's own alone. By way of the English language, group distinctions are maintained, with members of different groups only meeting in terms of more or less clichéd and stereotypical settings, topics and occasions. The important truths and the distinctive ways of talking about them, of elaborating upon them, are kept private to the group and become all the more valuable and significant for the dichotomy (Bernstein 1973; Rapport 1995).

There is an ambiguity, too, in the British class system which, Marilyn Strathern has placed at its very core: closed, introspective, caste-like groups whose individual membership is never quite certain or clear (1982: 270–71). British society is one of great process, however surreptitious and gradual, of regular movement of individuals from group to group. It is a society composed of individuals who act as autonomous units, continually breaching the boundaries of different groups in their independent progress from one to another. As individuals move, they change the histories, the proclivities, the eccentricities of the groups of which they become part, but they also come to adopt different working practices, different routines of interaction and different habitual community truths. Individuals learn to espouse the ethics of their particular momentary situations and to eschew others; the abiding, overriding morality is in the guarantee of their continual movement between 'ethical' working particularities.

In extremis, if individuals in British society are always on the move, and always see each stop within a group as a possibly temporary one, then their modal working community, the 'group' to which they in effect consistently belong, can be said to be themselves alone. As they continually trade one set of ethical practices for another, their longest-standing elaborations of meaning, and in this respect most true, remain private to themselves; thus that arch-figure of British transience, Oscar Wilde, could quip: 'A truth ceases to be true when more than one person believes in it' (1968: 434). Perhaps there was something characteristically British in my moving into Wanet – as I had moved previously between social relations, caste-like groupings and sets of expectations concerning what was true and right – and something characteristically British in the pragmatic, individualistic persona that came to the fore.

Conclusion: the Ethics and Ironies of Social Science

Social scientists have been portrayed as highly transient and marginal figures. What distinguishes them, perhaps, amid the complexity, plurality and fragmentation of contemporary society, is their embracing of movement. They make a virtue out of their social transience, and admit to the ethical irony, even subversiveness, accompanying their research. As Howard Becker summarises the case for sociology: 'a good study will make somebody angry' (1964: 267). The reason given for this is that, since context- or value-free research that is not contaminated by the bias of someone's particular point of view is not possible, and since the sociologist has multiple and conflicting loyalties – to sponsors and funders and subjects and colleagues and publishers and the state, and so on – the only choice concerns whose side to be on: taking sides as personal sympathies and political circumstances dictate. Admit to the limitations of one's vantage-point, then, it is advised, but continue the research: because the revelation of the diversity of individual life-worlds, the plurality of ethical-relational routines, and the revelation of normative deviance, fluidity and irony, within groups boasting behavioural and moral homogeneity and boundedness, and the relativising, the putting into perspective, of rules, interests, beliefs and selves locally regarded as a priori and absolute are of scientific as well as moral gain (Becker 1977).

Social scientists journey between situations and communities, talking relationships and selves, and consciously connect and compare these in order to garner information. They purposefully enter into different working practices, abide by diverse ethical relations (so that their behaviour from the standpoint of any one will seem inconstant, even hypocritical), come to learn meanings and truths that are constructed in inexorable opposition. This journey from self to self, ethic to ethic, without stasis, *as the activity of ethnographic fieldwork*, and its representation, through an interweaving of perspectives, without closure, *as the product of ethnographic fieldwork*, returns me, finally, to the notion of emergence. If to juxtapose ethical worlds is to contrast them, to show what each lacks in relation to the other, then this juxtaposition can also be constructive; because it invites each world to make space for the others. Juxtaposition of ethical worlds changes and extends those worlds, allowing the possibility of new viewpoints and new meanings. What might emerge is what Paul Ricoeur refers to as 'narrative hospitality': practising a generosity towards one another's stories of ethical proprieties which can be cosmopolitan (1996). At the very least it discredits rhetorical claims to 'final vocabularies' (Rorty 1992) and ethical absolutes: it shows human beings with the capacity to lead multiple lives, abide by diverse communitarian routines, at once, and lays claim to positing in this ironising capacity their true humanity.

What I have wanted to do in this essay is to bring into presence a juxtaposition of selves, ethical relations and discourses that did not exist before my fieldwork and my account of it. This bringing into presence is a strategic and a critical act. I decide upon representing a particular juxtaposition in a particular way, and hope not to leave ethical worlds quite as they were; I hope to place ethical worlds in positions of potential generosity relative to one another.

Nor is that the end of the story. If I offer a picture – in my experience of Wanet, in Britain and contemporary complex society – of epistemological and ethical pluralism, then there is nonetheless an ethics (and an epistemology) underlying all this, a foundational one, of an existential kind (Rapport 2002). It posits that movement is necessary and good, being able to put oneself in different social positions and exercise a generosity towards ethical difference. It posits the capacity of individuals moving between different life-worlds and different ethical systems, and continuing to make sense, and it posits the propriety of individuals being afforded the social space in which to exercise the ironic capacity to reflect critically on difference – and create difference afresh. Righting social reality ushers in an ethics of individuality.

References

Akeroyd, A. 1984. 'Ethics in Relation to Informants, the Profession and Governments', in R. Ellen (ed.), *Ethnographic Research*. London: Academic, pp. 133–54.

Becker, H. 1964. 'Problems in the Publications of Community Studies', in A. Vidich, J. Bensman and M. Stein (eds.), *Reflections on Community Studies*. New York: Wiley, pp. 267–84.

———. 1977. *Sociological Work*. New Brunswick, New Jersey: Transaction Books.

Bernstein, B. 1973. *Class, Codes and Control*. St. Albans: Paladin.

Collins, P. 2002. 'Both Independent and Interconnected Voices: Bakhtin among the Quakers', in N. Rapport (ed.), *British Subjects*. Oxford: Berg, pp. 281–98.

Dumont, J.-P. 1978. *The Headman and I*. Austin: University of Texas Press.

Marcus, G. 1980. 'Rhetoric and Ethnographic Genre in Anthropological Research', *Current Anthropology*, 21: pp. 507–10.

Okely, J. 1983. *The Traveller-Gypsies*. Cambridge: Cambridge University Press.

Rabinow, P. 1977. *Reflections on Fieldwork in Morocco*. Berkeley: University of California Press.

Rapport, N. 1993. *Wanet: Diverse World-Views in an English Village*. Edinburgh: Edinburgh University Press.

———. 1994. *The Prose and the Passion: Anthropology, Literature and the Writing of E.M. Forster*. Manchester: Manchester University Press.

———. 1995. 'Migrant Selves and Stereotypes: Personal Context in a Postmodern World', in S. Pile and N. Thrift (ed.), *Mapping the Subject*. London: Routledge, pp. 267–82.

———. 2002. 'The Truth of Movement, the Truth as Movement', in V. Amit and N. Rapport (eds.), *The Trouble with Community: Anthropological Reflections on Movement, Identity and Collectivity*. London: Pluto, pp 73–149.

Ricoeur, P. 1996. *The Hermeneutics of Action*. London: Sage.

Rorty, R. 1992. *Contingency, Irony, and Solidarity*. Cambridge: Cambridge University Press.

Strathern, M. 1982. 'The Village as an Idea: Constructs of Villageness in Elmdon, Essex', in A. P. Cohen (ed.), *Belonging*. Manchester: Manchester University Press, pp. 247–77.

Tyler, S. 1986. 'Post-modern Ethnography: From Document of the Occult to Occult Document', in G. Marcus and J. Clifford (eds.), *Writing Culture*. Berkeley: University of California Press, pp. 122–40 .

Vidich, A. and J. Bensman. 1964. 'The Springdale Case: Academic Bureaucrats and Sensitive Townspeople', in A. Vidich, J. Bensman and M. Stein (eds.), *Reflections on Community Studies*. New York: Wiley, pp. 313–49.

Wilde, O. 1968. *Critical Writings of Oscar Wilde*. New York: Random House.

PART II

WORKING ON/WITH/THROUGH MEMORY

Chapter 6

ETHNOGRAPHERS AS LANGUAGE LEARNERS: FROM OBLIVION AND TOWARDS AN ECHO

Alison Phipps

> Time present and time past
> Are both perhaps present in time future,
> And time future contained in time past.
>   ...
> But to what purpose
> Disturbing the dust on a bowl of rose-leaves
> I do not know.
> Other echoes
> Inhabit the garden. Shall we follow?
>
> T.S. Eliot, *Burnt Norton.*

From Language Learning to Languaging

I – for we have to begin this way, in this book – I am a language learner. I have always been a language learner. And yet, as Merleau-Ponty reminds us: 'The wonderful thing about language is that it promotes its own oblivion' (Merleau-Ponty 2002: 466).

I don't quite know how I got here but I'm standing in a lecture theatre in front of around fifty Portuguese academics and, with some nerves and deep breath, I'm starting off in Portuguese. This isn't an easy thing to do. I've been learning Portuguese for about two years and it's been something of a haphazard, evening class affair. 'Muito Obrigada para o convit. Desculpe, eu nao falo bem Portugues, mas falo um poco.' I say, haltingly, understanding the importance of meeting and greeting conventions in the language of my hosts, but knowing it costs me a fair amount of rhetorical pride, as I fumble around for a degree of fluency and the right words. I manage it, however, and this time it is already a hundred times better than my attempts last year, in the same place. How this has happened I don't really know. But clearly, magically it always seems, the week by week working with Portuguese words in a small class of learners has had some effect. And I've been here before, several years ago now, when I learned languages at school and university and watched as I became increasingly confident, fluent to the point of being able to live, quite comfortably, in the worlds of different words.

Once we 'have it', once we reach a certain level of ease and fluency in a language we forget what it felt like not to be a speaker of French, German, Xhosa, Farsi. In fact, more than that, we can't go back on the bodily knowing such speaking entails. We may be a 'bit rusty' but we still have the language we worked hard to reach, and it is only when we are faced with the prospect of speaking a new language that those feelings of foolishness and awkwardness return. It is one thing to learn a language in the classroom, to work through grammar books, vocabulary lists, the four skills of reading, writing, listening and speaking of the communicative language curriculum. It is quite another thing to be in a place where we can actually just live in the language, where we can, to use the term I have developed for this with my colleague Mike Gonzalez (Phipps and Gonzalez 2004) just 'language'. Like our enskillment (Ingold 2000) in other areas of life, 'languaging', is an active state of being where we engage with the whole social world, and not just the artefacts of a language classroom, in order to enter the social process that make and shape life as it is lived in that particular language. When language learners enter the social world of that language and start living in that language then they become 'enlanguaged' by those social worlds, and their ways of being and of dwelling change, often profoundly, though also imperceptibly, as a result.

Language Learners as Ethnographers

In 2001 Roberts et al. published a book-length study of a project to develop linguistic and cultural understanding in university students of modern languages using ethnography (Roberts et al. 2001). The book, *Language Learners as Ethnographers*, argues, persuasively, for an understanding of the task of language learning and the development of language curricula in ethnographic terms, showing how ethnographic method promotes cultural understanding and linguistic fluency 'In recent years, language learners have come to be described in terms of 'cultural' mediators, 'border crossers', 'negotiators of meaning', 'intercultural speakers' and such like. Language learning is becoming increasingly defined in cultural terms and these new names and targets for language learners imply a reconceptualisation of the language learning endeavour (Roberts et al. 2001). *Language Learners as Ethnographers* has had a considerable impact on the way in which modern languages are taught and conceived at advanced level in recent years. It demonstrates the way in which ethnographic methods can be incorporated successfully into an engaging programme of cultural study in modern languages (Byram 1997; Byram and Fleming 1998). As a trained modern linguist and anthropologist I have a dual relationship to this work. In modern languages I have seen paradigms shift, and have been part of trying to aid these shifts, in the direction of anthropological modes of learning and away from aspects of the literary canon of French, German, Spanish and Italian. I have witnessed 'culture' taking centre stage and 'high cultural' definitions be replaced by more anthropological understandings of culture as a way of life.

The integration of a lengthy period of residence abroad, for the purpose of language immersion, in modern language degrees now also serves as a time and space for students of modern languages to systematise their experiences of 'being abroad' through an introduction to the principles and practices of ethnography. A gift from anthropology to modern languages, ethnographic method has enabled the reflection and theorising of the cultural experiences of language and culture for the new generation of modern linguists.

This work begs the question, however, what of ethnographers as language learners? If language learners can develop ethnographic attitudes as part of their study then what of ethnographers who live and breathe languages in their fieldwork practices? How did they come by their languages? What phenomena were revealed as nuanced uses of language, dialect, register, grammar and lexis grew with time and practice and experience? How did their sense of self and their perceptions of culture and land and language change with the time required to learn and grow in other languages?

This chapter examines the role of language learning in ethnography autoethnographically. Rather than considering the work of language learning as a functional process that is detached from fieldwork, I reflect on my own experience of language learning and the role played by time and memory in experiences of language learning as a crucial, subjective element in my ethnographic work. I am interested to go back into the labyrinths of my language learning memories and to allow these memories to act in the ethnographic presents of my own fieldwork experiences. It is my contention that my language learning and my languaging – two separate things for our purposes here – shape my relationship to the field and to my different disciplinary contexts of modern languages, anthropology and education.

Furthermore, it is my contention that the politics of language learning and the necessity of languaging and of translation, are aspects of ethnographic and anthropological work that have indeed promoted their own oblivion. Ethnographers are also language learners. Much of the preparation for fieldwork undertaken by ethnographers includes the learning of a language. This may involve evening classes, it may involve travel over long distances to institutions where certain so-called 'minority languages' are taught systematically, it may involve the paying of a language tutor for 'conversation' or 'grammar lessons', on a one-to-one basis. In the field, after what for some will be troubling and others will be exciting encounters with the language of the field, there will be the testing times of 'languaging': the moment when, with the ethnographic body firmly in the field, there, the mouth will open and the first 'authentic' attempt at speaking will occur. And 'I' will be the one languaging – having a go, making an incalculable number of mistakes and having my speech and comprehension carefully, patiently shaped by those who attend to my languaging attempts at intercultural speaking, as intercultural listeners themselves.

Solidified Words

In ethnographic accounts, however, what we find solidified is the translated understanding, not the messiness of getting to a place where a word, a phrase can be trotted out as a piece of linguistic ethnographic data. As ethnographers, we use such linguistic data rhetorically, asserting with them, using them as a trusty tool to point to certain frames and understandings in the discourse of those we study. But when we do this we have already 'promoted the oblivion' of language. We have forgotten the work that has gone into getting to the place where we can distinguish this word or phrase from the morass of incomprehension and merging, gabbled Babel of sound that was indeed our first experience of the language. 'Speaking', says Ingold (2000: 292) 'should be treated as a variety of skilled practice.' Rather like music – and 'speech is', as Merleau-Ponty (2002: 217) reminds us, 'a kind of singing' – speaking is also hard to pin down, always in flow – like memory itself, going on to become.

Speaking another language, reaching literacy in another language, is a variety of skilled 'languaging' practice of a particular kind. However, it is a kind of skilled practice that, although present in the often multilingual accounts of ethnographies, stands on the page as already fully competent. The shaping of speech in another language is a relational, social practice and one that is perhaps the most exposing of the ethnographer's incompetence in the early days of fieldwork, and most indicative of the depth of comprehension later on. It is the medium through which other, attendant skills are learned. Ethnographers of pretty much anything or anywhere – be it herding or basket weaving in Ingold's examples, or theatre and tourism in my own – have also to learn the language and to language as an a priori act. Like the learning of any new skill, however, the learning of a language is an embarrassing affair and one which, in our tidied up narratives, we take care not to reveal. Ingold describes those learning in such a way as 'naïve speakers ... wholly immersed, from the start, in the relational context of dwelling in a world' (Ingold 2000: 409).

So, with the help of memory, and in an attempt to understand something of the subjective and eclectic character of these language learning memories for ethnography, I offer my own memories as an account of naive speaking. What follows is structured to follow my own recollections of language learning; first as a child and through schooling; then through immersion and study; then used in ethnography and finally in the ethnography of language learning itself. The representation is autobiographical and auto-ethnographic and follows the labyrinthine paths of where my language learning recollections have taken me. In the first volume of Proust's *A la recherche du temps perdu*, the taste of the madeleine transports Swann to a world of sensuous memories from his childhood:

> No sooner had the warm liquid mixed with the crumbs touched my palate than a shudder ran through me and I stopped, intent upon the extraordinary thing that was happening to me. An exquisite pleasure had invaded my senses, something isolated, detached, with no suggestion of its origin. And at once the vicissitudes of life had become indifferent to me ... or rather this essence was not in me, it *was me*. (Proust 1983: 48)

Such is, we now recognise, the palpable and disorienting play of memory on the body, as '*words gather their meanings from the relational properties of the world itself*' (italics in the original) (Ingold 2000: 409).

Remembered First Words

The Children's Encyclopedia was kept in a slightly musty cupboard in my grandparents' house in Blackburn. There were several volumes, hard bound – like a Ph.D. thesis, I now think – red, with gold lettering – important, enduring. It had been Mum's, if I remember rightly and when we went to stay I was allowed to explore the worlds between its pages. I'm sure I'd find much to appal me in the *Encyclopedia* now. I'm not even sure if they are still in our family possession. No doubt there is much of an imperial nature, some odd reflections on 'tribes' and 'primitive' peoples and always that classic 1950s striving towards a sense of civilisation. My favourite pages in the books were those with a sequence of pictures where a conversation was written out in French with an English translation below. 'Comment vous appelez – vous? Je m'appelle Jean.' I would spend hours on these pages. Trying to work out the words, trying to follow the clunky phonetic pronunciation and asking Mum and Dad what I should say. I have forgotten everything I learned from those books, except those pages. What has endured, in red and gold, for me is this language.

Every morning before going to school Dad would come into my room. He would throw back my bed covers and draw the curtains and say the same thing to me – day in, day out. 'Bonjour, comment allez-vous?' Dad didn't really speak French. Mum did. In the summer before starting secondary school, I was round at a friend's house playing and her older sister was talking about her German classes. She taught me how to say 'Ich heisse Alison' and 'Ich bin elf Jahre alt' and, memorably, 'Schwein' – which was somehow an important piece of vocabulary that made us all laugh.

And then – at long last – I had my first French and German classes. I had the same teacher for both. She was wonderful. To begin with I found it hard but I couldn't believe how exciting it was to discover new words and to make new patterns with them. I couldn't get enough. However inadequate some of the materials were, I will never forget the lesson about Hans Schaudi, the lily of the valley and his house in Cadolzberg where his dad made chocolate Easter bunnies – and Lieselotte, who was emphatically *not* his sister. The worlds that opened up were magical. I know now that I was learning using the audio-lingual method. Then I was just discovering new language worlds.

My teachers had all lived abroad in France or Germany. The energy of those years they had spent living the life of the language just rolled off them in waves – all of them – even the least inspiring teachers. Their connection to these places and to the people was always palpable. And they would generously open these relationships out to us and share them with us as teachers of languages themselves – giving up their precious holidays to pack us into minibuses, coaches or trains to make the long, overland journeys to places we'd never even known existed: Saint-Porchaire, Hofweier, Pont L'Abbé, Schutterwald.

The connections and possibilities of the language grew thick within me. I saved all my pocket money to go back to these now resonant places, not for travelling but for 'languaging' – for just being in the country, with the people, doing whatever it was that they were doing alongside them. I loved it all – the people, the ways of life, the social change – for the social changes were particularly acute for me out of the relative limits of my education. I learned about trains and about travel on my own, I learned to have conversations with people in carriages, about the excitement of feeling the language grow in confidence, complexity and connectivity with those I knew and met. My own connections became palpable – the post from abroad would be covered in stamps from France and Germany, with unusual copperplate handwriting, which bore traces, in the ink, of the old Gothic German script, and where, in the French, an 'r' looked to me like an 'm'. My grandfather – the one with the *Encyclopedia* – would patiently add the stamps to his collection, my French and German friends ending up on the same pages as his most prized penny black.

By the time I was sixteen, more than anything else, I wanted to be fluent.

Being Fluent

> Often an ethnographer bases much of her work on intensive discussions with a very few people. Rather than looking at the distribution of a few predefined variables in a large population, she is trying to learn the interrelationships of a large number of discovered variables among a few people. (Agar 2000: 137)

The discussions were intense and purposeful. They were about costumes, masks, songs and dances. They flowed in and out of the rehearsals. They took place in the largely empty auditorium where we waited for our turn. The common purpose was not my research purpose. The play was the thing: The *Schwäbische Schöpfung* by Sebastian Sailer and Martin Schleker. Hayingen was the village in the south of Germany where the play was to be performed. Ostensibly I was there as a rather unusually fluent ethnographer, amusing everyone by my ability to code switch between *Hochdeutsch* – High German – and *'s Schwäbische* – the particular inflection of the Swabian dialect spoken in this village, up on the Alb. Actually, by this time, I was also there as an actor, speaking and singing lines, in Swabian, ultimately for the benefit of an audience of around one thousand. You forget about ethnographic method pretty quickly when you are wearing a boned corset and a one-foot-high wig and standing in front of an audience that size. Actually you forget many things, relying on a different set of practised behaviours – memorised lines, movements, the blocking, the gesture, the timing.

In some ways this level of performance was an ultimate test of fluency. I was fluent enough to carry on 'intensive and purposeful discussions' with a few people, but performing in the language of the fieldwork rendered the distinctions I'd learned about, such as 'professional stranger' or 'going native', entirely redundant and paradoxical. Here I was, having 'gone native' – an actor amongst many, impossible to pick out as 'the ethnographer' by the audience, at least – subsumed in the same way as my co-actors, in the process of the performance. Yet I wasn't a 'native speaker'. I could pass in the language for quite a while, enjoy the flow and feel of the fluency I'd gained over many years of committed language learning and relationships with people that pre-dated the field.

But the story isn't simply an individual autobiography, smoothed and organised out of the actions of the ethnography and those related to it in a neatly bounded field. Events happen. The story is also shaped by larger-scale moments in history and our collective memories.

Collective Moments

I was lying in bed in my hall of residence that Friday morning. My radio alarm kicked in as usual with the news headlines. John Simpson's familiar tones were waking me up. What he was saying was infinitely memorable: 'I'm reporting to you from the top of the Berlin Wall.' If I check these words out in the BBC archive, it may just be that he said something slightly different. But this is now how I've solidified the story of 'where I was when I heard the news'. Germany, my Germany, German, my German – the language I had lived in and the language I was getting up for, for a 9 a.m. lecture that morning.

I'd already learned and lived the language before adding ethnography into the mix. I'd studied my languages, worked in a school in the area, before switching to ethnology for the purposes of my doctoral project, on open-air community theatre – *Naturtheater* – in southern Germany.

Perhaps this was the moment. It was *the* moment for so many: the commonly experienced moment of change, when everything changed and other worlds were possible, worlds of (re)unification, of rampaging neoliberal economics, worlds in which my godchildren would be born to *Ossi* and *Wessi* parents and I'd visit them in the US; worlds that would lead me to be able to write about the plays written by a contemporary Swabian dramatist, Martin Schleker, for the *Naturtheater*, which dealt with the problematic of the *Wende* – the changes – and of reunification, a problematic that had not even existed when I first encountered Hayingen.

When I was first trying to find a justification for the 'fieldwork' (*Feldforschung*) – as I learned to call it – that I wished to 'conduct' (*betreiben*) – in the open-air community theatres of Swabia – I was sent to literatures just emerging on 'anthropology at home'. 'Home', I discovered, was 'Europe', against all the other traditional field sites. Other anthropologists were doing 'fieldwork at home' at that stage (MacDonald 1993; 1997). As Europe formed, broke and re-formed again through the late 1980s and into the 1990s collective memories and events came to work their power on the individual narratives that were unfolding.

Maybe this media moment of encounter was it, the trigger, the moment for the narration of the role of memory in my ethnographic interests. In my published work on the topic, when first starting out, I don't mention how I came to the field. I don't insert myself into the field, my memories, accidents, stories. I launch straight into a defence of the field as significant, making claims for the *Naturtheater* as an important phenomenon and for amateur theatre as an important ritual process in the testing and forming of identities in twentieth-century Germany. The furthest I go in reflecting on my own position is where I note the need, for the purposes of my study, located as it was in both ethnology and German studies, to have regard for my own disciplinary 'safety' in the defense and casting of the work.

Today, I don't have to airbrush the story. Perhaps I didn't need to then, but either way it is an absence that amuses me, as I write of memory and the accidents of the field.

Getting Lost

We were camping, an international venture scout camp, high up on the Schwäbische Alb. There were a lot of delegates from England but, aged seventeen, I was the one with the most fluent German and, somewhat bemused – a state I came to associate later with doing ethnography – I found myself interpreting between German, English and Swabian (a dialect I had only just encountered at the camp) for around 300 people. To cut a long story short, I overdid it and lost my voice. I wasn't used to that much voice projection and that much talking. So I was sent off on an overnight hike for a couple of days. Just gentle conversation and the promise of a trip to the Hayingen *Naturtheater* when I returned. I was excited. I loved theatre. I'd been involved in open-air theatre at home recently and it had been magical, entrancing.

But we got lost … and missed the show.

Three years later, with a research grant and the start of a Ph.D. in the bag, I find myself sitting in the empty auditorium with the other villagers, waiting for the first rehearsal, of which I am to be a part, to begin.

But to what purpose
Disturbing the dust on a bowl of rose-leaves
I do not know.

When we walk down memory lane with ethnographic purpose we are 'Disturbing the dust on a bowl of rose-leaves'. Having lived with the memories in familiar ways we defamiliarise them through the specific action of 'intensive and purposeful' conversations with our pasts. The leaves look different in this context. I haven't considered these aspects for a while now, the dust has gathered on thought, much has appeared forgotten. Much probably is. And to arrive here, surrounded by musty books in the upstairs room, sitting on the floor by the book cupboard, shading my eyes against the sun in the auditorium, sitting bolt upright in bed as the radio tells me that my world has just changed overnight, is like getting lost in the labyrinth.

> Other echoes
> Inhabit the garden. Shall we follow?

'Quick now, here now.' There is an urgency to the tug of memory here. I want to keep exploring, looking for the moment, the origin, the romantic roots, searching for the story that will make sense for me, here now. 'Shall we follow?'

Perhaps we should. Perhaps something may be gained by 'walking the labyrinth' of memory, for anthropological reflection.

Walking the labyrinth has been a practice of myth and discipline in various places in the past, in ancient Greece, medieval cathedrals and more recently it has been rediscovered as a tool for 'spiritual' development and discovery. It involves the purposeful work of 'getting lost' or experiencing the self as rightly incomplete: 'The 'prescience of incompleteness' the 'sense of omitting facts' is the original matrix-phantom of scientific research. Such prescience, though suppressed or explained away for a long time, has been the major force behind the struggle against the positivistic conception of science' (Santos 1995: 134–35). My own story of getting lost is a story against a linear narrative of careful and systematic organisation and preparedness for fieldwork and for the story of my ethnographic work. My story is that of the error and the accident, the wrong road taken that turns out to be a road after all, just not the one expected. It involves a lost voice, and a lost way. Ethnographic narratives are riddled with such stories of events, surprise, doing the unexpected – classically Geertz's Balinese cock-fight (Geertz 1973), we might now conclude with insight, took much of anthropology away from the positivistic, structural-functionalist concerns and into a long and continuing interpretative turn, of which this volume represents a further outworking. But this continues to beg the question. To what purpose 'disturbing the dust on a bowl of rose-leaves'? To what purpose the autobiographical enquiry?

Labyrinths of Autobiography

I would emphasize the importance of developing an autobiographical
method in the social sciences as a way of testing new answers for questions
that are common to both science and literature: for example, the relations
between truth and design, between memory and invention, and between
description and imagination; the question of time structure; and finally the
question of the author. (Santos 1995: 129)

An autobiographical method is first and foremost a narrative method. It
involves the collection of fragments from the past, the assembling of
details in ways that enable a certain telling of a certain story. But to tell the
story ethnographically has usually meant following certain conventions
of reporting the facts from the field, respecting, ethically, the subjects of
the research, following a path laid out by a lineage of anthropologists and
their particular embedment in the social ideas of the day. It means
carefully annotated notebooks, highly prized and personal artefacts –
more precious to the fieldwork than any computer can ever be. It means
picking up these artefacts, with their careful descriptions of life and
language, and knowing them intimately.

It is easy to pick an episode, a moment in the past that, in the context of
where I am now – researching felt connections between languages and
anthropology – can act as an 'origin'. The encyclopedia seems as good a
memory as any. It shows me off as bookish, curious and fascinated by
languages. It's a nice place to start for a piece of 'vanity ethnography'. It
also acts as a post hoc authentic moment of experience from which a
narrative flows. Memories are labyrinthine; one triggers another as I
write. Writing triggers its own memories – this writing is not field writing,
is not the first writing in French, is not handwriting. The triggers to
memory – a request for a chapter on the place of memory in ethnography
– acts like the Proustian Madeleine, opening a past that had, I swear, been
forgotten until this moment, until asked to choose a moment from my
memory for this purpose.

And on and on it goes, the sidetrack, the route that Eliot describes so
well:

What might have been and what has been
Point to one end, which is always present.
Footfalls echo in the memory
Down the passage which we did not take
Towards the door we never opened
Into the rose-garden. My words echo
Thus, in your mind.

And here I am wondering, wondering what it would have been like if I'd not been fascinated by those red and gold books in my grandfather's cupboard; if I'd been more like my brother, fascinated by his reel-to-reel tape recorder with its luminous green recording light and the magic of the voices. And I'm being caused to wonder because of a particular time, place and project in anthropology today.

Santos maintains, reflecting on his own ethnographic experience in Brazil, that we call certain perceptions identities (Santos 1995). Here, as I insert the ethnographic 'I', I'm conjuring with identities – perceptions – and am drawn into a mode of discoursing that has followed from the linguistic and cultural turns in anthropology over the past twenty years – from Geertz to Clifford to Coffey, Coleman and Collins. The field is no longer what it was; the fieldwork rites of passage and the fetish of data Bourdieu (2000) describes don't form us in ways which fit as neatly and easily into the supposed certainties of clearly definable heres and theres of our past perceptions of ethnographic fieldwork. The autobiographical narratives set up an interplay between the exterior descriptions and the interior life. The language and languages of these experiences – those learned by ethnographers – are crucial to the felt life of these narratives, to their interiority and their exteriority. The question becomes, however, how to consider such narratives of language learning and languaging within an ethnographic report.

Echoes

My own field notebooks are full of my handwriting – they are mine because of the way my pen hits the paper, my boxes highlight script. They are mine because no one else quite writes their 'n' or 's' or 'x' in the way that I do. They are in my hand, of my hand – and that hand is also a languaging hand. My notes are in Portuguese, Italian, French, Chichewa, German, Schwabian dialect. My notes are multilingual and they tell stories, especially the recent ones, of how I have expanded myself into another language. My notebooks are vocabulary books, they are grammar books, exercises and sheets, attempts, coming in the third or fourth notebook, to write several sentences and to do so in ways that are coherent, accurate even, and which demonstrate that I can actually do things with words, that I can live a bit in this language. I look after these notebooks – these artefacts of language learning – aware that I have been on this road before, in my learning.

I pack my dictionary, my grammar guide, my vocabulary book, my exercise book and my field notebook. It's like being at school, only, now, because I'm learning about learning languages whilst learning languages it has all become much more complex and I'd risk mixing things up if it weren't for the careful colour coordination of each different one.

Memories of learning languages, together with the Portuguese I'm learning now, come flooding back to me as I prepare for each class. Like an echo.

And it is in this place of remembered 'languaging' and language learning, in the interstices of expression between what is the *interiorised* thinly remembered present and the *exteriorized* thick description of the field, that the question pertinent to this volume may lie. 'My words echo thus in your mind,' says Elliot, after confessing to not knowing the purpose of such memorial work. Echoes are what this work brings up. Echoes are where – to return to Ingold's point – *'words gather their meanings from the relational properties of the world itself'* (italics in the original) (Ingold 2000: 409). They may be to no purpose. Echo sites are traditionally seen to be special, magical, often ritual sites. In contemporary modern contexts, places that echo are also tourist sites – attracting people who stand and play with the sounds made by the temporal journey of their voices. Echo, in Greek mythology was a duplicitous nymph, punished to only ever repeat what others said because of her incessant chatter, which was aimed at distracting Hera from the affairs of Zeus. In Roman mythology, Echo was torn to shreds by Pan, who denied Echo's love, scattered her into pieces that would be left for us to hear.

What both the symbolism of these myths and the symbolism of the sites point to are the seduction and the scattering that come with echoes as they gather new meanings from the relational properties of the world. Here is the warning for the autobiographical mode – the seduction of self, of one's own incessant voice, of hyper-reflexivity, of the way memories can return with, as Freud amply taught us, more than we bargained for. In making an echo, there is a pause after the calling out, a remembering of the call and then the hearing of it again but already modified, amplified, and taking a different form. What we have are words – language and languages – but working in different ways, already out of mouths before we have time to think again, returning to us 'en-stranged'. That is to say, they are still ours, not estranged – but somehow no longer of us as they were before; they return but with something perhaps ethereal, public, with a meaning made, gathered; not inside, and not against the rock, but in-between, and through time and the air.

What waiting for the echoes and working with the echoes may allow is a way of reflecting on the languages of experience and their sensory confusion and 'en-strangement'. For languages, lived and learned, offer a kind of synaesthesia, a web of connections that we would otherwise not be 'en-stranged' enough from ourselves or from the field; the rock, to make: Merleau-Ponty maintains that 'when I see a sound, I mean that I *echo* the vibration of the sound with my whole sensory being' (2002: 234) (my emphasis).

Field sites are resonant – in the present, in memories and for the future. The resonance – or sound they make – is, amongst other sounds, one of languages, learned for the purpose of a resonant ethnographic report, the resonance of gathered, relational meaning and understanding. But this meaning, gathered in languages, learned prior to and in the field, is not something that can simply be taken as given and as not significant to the relational work of making ethnography resonate.

Language may indeed promote its own oblivion. An echoing ethnographic practice may not.

References

Agar, M. 2000. *The Professional Stranger: an Informal Introduction to Ethnography.* London: Academic Press.

Bourdieu, P. 2000. *Pascalian Meditations.* Cambridge: Polity.

Byram, M. 1997. *Teaching and Assessing Intercultural Communicative Competence.* Clevedon: Multilingual Matters.

Byram, M. and M. Fleming. 1998. *Language Learning in Intercultural Perspective: Approaches through Drama and Ethnography.* Cambridge: Cambridge University Press.

Geertz, C. 1973. *The Interpretation of Cultures.* London: Fontana.

Ingold, T. 2000. *The Perception of the Environment: Essays in Livelihood, Dwelling and Skill.* London and New York: Routledge.

MacDonald, S. 1993. *Inside European Identities: Ethnography in Western Europe.* Oxford: Berg.

———. 1997. *Reimagining Culture: Histories, Identities and the Gaelic Renaissance.* Oxford and New York: Berg.

Merleau-Ponty, M. 2002. *Phenomenology of Perception.* London: Routledge.

Phipps, A. and M. Gonzalez. 2004. *Modern Languages: Learning and Teaching in an Intercultural Field.* London: Sage.

Roberts, C., M. Byram, A. Barro, S. Jordan, and B. Street. 2001. *Language Learners as Ethnographers.* Clevedon: Multilingual Matters.

Santos, B. de S. 1995. *Towards a New Common Sense: Law, Science and Politics in the Paradigmatic Transition.* London: Routledge.

Poetry

T.S. Eliot, extracts from 'Burnt Norton', *The Four Quartets*. London: Faber.

Prose

Proust, M. 1983. *Swann's Way: The Remembrance of Things Past.* Penguin: London.

Chapter 7

LEADING QUESTIONS AND BODY MEMORIES: A CASE OF PHENOMENOLOGY AND PHYSICAL ETHNOGRAPHY IN THE DANCE INTERVIEW

Jonathan Skinner

From Sauce to Salsa: Towards a Sensuous Anthropology

In the same year that we were told that ethnography was in an 'experimental moment' (Marcus and Fischer 1986), one that should remain endlessly experimental, Paul Stoller (1986) was introducing us to an anthropology of the senses. Stoller used cuisine as an entrée to the senses, arguing that anthropologists should give readers or viewers 'a sense of what it is like to live in other worlds, a taste of ethnographic things' (1986: 156). Stoller's ideas stem from the work of the phenomenologist Merleau-Ponty (1962), who, suggests that the task of representation is creative in itself, a task that requires the writer to engage the readers and to write evocatively – a stance echoed by postmodernist ethnographic writer Stephen Tyler (1986), who wants all ethnography to be an evocative, meditative vehicle for reflection and understanding. For me, this approach can and should be extended into the data-gathering side of ethnography and should not just be withheld for the writing. This means that the anthropologist's self becomes one of the key resources in ethnography, nowhere more so than in the anthropology of dance where it is vital that the writer dances and so shares the experience of the dance, joins in with the dancers and embodies the dance for: '[i]t is by dancing that one can fully understand dance … [Dancing] requires an observing participant rather than anthropology's orthodox participant observer,' as Daniel suggests (1995: 21, 22) in her study of rumba in Cuba.

Fellow Caribbean anthropologist and dancer Deborah Thomas (2002: 512) suggests that performance is a useful 'point of entry' with other – often unfamiliar – people. These points of entry can be both emic and etic, but, if we follow the dance theorist Sondra Fraleigh (1987: xv, 56), dance unites the dancer and the audience in a 'lived metaphysic', and is thus best experienced from the inside (phenomenologically – that which seeks 'the irreducibles of subjectivity'). This is the best way of researching our thinking, remembering and moving body; do not thinking and learning come about through movement – is not movement the mother of all cognition (Sheets-Johnstone 1966)? And should not our ethnographic writing reflect its inherently mobile and unfinished state (Clifford 1988)? This physical 'movement' is a form of knowing itself (Sklar 2000), and one which, through the body, is capable of generating ideas, 'thought forms' as well as a somatic memory, 'bodily writing' in dance, for example.[1] Dance anthropologist Sally Ness (1996: 135) makes the valid point that an ethnography of dance deliberately makes 'cairns-in-memory' of movement. She also adds the significant rider about the writing of ethnography as the release and dismembering of recollected experiences as they are turned into text, made static and disembodied as the body logos is translated into symbolic logocentrism. It is important, then, to consider the interview material we 'in-corporate' into our ethnographic texts and to reflect upon not only how it has been gleaned, but also how it has been affected physically by the complex and varied experiential relationships between interviewer and interviewee during the process of eliciting primary research findings. Touch, for example, is a sense with an especial modality of perception in that it blurs subject and object, bringing them together. It is unlike sight which distances and objectifies self from other. Touch along with smell and taste have, so Stoller (1986: 8) notes, become typically the lower-order senses, relegated by empiricism below sight and sound senses, the two mainstays of anthropological participant observation. This chapter is an attempt to address the apparent ethnographic bias for 'outer forms' at the expense of 'inner states' (Appadurai 1990). I aim to do this by concentrating upon the relationship built up with an informant, one gained through physical knowledge of them, knowledge that facilitated the data-gathering function of ethnographic fieldwork, knowledge which crosses 'the outer' and 'the inner' and breaches the walls between the rational and the romantic. Thus, from this one example, an interview with Sarah following one particular salsa dance with her at a nightclub in Sacramento, California, I argue for an attention to the process of relating to and with the subject (self and dancing 'other', in this case), a critical and neglected part of the data gathering exercise.

Let me first situate this chapter further in the ethnographic research and interview literature: it belongs in Denzin and Lincoln's (1994) 'Sixth

Moment' of qualitative research (following positivist, modernist, blurred, crisis and diversity moments). It is also part of an 'inside-out writing' genre which embeds the vulnerable self before engaging the other (Behar 1996). This is 'auto-ethnography', the textual engagement with both the ethnographer's self subject and the ethnographic other object, a formerly 'forbidden narrative' (Church 1995) which challenges us to think about the process of reading and writing and has the potential to bring new insight to the field and the nature of fieldwork, and new relations and collaborations with the reader (Jones 2002). In keeping with the nature of this chapter, it is also written with an attention to phenomenological and ethnographic modes of description and analysis after Lindsay's (1996) skilful essay on learning hand drumming. There, Lindsay writes about practical engagement in an activity, embodiment and practice as ways of being-in-the-world: hand drumming as a way of losing oneself to the world ('coextensive' (Sartre 1955), 'the absent body' (Leder 1990), in 'flow' (Csikszentmihalyi 2002), creating new 'habitus' (Bourdieu 1977)).

It is through the ethnographic interview that this chapter makes its point. The interview is worthy of scrutiny because we live in an 'interview society' (Atkinson and Silverman 1997), one that not only relies upon the interview as a primary source for social science investigation, but also relies upon the interview as the reflective gaze through which society knows itself. The interview – 'a conversation with a purpose' (Robson 1993: 228), 'a professional conversation' (Kvale 1996: 5) – is a coming together of two (and sometimes more) people. Preferably the interview is a mutual 'inter-view' (Finch 1984), and not 'a one-way pseudoconversation' (Fontana and Frey 2003: 82) as the researcher elicits research information, acting out a relationship but without really relating (Benney and Hughes 1956). This chapter is a learning case study from an ethnographic interview: semi-structured, spontaneous and situational, gendered, intimate and reflexive, personal and phenomenological – and, above all, one based around muscle and cerebral memories.

Sarah's Story

Interview Beginnings

Brilliant. Well, if you could tell me about your background and how you got into the salsa or dancing in general, that would be great.

I used to dance classical ballet when I was a teenager and I was in the XXX Ballet.

Oh, wow so you were actually in a ballet …

I was in the professional school for two years when I was fourteen, fifteen, sixteen. And then I was not accepted. They said I was too tall and I didn't look like a little boy [laughter]. And so they wouldn't offer me a position in the company.

Yes

And that was my whole life. And so I quit. I joined the military. I met my husband, had children and didn't dance.

Right

And about three years ago I er, um, I got a divorce unfortunately. And I, it messed up my whole world. And I met someone who asked me what I used to do before I got married. And I said 'dancing'. That's what made me really happy. And um, he said, 'Well, why don't you dance salsa?' And I took some classes and I, I really love it.

So this is what you been doing it for three years now?

Sarah is an anaesthetist who teaches salsa lessons in the OR when the patients have gone under. She is a divorcee with children, a woman who has had a difficult and abusive past, one from which dance has often been the saving grace, her therapeutic narrative. This is verbatim from the start of a thirteen minute interview with her snatched between dances at Cotton's Nightclub. It was the very first time that we had met or seen each other. We had danced and then she had asked about my accent and then what I was doing in Sacramento. I explained that I was starting a research project on salsa in Sacramento, and she offered herself as an interviewee. She also suggested that we go to the cafe tables outside the nightclub entrance where there would be a little more privacy and the sound levels would be masked. It was a public space, but one that I would not have thought to suggest to someone I did not know better.

In this start of the interview, I show an enthusiasm for the task at hand as well as a sharp interest in her narrative. There is a relaxed rapport between us which, later, Sarah revealed as a mild infatuation on her part. Certainly, during the dancing, there was light flirting from both sides, the interviewer responding to circumstances to get the interview, aware that the flirting was not going to go anywhere and that it was being well taken and not doing any harm. If anything, I was the passive participant in the entire interview process. There is candour in the interview, and Sarah's narrative spins forward in the context of dance: she danced semi-professionally, quit and whilst not dancing joined the military, married, had children and divorced, and then she came back to dance. In personal narratives of people who are or have been ill, Bury (1982) has noted the 'biographical blip' as their liminal ill time. In this case, it is as though Sarah's biographical blip was when she was not dancing. It was her divorce that precipitated her return to dance, dance that gave her comfort and solace during a difficult time in her life.

In this second more extensive quotation below which followed almost immediately after the first extract, I follow up on Sarah's opening comments. This is one of the advantages of the unstructured interview approach: there is space (freedom) to respond to the twists and turns of a conversation. This is the interviewer working as opportunist. Here, Sarah has been exceptionally candid inbetween her flirtatious sallies. Recalling the interview, I felt that Sarah was open and opening up to my questions but that in jest, and with her confidence, she was able to protect herself. I therefore opted to respond to her answers by probing deeper rather than moving on or glossing over them. This, I felt, at that moment, was a risky strategy. Direct and very personal questions have the potential to be perceived as intrusive, inappropriate and rude and could have resulted in the termination of the interview. And yet such questions would be in keeping with the contents and character of the interview and her previous – and perhaps slightly challenging to the interviewer – answers. To not respond to her answers, then, would result in my masking my real questions and would shift the interview back down to the level of data collection rather than empathetic and pointed conversation with a purpose. This would be me 'backing down'. The route I opted for was very productive, in my mind, resulting in further intimate comment and challenges to the interviewee which were robustly answered.

Probing the Interviewee

If I may, could I ask you, I mean, is, is the dancing, um, something that sort of takes care of the hurt or the feelings? I mean, is it a sort of a salve for the, for the...
OK, I'm gonna give, I'm gonna be really candid.
OK.
I, I didn't have a very good childhood. I was, I, my parents died, both of them before I was five and two brothers the same year and I was adopted into a family. It was not good. It was quite abusive and I used to dance – ballet was my escape from reality. And, and I suppose that, that after my divorce I sort of, that drew me back. It's the same thing. When I come here I don't come here to meet men or, and when people ask to dance merengue or – my friend and I and a lot of us, we don't dance merengue – not because we don't like it but because a lot of the men that can dance just want to, they just want to touch you.
Right.
I don't want it. That's not why I'm here. I wanna dance. I wanna feel the music and
Yeah.
– escape reality
Sure.

– to something better, more pure than –

Sure. But if the dancing was escapism for sort of hurt, presumably through the divorce you worked through things; now there is less hurt so there is less need for the dancing?

No. It brings me joy now. It, it's not just that. Even when you have a bad day or a bad week whatever, and you come and dance and you just feel better.

Sure. I mean, can I push you a bit further, a bit more on your feelings when you're dancing. What's the experience like, dancing with different people? Is there a...? What styles are there?

I don't know. I like salsa, and I like a strong lead obviously.

Uhuh.

I don't know how to describe it. I tried to describe it once to somebody and it comes out wrong. I can't think of a way.

Mmmm.

To me, its almost better than sex. When I say that to men they don't get that. They just say that you must not have had good sex. But that's not true. It's, so, the next better word I would say is like nirvana. I don't know what it is. It's like ...

Right.

It's like peace and joy and everything at once.

Sort of –

That's how I feel.

Psychologists have talked about a state of flow. Or where, where, where you lose a sense of self –

– Yeah.

where you just go with the moment and there isn't any past, present, future type of thing –

– Exactly!

Clearly, for Sarah, dancing is her escape. When dancing, Sarah tunes out from all the realities of life going on around her and to her. Through dance, Sarah escapes into her fantasy world. Towards the end of this excerpt, I asked Sarah what it felt like to dance, her experience of dancing. Sarah's answer is that she gets lost in the music and the flow of the movements. For her, dancing is close to her sexual experiences. In dance, she experiences 'peace and joy and everything at once'. It is her nirvana or, as I prompt, a state of flow for her. Having pushed her earlier on the topic of dance and her divorce, I felt reassured when Sarah made her final replies of 'Yeah' and 'Exactly'. Congruence had been maintained between us, and I was reading Sarah's replies within the Barrett-Lennard (1981) empathy cycle model as further confirmation: I was 'checking', intentionally, that communication between interviewer and interviewee was continuing, and using her negative or positive responses to my comments as the measure. They were very positive ('Yeah', 'Exactly!'). I was probing someone's memories – which is essentially what an interview is about. And it should be noted that such an interview is alive, active, transformative and, in its narration, there is an inevitable change to the interviewee's memories: healing, reinforcement, reappraisal, remembering and re-authoring in the telling of stories. To paraphrase Hertz (1997), an interview results in the interviewee retelling their past experiences whilst the interviewer lives and negotiates their present. The interview experience can thus transform self and other as the anthropologist Vincent Crapanzano (1980) found during his interviews with Tuhami: a shift from an 'I–thou' interview relationship into a 'we' relationship (Seidman 1991: 73). A reflexive and auto/biographical narrative route of memory and empathy with ethnographic subjects is duplicitous in its simplicity if it just attends to the narrated moment (see also Eichberg 1994).

Other issues covered in the interview ranged from 'the feel and experience' of salsa dancing, the salsa community and whether or not immigrants were recreating their homeland in their 'everyday' evenings, to female intuition as to male dancer motivations on and off the dance floor. After the interview, during which Sarah had talked about refusing to dance merengue with the men because it was an excuse for them to touch the women, we returned to the dance floor area in Cotton's. They were playing a merengue piece. I joked that it was a pity that it was merengue which she didn't like to dance because of the men. She asked me to dance to it. This request and the enjoyable dance following it I read as signs that the interview had been a success, and that Sarah did not regret her comments and confessions. We resumed a flirtatious banter which continued over the weeks of my research visit. It was only later in a follow-up interview and in some email exchanges that I remembered to ask her about the effects of the dancing prior to the interview. Then, she told me by email how she knew I was genuine; from our initial dance together, she had felt that I too – like her – loved to dance, and from that she sensed that we had had a connection from the start, that we knew each other and responded to each other's perceived intentions. These feelings came from the bodily negotiations of two dancers with a physical skill which they recognised in each other. We had 'read' in each other a 'kinaesthetic empathy' (Parviainen 2002: 20) as our bodies distinguished, comprehended and catered for movements not our own, 'a fragile activity' akin to Ness's (1996: 135, 136) description of dancing with a dance partner: '[i]nnumerable minute adjustments of pressure, speed, and direction, were registered, "heard" and understood performatively through the linking of our hands'. This is how we came to know each other, to rely and trust each other unlike those who interact with us in our daytime relationships. This experience, growing to know the other, Bollen (2001: 291–300 after Diprose 1994) describes as a 'syncretic sociability', an indistinctness between bodies: the transfer and imitative generation of gestures and movements which, in phenomenological terms, can lead to a decreased intolerance to others. In sum, in dance, in the openness of relations with others, we become 'less like ourselves and more like each other' (Bollen 2001: 300). It was the imitative synchronicity of our dancing connection that made Sarah welcome the interview, even offering to go outside to find a quiet spot – something neither she nor I would suggest to a stranger. And this synchronicity allowed her to be so candid and open to a stranger: because I was not really a stranger after all our kinaesthetic negotiations, appropriations and accommodations. I was her dance partner in her monthly moment of peace and bliss and nirvana. Because we had danced, there was a commonly shared notion – or assumption – between us that we knew each other. 'When you touch someone, when you experience someone, it makes you more comfortable with them' were the memorable words which she later emailed to me. This comment substantiated my interview hypothesis that dancing with someone does more than make them feel obliged to agree to be interviewed by you, that dancing with someone relaxes and connects with them, embodied minds reaching out and entangling.

Reflexive Memories, (Post)Modernisation and Dance Ethnography

If Sarah is dancing to achieve nirvana, and if she is dancing just for herself, then she part exemplifies Daniel's (1996) comments about women dancing for themselves, performing an 'autosexuality', with the man as mere appendage. This example of 'women dancing back' (Gotfrit 1988) shows that it is possible to know oneself differently through dance, that dancing can precipitate a powerful sense of longing – the recovery of past pleasures and past times, to feel desire and to feel desired, both sensations courted and orchestrated on and around the dance floor, played with – safe flirting and safe sex that are almost better than the real thing as Sarah would lead us to believe. This is the time that Sarah throws caution to the wind and reduces her levels of self-regulation. This is the time that I myself also felt most comfortable in an alien environment, I the academic migrant fulfilling my own research hypothesis about migrants and their salsa-dancing 'everynight' behaviour recreating their comfort world through physical memory pursuit. This was when I could physically relax. This dancing activity became my familiar home: I embodied my home, safe in salsa. To return to Sarah, this is her response to living in an age of reflexive modernisation when self-monitoring is the powerful norm. Her behaviour ties in with modernist ideals of self-transformation, learning aspirations for the night out to be constructive, structured and only slightly 'edgy', and knowledge acquired to be decontextualised so that these cosmopolitans can use it wherever and whenever they wish (see Hannerz 1990; Lash et al. 1994). The idea of reflexivity as self-monitoring process not only is a thesis relevant to the dancing cosmopolitans of Sacramento, but also fits well with the dancing ethnographer's methodology. Jill Flanders Crosby (1997: 73, 75) found 'motional harmony' from dancing with her Ghanian dance informants before the drums, from sharing meanings and experiences with them, and she suggests that her practice-based anthropology resulted in 'alternate insights and deep perspectives' besides the development of her empathetic kinaesthetic perception in her dance skills. By way of analytic perception, Flanders Crosby 'knew' that her jazz dancing was wrong despite the accuracy of her body patterns and steps. It did not feel right to her until she learned the nuances and meaning of the dance. Likewise, it was only by opening himself up to the habitual nuances of *bata* drumming and the tangible pull of the rhythms that Lindsay (1996: 201–5) felt he had gained 'sensual practical understanding': 'We had learned enough to actualize the identity of gestures and sounds, and the result was uncanny. It was as if we were dancing, wrestling, fencing without visible signs of contact. In reaching out to grasp a rhythm not entirely of its making, my body had become invisible to me, although it maintained a sensual presence' (Lindsay 1996: 201).

These are critical moments when we express ourselves, linking inner worlds of desire for companionship, attractiveness and glamour with outward behaviour. They are also moments when the physical can act as transformative agent for the inner self – self-knowledge, awareness, kinaesthetic perception and even our intellectual development, as Rapport (Rapport with Vaisman 2005) noted recently when tracing his personal and intellectual convictions back to turning points in his life when he was literally turning the soil during fieldwork in rural Wanet.

Memory thus features strongly in this chapter whether it be the interviewee's past narratives about dance and divorce, or the dancers' search for their ideal or idealised time, often their long lost youth. These memories are 'punctual' (Deleuze and Guattari 1999) in that they refer to a specific point on a timeline. Because they refer to times often forgotten till cued or stimulated, these memories are reterritorialising. When associated with becoming, with the future and fantasy proto-narratives of the self, they become anti-memories. The memories and anti-memories crowd into the interview, just as they cloud the relationship between the interviewer and interviewee. As Tietel notes, after an unfortunate encounter with a respondent irked by his interviewer's apparent low status and lack of background knowledge, interviews frequently include the cognitive level of understanding but leave out the affective in the transcript, write-up or analysis. Tietel (2000: 3) concludes from his interviewing experiences that 'special attention has to be given to affective reaction, to the feelings, fantasies and (counter) transferences that crop up in the researcher during his contact with the members of the organisation'. We can add an awareness of these affective reactions going on with 'the researched' to this as well. These reactions all derive from memories from previous experiences and interactions and can manifest themselves in the language – verbal or non-verbal – of the interview, in the choice of words, in the mannerisms and postures adopted. They can also remain contained beneath the surface of the interview: the suspicion, caution and gender issues (Lee 1997); the confidence, desires, loathing, contempt, affection, sympathy and empathy held by the interviewer or interviewee for each other; the projections and fantasies played out in the head (Sarah's mild infatuation, my memories of jive dancing with other flirtatious divorcees on the dance floors of Dundee, Edinburgh and Oxford – the smell of 'Dutch courage' from their mouths, the rough clutching hands, the laughing group having a night out at the expense of the regular dancers around them).

In this case study, any possible evidence of counter-transference would be in my acknowledgement and experience of the power of dance to act as a salve. It was direct experience with this as I once danced through the loss of a relationship – filling my time on the floor – that led me to probe Sarah in my questioning. Rather than treating counter-transference as a neurosis, bias or weakness in the interviewer, it can be used as an important tool in the analysis of the interviewee (Heiman 1950). A sensitive and engaged interviewer is more likely to establish a deep rapport with their interviewee, to gain quality, 'meaningful' material and to be able to verify the accuracy of the material longitudinally in an extended relationship with the interviewee.

But memory can be less elusive than the cognitive fantasies, creations and distortions of representation. Memory can be enacted physically through the unleashing of 'bodynotes'. If a text is a stored representation to be awakened by the reader's mind, then it is possible for the human body to store muscle memories of learned movements, ranging from the ability to hold the body inverted in capoeira (Downey 2005), to flow into the drums and create particular sounds with the hands slapping (Lindsay 1996), or even to perform a salsa shine shoulder shimmy to vibrato music, whether deliberately or quite by accident, as I found out during a tango class I recently took, much to the bemusement of my instructor and amusement of my dance partner. The 'bodynote' is a variant I am coining from Ottenberg's (1990: 142, 144) term the 'headnote', the notes in his mind of other people whom he found turning into a projection of himself, his memories of his field research amongst the Afikpo which he found to be subject to change with the changes in his personal and marital life. For me, the bodynote is a muscle memory, such as a dance step or dance lead. It is stored and then acted out as immanent motility and memory made manifest.

For Ottenberg (1996: 146), his headnotes and his written notes are always in constant dialogue with each other. The headnotes are always considered to be the more important. Bodynotes, like headnotes, are the unseen. They are the potential for certain movement. They are the memory of a dance lesson or dance class which can reappear consciously (I intentionally lead the woman into a 'J' turn by signalling with my left hand or into a 'cross-body lead' by pushing with my left and pulling with my right whilst opening a space with my feet for her to cross past me) or unconsciously (my feet run through patterns of shines (solo footwork) which I have previously learned or seen others do). With Sarah, we dance the salsa and then the merengue. The dance is a getting to know each other, adjusting and calibrating bodies and body knowledges: for instance, I can dance a cross-body lead with her without any difficulty – a standard salsa move, but I could not lead her into complex moves and sequences with lifts or drops with a fingertip lead and little experience together. Both the dancing and the interview, I would suggest, are our 'memory-work', a term Sironen (1994) uses for her exploration of her own sporting and body history.

The Dancing Body Phenomenon

Memories, then, are key to the interview, in both its form and its content. Memory informs the behaviour of the interviewer and interviewee, infringes upon their temporary relationship and is the subject matter of the interview itself. And there are, indeed, different types of memory: the long- and the short-term, also characterised as the semantic and the episodic (Whitehouse 2000) – the former cultural (how to behave or interpret a road sign or dance lead) and the latter personal (an autobiographical memory, such as the recollection of a specific moment during Sarah's divorce); and memories can be 'physical', stored muscle memories, bodynotes conditioned into us or memories supposed to be found in the blood (for Stoller (Stanton 2000: 265), '[t]he body … is the repository of cultural memories – memories "of the flesh" … "sedimented into the body"'; 'blood memory' (Gottschild 2003: 279)). Phil Johnson (2004: 115, 126), for example, in his study of clubbing in London, goes so far as to suggest that the bodily techniques of clubbing, the habitus of the dance, became embodied in the dancers as a 'socio-emotional memory', 'knowledge in the flesh'. Implicit in his use of Bourdieu is the mistaken assumption that body movements represent convincing and uncalculating truths as opposed to imagined and virtual gestures (Langer 1953: 177–78). Both Sarah and I were playing roles during the interview, as well as during the dancing before and after the interview.

Whilst this chapter is a report on interview research in Sacramento, an enquiry into the dancing body and how physicality and perception affect the interview, it is by necessity also an investigation into the nature of perception and perception's place in social interaction. So far, I have argued for an increased attention to 'memory' in ethnographic practice, the interviewer's as well as the interviewee's particular memories. The relationship between the interviewer and the interviewee is also important, not just in structuring the interview, but also for assessing the psychodynamics of the interview. This takes us away, then, from the socially structured notion of collective movements and memories, of Bourdieu's (1977: 78, 95) habitus ('an endless capacity to engender products – thoughts, perceptions, expressions, actions – whose limits are set by the historically and socially situated conditions of its production'), best summed up as 'history turned into nature'.

An attention to perception and the senses in ethnographic practice suggests that anthropologists should connect with phenomenology, the study of phenomena; the radical empiricism of William James, as indeed Stoller (1989: 155) recommends us to do at the end of *The Taste of Ethnographic Things*. But I am not calling for an unreserved shift into a phenomenological approach to ethnographic research and interviewing in particular. A phenomenological approach is one that has the objective of describing 'things as they are' (Jackson 1996). Phenomenology, however, I would declare, is the practice of understanding consciousness from within, the nuances and meanings of everyday practice which Bourdieu rules out as unnecessary for his analysis with the introduction of his habitus concept which stresses the automatic and impersonal nature of everyday practices and experiences. Phenomenology is well suited to anthropology in its anti-ethnocentric tenets and its mutual desire to locate the human condition from inside. As a philosophy and a practice, phenomenology seeks presuppositionless principles for Husserl; it traces inner perception for Bretano; it explores imaginative and personal meanings according to Sartre, and the limits of human intentionality for Levinas. And for Merleau-Ponty (1962: xi), a transcendent phenomenology is about accessing the primary consciousness of what words and things mean. This mode of 'analytic reflection' (Merleau-Ponty 1962: xi) is sheer description *sans* explanation or interpretation, if that is at all possible?[2]

A phenomenological turn, or return, might be seen to reverse the approach taken during the recent crisis in representation in the social sciences and ensuing shift from description to communication. It is, however, a descriptive approach to be adopted with reservation.

In his sophisticated guide to qualitative research interviewing, Steinar Kvale (1996: 53) writes that the phenomenological interview approach 'attempts to get beyond immediately experienced meanings in order to articulate the pre-reflective level of lived meanings, to make the invisible visible'. Whilst I agree with his suggestion that the phenomenological is a focus upon the experienced and the felt, as Merleau-Ponty has stated, Kvale too goes on to reduce the phenomenological to the descriptive in the interview setting. I do not believe that it is possible to obtain such a core ambition. True, the senses, memories and perception will always derive in part from some sociocultural conditions, but they will always be predominantly experienced biographically. This is why we should continue with an ethnography of the particular rather than the whole, 'to describe human consciousness in its lived immediacy' as Jackson (1996: 2) refers to phenomenology, and then to go on and analyse that consciousness, to explore the other's behaviour at the same time as my own behaviour – the 'inter-experience'. This is 'tactile humanism' (Abu-Lughod 1993) rather than 'participant objectivation' (Bourdieu 2003). In other words, my tendencies lie towards the use of phenomenology as a 'social phenomenology' (Laing 1967) rather than Merleau-Ponty's asocial phenomenology. Knowledge in the flesh has to be partial and personal by its very nature. This is why Downey (2005) in his phenomenological study of capoeira expresses sound perception as 'grainy' in keeping with the experience, one learned through apprenticeship, not one stripped of all cultural influence and interpretative language or imagery. This is also why Jackson (1996: 41) turns to the social poetry of William Carlos Williams and Ralph Waldo Emerson at the end of his introduction to the phenomenological approach in anthropology, to the evocation of lived experience not as systematic description but as social metaphor. And this is why Lindsay (1996: 204) characterises his drumming learning as an apprenticeship in African and Afro-Caribbean music traditions with imaginative polyrhythmic pushes and pulls. None of these writers, in any of their work, have the sole goal of reducing their experiences and inter-experiences to their descriptive elements. Phenomenology might well be the 'presuppositionless philosophy' that Wagner (1970: 3) describes, but the phenomenological turn can include memories and interpretations with the experience of motion, 'phenomena such as believing, remembering, wishing, deciding and imagining things; feeling apprehensive, excited, or angry at things; judging and evaluating things; the experiences involved in one's bodily actions' according to Hammond et al (1991: 2). In sum, I am suggesting that meaning and intent belong to the philosophical interest in the subject's *Lebenswelt* (Husserl's 'life world', Heidegger's 'being-in-the-world'), and so internal mechanisms of causation and, psychological and psychoanalytic perspectives, are neither independent of – nor alien to – the desire to fathom the basic experience of the lived world.

Paso Doble Denouement

After dancing with Sarah, she felt comfortable talking with a 'relative' stranger about her feelings towards dance and her dance leads. Echoing Flanders Crosby (1997: 74), these dance descriptions come from the viewpoint of the participant rather than any observer, 'they emphasize the quality of being inside the experience as opposed to visual shape'. I can attest to this on other occasions when I have both joined in dance classes and dances, and video-recorded them, and in the latter I have felt a very different experience: disengaged and uninvolved, restricted in gaze, critical without empathy, a voyeur. In the former I have felt quite the opposite, completely 'enthralled', as Downey (2005: 504) was during his capoeira. In terms of the interview, our dancing together and our shared assumptions about each other and our commitment to the salsa dance and the motives and experiences of dancing salsa, allowed us to move through what in other circumstances would have had to be a number of successive meetings and interactions. We bonded through salsa and so were able to have more of a candid conversation about our dancing than had I followed the traditional 'rape research model' in the social sciences of field penetration and withdrawal. If social science research involving the researching interview of subjects and subsequent writing about them is an Orientalist exercise in knowledge production, then the above case study in interviewing, memory and the senses/phenomenology goes some way towards neutralising such power inequalities.

The following year, Sarah read and commented upon this chapter and told me that some social services training on her medical courses had instilled in her counselling techniques in her conversations, a continual checking and rechecking of questions and responses similar to my social science interview and counselling training. Before, after – and during – the interview, we had been literally dancing around each other.

Notes

1. This somatic memory has been said to include the political oppression of a nation found in Argentinian tango (Taylor 2001).
2. Moran (2000: 3, 20) points out, after Heidegger, that it is not possible to make a description without interpretation, the former being a derivative of the latter. Moreover, contra Merleau-Ponty, Farnell (1999: 148) makes the valid

point that experience through participation is necessarily filtered through the semantics and structure of bodily language and the imagination.

References

Abu-Lughod, L. 1993. *Writing Women's Worlds: Bedouin Stories*. Berkeley: University of California Press.

Appadurai, A. 1990. 'Topographies of the Self: Praise and Emotion in Hindu India', in C. Lutz and L. Abu-Lughod (eds), *Language and the Politics of the Emotion*. Cambridge: Cambridge University Press, pp. 92–112.

Atkinson, P. and D. Silverman. 1997. 'Kundera's Immortality: the Interview Society and the Invention of the Self', *Qualitative Inquiry* 3(3): 304–25.

Barrett-Lennard, G. 1981. 'The Empathy Cycle: Refinement of a Nuclear Concept', *Journal of Counselling Psychology* 28: 91–100.

Behar, R. 1996. *The Vulnerable Observer: Anthropology that Breaks your Heart*. Boston: Beacon Books.

Benney, M. and E. Hughes. 1956. 'Of Sociology and the Interview: Editorial Preface', *American Journal of Sociology* LXII (2): 137–42.

Bollen, J. 2001. 'Queer Kinesthesia: Performativity on the Dance Floor', in J. Desmond (ed.), *Dancing Desires: Choreographing Sexualities On and Off the Stage*. Madison, Wis.: University of Wisconsin Press, pp. 285–314.

Bourdieu, P. 1977. *Outline of a Theory of Practice*. Cambridge: Cambridge University Press.

———. 2003. 'Participant Objectivation', *Journal of the Royal Anthropological Institute* 9(2): 281–94.

Bury, M. 1982. 'Chronic Illness as Biographical Disruption', *Sociology of Health and Illness* 4(2): 167–82.

Church, K. 1995. *Forbidden Narratives*. London: Gordon and Breach Publishers.

Clifford, J. 1988. *The Predicament of Culture: Twentieth-century Ethnography, Literature and Art*. Cambridge, Mass.: University of Harvard Press.

Crapanzano, V. 1980. *Tuhami: Portrait of a Moroccan*. Chicago: University of Chicago Press.

Csikszentmihalyi, M. 2002. *Flow: The Classic Work on How to Achieve Happiness*. London: Random House Group.

Daniel, Y. 1995. *Rhumba: Dance and Social Change in Contemporary Cuba*. Bloomington and Indianapolis: Indiana University Press.

———. 1996. 'Tourism Dance Performances: Authenticity and Creativity', *Annals of Tourism Research* 23(4): 780–97.

Deleuze, G. and F. Guattari. 1999. *A Thousand Plateaus: Capitalism & Schizophrenia*. London: Athlone Press.

Denzin, N. and Y. Lincoln (eds). 1994. *Handbook of Qualitative Research*. London: Sage.

Diprose, R. 1994. 'Performing Body-identity', *Writings on Dance* 11/12: 6–15.

Downey, G. 2005. 'Educating the Eyes: Biocultural Anthropology and Physical Education', in J. Skinner (ed.), Special Issue: Embodiment and Teaching and

Learning in Anthropology, *Anthropology in Action: Journal for Applied Anthropology in Policy and Practice* 12(2): 56–71.

Eichberg, H. 1994. 'The Narrative, the Situational, the Biographical: Scandinavian Sociology of Body Culture Trying a Third Way', *International Review for the Sociology of Sport* 29(1): 99–113.

Farnell, B. 1999. 'It Goes Without Saying – But Not Always', in T. Buckland (ed.), *Dance in the Field: Theory, Methods and Issues in Dance Ethnography*. Basingstoke: Macmillan Press, pp. 145–60.

Finch, J. 1984. '"It's Great to Have Someone to Talk to"': Ethics and Politics of Interviewing Women', in C. Bell and H. Roberts (eds), *Social Researching: Politics, Problems, Practice*. London: Routledge, pp. 70–87.

Flanders Crosby, J. 1997. 'The Dancer's Way of Knowing: Merging Practice and Theory in the Doing and Writing of Ethnography', *Etnofoor* X(1/2): 65–81.

Fontana, A. and J. Frey. 2003. 'From Structured Questions to Negotiated Text', in N. Denzin and Y. Lincoln (eds), *Handbook of Qualitative Research*. Thousand Oaks, Calif.: Sage Publications, pp. 61–106.

Fraleigh, S. 1987. *Dance and the Lived Body: A Descriptive Aesthetics*. Pittsburgh: University of Pittsburgh Press.

Gotfrit, L. 1988. 'Women Dancing Back: Disruption and the Politics of Pleasure', *Journal of Education* 170(3): 122–41.

Gottschild, B. 2003. *The Black Dancing Body: A Geography from Coon to Cool*. New York: Palgrave Macmillan.

Hammond, M., J. Howarth and R. Keat. 1991. *Understanding Phenomenology*. Oxford: Basil Blackwell.

Hannerz, U. 1990. 'Cosmopolitans and Locals in World Culture', in M. Featherstone (ed.), *Global Culture: Nationalism, Globalization and Modernity*. London: Sage Publications, pp. 237–51.

Heiman, P. 1950. 'On Counter-transference', *International Journal of Psycho-analysis* 31: 81–84.

Hertz, R. 1997. 'Introduction: Reflexivity and voice', in R. Hertz (ed.), *Reflexivity and Voice*. Thousand Oaks, Calif.: Sage, pp. vi–xviii.

Jackson, M. 1996. 'Introduction', in M. Jackson (ed.), *Things As They Are: New Directions in Phenomenological Anthropology*. Bloomington: Indiana University Press, pp. 2–50.

Johnson, P. 2004. *Inside Clubbing: Sensual Experiments in the Art of Being Human*. Oxford: Berg.

Jones, S. 2002. 'The Way We Were, Are, and Might Be: Torch Singing As Autoethnography', in A. Bochner, and C. Ellis (eds), *Ethnographically Speaking: Autoethnography, Literature and Aesthetics*. Oxford: Altamira Press, pp. 44–56.

Kvale, S. 1996. *Interviews: An Introduction to Qualitative Research Interviewing*. London: Sage Publications.

Laing, R. 1967. *The Politics of Experience and the Bird of Paradise*. Harmondsworth: Penguin Book.

Langer, S. 1953. *Feeling and Form*. London: Routledge and Kegan Paul.

Lash, S., U. Beck and A. Giddens. 1994. *Reflexive Modernisation*. Cambridge: Polity Press.

Leder, D. 1990. *The Absent Body*. Chicago: University of Chicago Press.

Lee, D. 1997. 'Interviewing Men: Vulnerabilities and Dilemmas', *Women's Studies International Forum* 20(4): 553–64.

Lindsay, S. 1996. 'Hand Drumming: an Essay on Practical Knowledge', in M. Jackson (ed.), *Things as They Are: New directions in Phenomenological Anthropology*. Bloomington: Indiana University Press, pp. 196–212.

Marcus, G. and M. Fischer. 1986. *Anthropology as Cultural Critique: An Experimental Moment in the Human Sciences*. Chicago: Chicago University Press.

Merleau-Ponty, M. 1962. *Phenomenology of Perception*. London: Routledge and Kegan Paul.

Moran, D. 2000. *Introduction to Phenomenology*. London: Routledge.

Ness, S. 1996. 'Dancing in the Field: Notes from Memory', in S. Foster (ed.), *Corporealities: Dancing Knowledge, Culture and Power*. London: Routledge, pp. 129–54.

Ottenberg, S. 1996. 'Thirty Years of Fieldnotes: Changing Relationship to the Text', in R. Sanjek (ed.), *Fieldnotes: The Making of Anthropology*. London: Cornell University Press, pp. 139–60.

Parviainen, J. 2002. 'Bodily Knowledge: Epistemological Reflections on Dance', *Dance Research Journal* 34(1): 11–26.

Rapport, N. with N. Vaisman. 2005. 'The Embodiment of Learning and Teaching: the Enigma of Non-arrival', in J. Skinner (ed.), Special Issue: Embodiment and Teaching and Learning in Anthropology, *Anthropology in Action: Journal for Applied Anthropology in Policy and Practice* 12(2): 1–10.

Robson, C. 1993. *Real World Research: A Resource for Social Scientists and Practitioner-researchers*. Oxford: Blackwell.

Sartre, J. 1955. *Being and Nothingness*. New York: Philosophical Library.

Seidman, I. 1991. *Interviewing as Qualitative Research*. New York: Teachers College Press.

Sheets-Johnstone, M. 1966. *The Phenomenology of Dance*. Madison: University of Wisconsin Press.

Sironen, E. 1994. 'On Memory-work in the Theory of Body Culture', *International Review for the Sociology of Sport* 29(1): 5–13.

Sklar, D. 2000. 'Reprise: On Dance Ethnography', *Dance Research Journal* 32(1): 70–77.

Stanton, G. 2000. 'The Way of the Body: Paul Stoller's Search for Sensuous Ethnography', *European Journal of Cultural Studies* 3(2): 259–77.

Stoller, P. 1989. *The Taste of Ethnographic Things: The Senses in Anthropology*. Philadelphia: University of Pennsylvania Press.

Taylor, J. 2001. *Paper Tangos*. London: Duke University Press.

Thomas, D. 2002. 'Democratizing Dance: Institutional Transformation and Hegemonic Re-ordering in Postcolonial Jamaica', *Cultural Anthropology* 17(4): 512–50.

Tietel, E. 2000. 'The Interview as a Relational Space', *Forum: Qualitative Social Research* 1(3), http://www.qualitative-research.net/fqs-texte/2-00/2-00tietel-e.htm, accessed 14 December 2005.

Tyler, S. 1986. 'Post-modern Ethnography: From Document of the Occult to Occult Document', in G. Marcus and J. Clifford (eds.) *Writing Culture: The Poetics and Politics of Ethnography*. Berkeley: University of California Press, pp. 122–40.

Wagner, H. 1970. 'Introduction', in A. Schutz, *On Phenomenology and Social Relations: Selected Writings*. Chicago, Ill.: University of Chicago Press, pp. 1–52.

Whitehouse, H. 2000. *Arguments and Icons: Divergent Modes of Religiosity*. Oxford: Oxford University Press.

Chapter 8

DUALLING MEMORIES: TWINSHIP AND THE DISEMBODIMENT OF IDENTITY

Dona Lee Davis and Dorothy I. Davis

Memory is an intriguing, complex and multifaceted phenomenon. Memory is poetically depicted as subjective time travel (Tulving 2002), the present of things past (Rapport and Overing 2000: 7), a mental mirror (Kotre 1995), a labyrinth that takes a different turning each time we come back to it (Teski and Climo 1995: 1), and a conundrum of record and resource (Boyarin 1994, Kotre 1995). More prosaically, memory is depicted as everyday forms of social process and action (Garro 2001). Memories also link us to our earlier selves (Lowenthal 1985). Themes of identity, person and selfhood permeate the memory literature (Fivush et al. 1995). Memories impart interesting or important information about events that bridge people's inside and outside worlds (Mageo 2001).

This chapter draws on both the more exotic and the more prosaic aspects of memory. As anthropologists and as identical twins, we present an analysis of memories among two pairs of adult, identical twins that focuses on some of the early developmental identity challenges faced by twins. In the popular science and academic literature identical twins are depicted as truncated or compromised selves, whose embodied likeness and mutuality impede the development of their individuality. As such, they are placed on fault lines (Conklin and Morgan 1995) of Usan constructions of embodied identity and self and personhood.[1,2] We argue, however, that, although identical twins may face some unique challenges as they construct and legitimise their identities, presentation and analysis of their memory narratives show that twins'('s) self-styling develops in accordance with cultural expectations. Nevertheless, the dual, positioned and dialogically co-constructed personal memory narratives of identical twin pairs do provide an interesting lens through which to view memory as a form of social action (and interaction) embedded in wider cultural meaning systems.

Although it is probably not what they had in mind, ours is truly an exercise in what Collins and Gallinat (this volume) term 'double vision'. In its minimalist guise, a twin dyad, we explore thresholds marking individual, personal memory from collective memory. As identical twins ourselves, we have first-hand, everyday and lifetime knowledge of the juxtaposed, embodied, existential worlds of identical twins. In what follows, our own memories and experience, combined with those of other sets of twins, become a resource for putting the I and the we back into the doing and writing of ethnography.

Doubling Visions: Twinship and Twinscapes

As anthropologists and identical twins, we for the first time in our anthropological careers play the native card and become subjects and objects of the anthropological gaze as well as subjects and objects of our mutual and individual memories. We eclectically draw from and combine perspectives of person-centred (LeVine 1982; Hollan 2001) minimalist (Rosaldo 1986; Jackson 1998), and identification (Visweswaran 1994; Behar 1996) ethnography with perspectives of autobiographical (Bartlett 1932; Rubin 1986, 1996) and co-biographical memory (Abelson and Schank 1995; Fivush et al. 1995) theorists. We focus on memory both as a form of social action (Garro 2001) and as a form of narrative or memory story (Baumeister and Newman 1995; Bruner and Fleischer Feldman 1996).

Memory lies at the very heart of reflexivity (Behar 1996). The practice of reflexive self-ethnography or identification theory desegregates boundaries between self and other (Visweswaran 1994; Behar 1996). As twins talking to twins about their lives as twins, we not only bring our subjects to authorship but also draw on our shared worlds and an intimate knowledge of each other to reflect on our own self-makings. We are, at the same time, researchers and informants. The very process of researching and writing this piece is a dialogue of self and other that enacts the very dynamic we seek to analyse. Our goal is not to expose our own vulnerabilities (Behar 1996), but to make a contribution to the memory literature at three of its weaker links. These are: (1) memory as material and embodied; (2) memory as social action and interaction; and (3) memory as shaped by social and cultural processes (Garro 2001; Hollan 2001).

Any discussion of identical twins'('s) memories must take into account the embodied and material aspects of memory. With our informants we have a shared, embodied, dyadic, experience of growing up with a most significant other who shares your face and looks just like you. Others, including your own family members, either confuse your two embodied, personal identities or conflate them into a unit identity such as 'the Davis twins'. We use the term twinship to characterise the twin bond or intimate, social and psychological relationship between twins. Twinship, as we use it entails an insider's (within the twin dyad) perspective. Yet the experience of being twins is not only shaped by twinship. The wider social and cultural contexts also shape the lived worlds of twins. Your twinship may exist in a wider world that views twins as genetic freaks of nature, as good and evil, as good for advertising, etc. These meanings and beliefs or cultural models of identical twins have practical implications concerning what is expected of you and how you live your life. We use the term twinscapes to refer to the singleton (non-twin) view of twins, as well as to twins as situated in the wider, cultural domains of social practice and meaning.

Background: Intertwining Memories

Data for this study come from three narrative-based case studies in which twins reminisce about their childhood as twins. The first case features Tina and Gina, identical twins we interviewed at the 2003 Twinsburg Twin Festival. The second and third cases turn the ethnographic lens on our selves. Case two comes from our Twinsburg research assistant's (Cody 2004) interview of us. While the first two cases capture the more exotic aspects of memory, twinship and Usan twinscapes, case three draws from our own more mundane, everyday memories and comes from narratives explicitly prepared for the purposes of this chapter. Before our personal travels down memory lane begin, however, we take a short detour through the relevant memory literature in order to give our twin memory project an academic as well as a reflexive tone.

The terms autobiographical or personal memory refer to the capacity of individuals to recollect their everyday ordinary lives (Bartlett 1932; Baddeley 1992; Rubin 1996; Garro 2001). Autobiographical memory can be episodic, as in the recall of a single event, or repisodic (Kotre 1995), as in memory of extended situations or typical patterns (Neisser 1988; Garro 2001). Self-stories as a form of autobiographical memories are viewed as the essence of self, self-theories, self-reference, self-definition and identity. Self-stories answer the question of who we are (Rubin 1986, 1996; Kotre 1995: 103) and provide information about our lives from which we are likely to make judgements about our own personalities (Singer and Salovey 1993).

The minimal components of autobiographical and personal memory include verbal narrative, visual imagery and emotion (Bruner and

Fleischer Feldman 1996). Autobiographical memories are constructed through narrative (Abelson and Schank 1995; Kotre 1995; Kirmayer 1996; Rubin 1996). Memory creates narratives and narrative creates memory. Narrative encodes possible ways of knowing and acting, as well as a philosophy of life integral to what a person brings to self-definition or being and acting in the world (Bruner 1994; Abelson and Schank 1995; Baumeister and Newman 1995; Garro 2001). As forms of social action and interaction (Fivush et al. 1995; Garro 2001), personal memories are situated and positioned. They have a location and a point of view (Abelson and Schank 1995; Garro 2001). Autobiographical memories have an audience and enact personal motivations and agendas (Baumeister and Newman 1995). Personal memory is acquired through embodied experiences actually felt by the person and associated with movement and sensory perception (Barclay 1993; Hollan 2001).

As twins and anthropologists, we have four major issues with the literature on autobiographical memory. First, the authoring self and the self described in personal or autobiographical memories are an individual self. Few memory studies feature a dyadic component. Even when terms such as co-constructed and co-biographical (Barclay 1993; Abelson and Schank 1995; Fivush et al. 1995) are used to refer to the recounting of events with others who shared the experience, a standard Western sense of self is assumed. In Western folk theory this is an a priori, essential, embodied, bounded, unique self that is set in contrast to other embodied, bounded, unique selves (Bruner 1994). Secondly, even though memory is recognised as having multiple actors (Conway 1996), the socially textured, interactive dimension of personal memory – as felt relations to others (Haraway 1991), social interactions and social acts used to accomplish everyday, mundane, tasks in the real world (Rubin 1996; Garro 2001) – is rarely addressed. Thirdly, with the exception of memory and embodiment of trauma (Antze and Lambek, 1996, Young 1996), the body as a focus of analytic attention in the memory literature lies largely within the neuro- and cognitive science literature (Tulving 2002). One finds little discussion of how experience is embodied or how the senses and perceptions of the body are culturally elaborated into the experience of self and other (Hollan 2001). This point about culture brings us to a final, fourth, critique of the memory literature. Although personal memories are recognised to be embedded in wider cultural institutions, social relations and meaning systems, little attention is given to explaining how cultural factors come into play or to explicating what happens when there are contradictions between personal experience and expectations based on shared cultural models (Bruner 1990; Antze and Lambek 1996; Rapport and Overing 2000).

The following analysis of identical twins'('s) identity narratives supplies a corrective to these gaps in the memory literature. The three cases that follow are examples of joint reminiscing. They are dyadic, dialogic, co-constructed and co-biographical. Western constructions of selfhood are challenged. Twin selves are less bounded and ego-centred. Their lived worlds are intimately and intensely shared. Among identical twins in Usan culture, a range of potentials for self constructions, past and present, are brought into play (Goffman 1959; Markus and Nurius 1986; Gergen 1994). Instead of self-defining memories (Singer and Salovey 1993), we prefer the terms self-styling or mutually self-styling memories, since they raise situational issues of what self is being defined, by whom, for whom and to what effect or purpose. Our notion of social action both is interactive and spans different time frames. By focusing on the microcosm of twinship and relating it to the notion of twinscapes we hope to put some ethnographic meat on the bones of culture and memory theory. First, however, we need a further word about cultural contradictions and the embodiment of identity in identical twins.

When Connerton (1989) commented on the importance of bodily practice and habits of the body in the formation of collective identity, he was not thinking of identical twins. Neither was Csordas (1990, 1999) when he used the term embodiment to refer to the body as the existential condition of life, the site of apprehension of the world and the subjective and intersubjective ground of experience. Certainly Proust (cited in Connerton 1989: 2) was not thinking of identical twins when he notes that on seeing someone we know we pack the physical outline of the person we see with all the notions we have already formed about them. Identical twins bring a new twist to the notion of embodied identities. Identical twins challenge us to figure bodies from the inside out as well as the outside in. Growing up within the twinscapes of Usan culture, identical twins face cultural contradictions about embodied identity and challenges for self-styling that are not experienced by singletons. They face a development task of interactively disembodying (or detwining or splitting) their identity(ies). Identical twins, particularly in early childhood, must find their own individuality. They must disembody their collective and shared identity to meet the self-development demands or expectations of the wider culture. Within the transcendent and interconnected 'we-ness' of twinship, each twin has to disembody her identity by communicating to others that 'I' am more than just someone who looks like her. We call this dualling.

Dualling Memories

When we originally conceptualised this chapter, we felt quite clever in arriving at the title dualling memories as a fairly straightforward play on words. We are not so sure of that any more. Dualling implies a collaborative, co-biographical effort, shared experiences and a common stock of knowledge (Schuchat 1995). Dualling implies past and present. The homonyms of dualling/duelling also refer to memory as positioned social interaction and knowledge. This encapsulates the notion that memories may be contested. Through the dyadic lens of twinship, we want to capture, within narratives, the process in which the single becomes dualed and the process in which the dualled becomes single. Although twins simultaneously share an immense amount of space and experiences, as the three cases show, it is more than propinquity that binds us together. Twins' collective identity, mutuality and permeability of self-boundaries challenge Western dualistic epistemologies of self and other as well as mind and body. Yet self-styling among twins also includes disembodiment or dualling of identity, a closing off of the body boundaries from those of the other twin. Twins'('s) identities are thus based on a duality of being the same and being different. Dualling in this chapter also implies an academic co-authorship, where we are both researcher and informant. As fifty-nine-year-old twins, with the help of Tina and Gina, we find ourselves, as co-authors, in it together again, mining our collective and individual memories, 'we-ing' and 'I-ing' ethnography as we re-imagine self and other from yet another standpoint of life.

Childhood Memories of Being, Being There and Becoming Different

We use three case studies to explore how childhood memory narratives, as self-styling, embodied forms of social interaction, are embedded within both the twin dyad and the wider Usan cultural context. Each case illustrates a different approach to what we have called the dualling and disembodiment of identity. The cases are examples of a living narrative (Ochs and Capps 2001: 2). They are ordinary social exchanges (rather than polished narratives) in which interlocutors build accounts of life events without knowing where they will lead. A critical feature of narrative is that it forges links between the exceptional and the ordinary (Bruner 1990) or rationalizes puzzling elements to render material acceptable and understandable (Garro 2001). Twins, because they lie on the fault lines of Usan person and selfhood are a particularly suitable subject for a narrative analysis of how culture shapes memory as it contributes to what a person cares about, pays attention to and remembers (Garro 2001).

When interviewing twins at Twinsburg, we were frequently told stories of early childhood identity confusion. We were also told 'favourite twin stories' about how identical twins colluded with each other to play tricks on those (parents, teachers, friends) who could not tell them apart. In mutually reminiscing about their lives together, twins' autobiographical memories also included a 'split episode' or an individuating event such as getting married or leaving home for work or school. The three cases that follow illustrate these themes. In the first, Gina and Tina describe a traumatic emergency room incident where their remembered identities become conflated in an imagined reality of 'being there'. In the second, our Twinsburg research assistant, Kristi Cody (2004), asks us each individually for our first memories. She gets two 'blanket stories', about shared worlds and trickster twins. The first two cases embody what are everyday commonplace memories among twins, but their mystical (or pathological) content also reifies the more exotic twinscapes of Usan culture. The third example also comes from ourselves. Case three is a kind of split story where we reminisce about two very different ponies that entered our life worlds around age seven. We describe how our ponies enabled the disembodiment of a collective identity and set us on the path to more individual or individuated identities. Together the three cases show how life is situated and contextualised and identities are improvised from the resources at hand (Holland et al. 1998).

In writing this chapter, we subject our own memories (and those of Tina and Gina), as twins, to several lines of analysis that reach beyond our previous fieldwork experiences or training in anthropology. We feel secure in our expertise as twins and our ability to share and relive our own experiential worlds of being twins with other sets of twins. The phenomenon of memory and literature on memory, however, constitutes uncharted territory for us. Participating in this project we have seen numerous ways that anthropology can contribute to the memory literature. Each case study, although thematically interrelated, as cultural analysis, will engage the memory literature in a slightly different way

Case One: On Body, Being and Being There

The past is what you remember, imagine you remember, convince yourself you remember or pretend to remember. (Harold Pinter, quoted in Adler 1974: 462)

Case one comes from our interview with Tina and Gina.[3] At the time of our interview (2003), Tina and Gina were thirty-six years old. Gina recently received her Ph.D. and Tina has an MA. They are both college instructors and work at different schools of business. Each twin is married with children and they currently live within six miles of each other. They are very close and both feel that they are at a stage of their life where they have a special appreciation of being twins. Their memory narrative illustrates what Kotre (1995) describes as the curious mix of past and present and memory and imagination. The following narrative comes as an answer to our final interview question: 'Tell us some of your favourite twin stories.' Gina and Tina regard this as a fairly typical twin story. The story enacts a form of intragroup (both within the dyad and among twins) memory that validates the status quo (Mageo 2001) of twinship and marks them off from the singleton-dominated world. It is an experience that places twins on the fault lines of Usan culture in that it raises some interesting issues about selfhood and the embodiment of memory.

Tina: When I was three or four …

Gina: … two or three …

Tina: three, let's agree on three. OK? We were playing hide-and-seek, and our brother jumped out and I put my hand through a china cabinet. Just, you know, a piece of plate glass there. I push my hand through and had to go to the emergency room. [I] Had blood all over. She [Gina] had a tear on her shirt and it had blood on it. She kept crying that her shirt was bleeding. I had cut three major arteries, but she says *her* shirt was bleeding and she was crying. Here, I was in the hospital and they were stitching me up. I'm lying there and I'm looking over there and I see Gina. And I say, Mom, I just want Gina. Can't I go over to Gina? Can't they sew it up over there with her?

Gina: And I was watching her and she was very upset.

Tina: And, when we were nine or ten, we were talking about it. Oh! Do you remember?

Gina: I remember them standing you up and I said she has glass in her feet. She's got glass in her feet.

Tina: They kept standing me up and I'd cry.

Gina: She'd cry.

Tina: They would stand me up again and I'd say it hurts; it hurts; it hurts.

Gina: And I said she has glass in her feet.

Tina: They took the glass out and put two big Band-Aids there.

Gina: She's got big scars there.

Tina: When we were nine or ten we were talking about it. I wanted her there and had my eye on her when they put in the stitches.

Gina: I watched them do it. But then we were thinking this is kind of weird. Why would they let me watch them sewing her up? We were older than that though, I think we were older than that (nine or ten). I think we were eleven or twelve when we were telling that, 'cause I was saying 'I think that's pretty sick. They were letting me watch them sewing her up.' And our Mom goes, 'You weren't even in the same room, Gina. You were out in the waiting room crying hysterically. There was no way they would let you in there. You were not there.'

Tina: So that was our only twin psychic type of thing, which we don't buy into. Ha Ha.
Gina: I still have the visual memory of the seat, everything, watching her. It was real. That's our only weird thing.

Tina and Gina's memories of the trauma and of each other in the emergency room, although not veridical, are vivid and real. Their memory narrative positions them both as apart and together. The narrative is dualling in the sense that it is co-told and boundaries of self and other in terms of embodied experiences are permeable. The narrative is duelling as fact and fiction are played against each other, as are memories from different life stages and the mother's versus the twins'('s) memory of the event. This memory contains elements of self and not self, because the narrative story is both self and twin/twinship defining. Embedded within the narrative are embodied dualities of connectedness and separation. On the one hand, this living narrative supports Usan twinscapes of identical twins having overlapping, confused or conflated identities and a more exotic but also stereotypical notion about a mystical, embodied, psychic, unity of the twins (Johnson 2004). The more psychologically inclined (Schave and Ciriello 1983) might argue that Tina and Gina's confused self-styling narrative represents some unresolved identity conflict or failures in individuation. On the other hand, Tina and Gina accept the rationale that Gina would not have been admitted to the emergency room and state that in later childhood they came to accept their mother's version of events. Nevertheless, the memory remains real to both of them.

Gina and Tina's case offers some interesting challenges to the memory literature. According to Lowenthal (1985: 195) memories can never fully be shared: 'For someone else to know about my memory is not the same as having it. We can no more share a memory then we could share a pain.' Yet, in their narrative and in their memories, Tina and Gina do share (as real) Tina's pain and frightening experience. Even accepting the mother's version, if not in the emergency room, Gina was crying hysterically in the waiting room. Their emotional distress was mutual and interactive. Tina and Gina both felt it was natural for Tina's distress to also be felt and embodied in Gina. The twin twist (as a twin memory story) here comes not from confusion of identity, as Gina knows she is Gina and Tina knows she is Tina, but from the shared distress as well as the vivid sharing of the false emergency room memory, which features the disembodiment of Gina (in the sense that she is in two places at the same time). The point they make is that twinship is a special relationship, a sense of attachment, empathetic connectedness and sharing that conflates or joins both mind and body and self and other. Yet also embedded within this story of shared worlds and empathetic connectedness is a story of discovering difference, individuality and bodily boundaries. Tina and Gina do not buy into an extrasensory perception (ESP) explanation. At an older age they come to re-examine this memory and concur with their mother's version of what actually happened. Twins with their shared worlds and identical faces and embodied likeness have identity challenges that are not 'faced' by those in the singleton world. Nevertheless, within their short narrative, their dyadic bond becomes re-contextualised in the wider cultural milieu that stresses the importance of an embodied, bounded, individual self.

Case Two: Trickster Twins and Blanket Identities

> Intragroup memories provide a kind of protective shell that solidifies group identity (in contradiction to others) and represents a unified front to the world. (Mageo 2001: 13)

According to Bruner and Feldman (1996: 292), autobiographical memory creates a life story around a self under particular constraints that are shared with no one else. Memory is subjective in that it is uniquely ours. Even memory among those in a close dyadic relationship (husband and wife) shows a kind of Rashoman effect and becomes told as two different stories. Yet because of their situated closeness in early childhood, as in the case of Tina and Gina, twin memories evoke an enormous archive of shared experiences. While interviewing twins at Twinsburg we found that among the personal fables (Kotre 1995) of twinship were first memories as twins. There seems to be a folk theory among twins that because they spent so much time in each others company, they can remember things from an earlier age than singletons. Early childhood memory is a topic of considerable debate. Our 'blanket case' addresses issues of primary and secondary memory.

Since we were identical twins interviewing identical twins at Twinsburg, we thought it appropriate to be subjects of our study. Our student research assistant, Kristi Cody (2004), interviewed us, using her own interview schedule. She asked us, without consulting each other, to email her a short narrative of our respective first memories of being a twin. These memories came as a big surprise to the three of us and make up case two. The similarities of our memories will be familiar to twins or to those close to them. It is a kind of twin trickster tale where twins collude in using their physical similarity to switch identities or confuse others. But sometimes it is just the two twins collectively occupying the same space at the same time, sharing agency or acting together, positioned as a unit that anchors the tale.

Dorothy: This question is not easy to answer. I have many early memories of stuff that Dona and I did together. I remember playing hide and seek under a blanket with Dona. Dona and I are hiding from our older sister, Pam. We were young enough to think that she really didn't know where we were when the blanket was over us ... whatever Piaget development stage that is???

Dona: When we were babies, Dorothy and I shared a room. We each had cribs on opposite sides of the room. There was a big space in the middle. Our Mother must have put us down to play because I remember being on the floor with lots of blankets. I think we were crawling but not walking. My older sister, Pam, brought her red haired friend to see us. They opened the door to see us. Dorothy and I were hiding under the blanket. We were laughing because they couldn't see us. They made a big deal about 'where could the twins be, where are they?' We thought we had fooled them. It was a conscious act of collaboration and planning even if we were stupid enough (speaking in a Piaget sense) to think that no one knew that the two giggling lumps under the blanket were us.

Our written memory (or should we say memories?) of being together under the blanket contains a vivid imagery of a single incident. This is called a flashbulb (Fitzgerald 1988) or flashback (Rubin 1996) memory. According to Kotre (1995), first memories exist on the border between memory and dream and there is no research that can tell one from the other. Most memory experts assert that language must precede memory (Hudson 1986) and memory for those less than three years old is non-existent. As 'crawlers', for us it is therefore unlikely that this could be a direct memory. Kotre (1995) like the two of us, refers to Piaget, stating that it is difficult, if not impossible, to recover memory through the eyes of a child who has not yet acquired the cognitive skills we reflexively take for granted as adults. Among these skills is the ability to employ conventional narrative structures for memory. Although we cannot remember being told this as a story, it is most probably a secondary memory or a version of a story told to or about us by family members, or what Lowenthal (1985: 96) refers to as 'the remembering things from the remembering of them'. Even if this was a family story, we both sincerely doubt that it had a Piaget caveat in the family's telling. Perhaps the blanket case shows us that you can take the memory out of the anthropologist but cannot take the anthropologist out of the memory.

Earliest memories as personal fables or myth makers, however, do establish the place where you began (Kotre 1995). They reveal a person's attitude towards self and others and life in general (Huyghe 1985). Our twin trickster story is not a story of confused identity; it is a story of being in it together. The blanket is our protective shell. It unites us in our own environment. Dualling here means that both first memories are the same.

But it also means that the memory narrative co-embodies and unties us and at the same time it closes us off from the outside world. We are the giggling lump under the blanket. Our memory entails a sense of self and other as collaborators in action but also a sense of self and other as insiders, under the blanket, and outsiders, our mother, our older sister and her friend. Twinship for us was in many ways a joint enterprise. Like many twins, we shared a room, we shared a life and we were always together.

Yet memory experts like Kotre hold that, although the memories date back to childhood, they are really about a person's entire life, especially the present conditions of life (Kotre 1995). These are culturally shaped. Although describing a joint endeavour, the process of remembering in our narratives is contextualised and marked by each narrator's use of 'I' and personal identifying names. It is also dualled as a tale told by two individuals about us and them. Moreover, the blanket memory joins the children under the blanket with the present-day academics. This memory is also positioned in contemporary social relationships. Audience is important here too (Hirst and Manier 1996; Rubin 1996; Mageo 2001). It is a case of two rather pedantic professors that have a tale to tell a student. Narrative is created by the process of retrieval and influenced by our goals at the time of recording as well as retrieval (Rubin 1996). Like Tina and Gina and ESP we are quite sanguine about the similarity of our narratives. It's just part of being twins. What does on reflection bother us is that neither one of us is very keen on Piaget's theories.

Case Three: Material Memories and the Emponyment of Identity

Dorothy: You are your pony.
  Dona: I loved Bobby Boy with all my heart. He was mine, mine, mine, mine.

Dening (2001: 209), when he states, 'I recognize myself in the mirrors of otherness around me,' was probably not thinking of twins riding their ponies, nor was Haraway (1991) when she comments that intragroup memory involves states of embodiment and felt relations to others. Yet self and family narratives of us as twins and as individuals feature repisodic memories of our respective ponies as instrumental in effecting the type of persons we would each become. We call this the emponyment of identity. For each of us our pony became a significant 'other'. For the first time in our young lives, sitting on our respective ponies, our father could actually tell us apart. Yet the ponies mean much more in that they have emerged as condensing narratives of how we are and have become, same and different.

> Dona: The horse thing was very much a part of our identities. They [our ponies] were in the family until we were twenty-seven and embody memories of our early childhood and adolescence.
> Dorothy: Dona and I both see that our involvement with our ponies and challenges they presented as being integral to our personality development. These ponies were our pets from second grade all the way through college.

Data for case three come from two largely chain-of-consciousness autobiographical essays we each independently wrote about our ponies. We approached the project as homework (Visweswaran 1994), or an opportunity to develop our own self-styling narratives. After writing the initial essays, we commented on each other's essays in order to give a collaborative, processual and negotiated dimension to the project. Our analysis of the emponyment of identity starts with a discussion of material and embodied memory and ends with a discussion of family, individuality and shared and non-shared environments.

Material memory receives little attention in the personal memory literature. The term material memory (Lowenthal 1985; Middleton and Edwards 1990) refers to artefacts, pictures and literature as well as to the physical environment. Photographs are a kind of material memory (Kotre 1995). Probably over 90 per cent of our pictorial history, up until late adolescence, captures us on a pony or later a horse. A picture of us at our first Christmas shows us, at nine months old, sitting together under the Christmas tree, dressed exactly alike, in footed pyjamas with cowboy hats and gun belts and each holding an identical stuffed black horse set on wheels. Like many middle-class twins raised in the 1950s, our parents felt that the only way to treat us fairly was to treat us equally. Our physical similarity was reflected in the duality of a material world that included our toys, clothes and other objects, such as identical twin beds.

When we were seven years old, we were each given a pony of our own, resulting in the formation of new dyads and the emergence of new quadratic relationships. Although our father initially set out to find us two similar, if not identical, ponies, he ended up buying two very distinctive ponies. Our ponies were the only material things we had ever been given that did not arrive at the same time and were not exactly alike. In case three, dualling involves same (getting a pony and riding them together every day) and duelling involves difference (the ponies themselves).

> Dorothy: Bobby Boy and Pepper were as different as night and day.

Dona: Bobby Boy and Pepper were the first parts of our lives that were different. We were both to be equally adept riders but with very different mounts.

Dorothy: We spent our formative years on those ponies.

Attachment, literally and figuratively, to our ponies anchored for each of us as a sense of mutual embodied identity of twins with ponies that included the embodiment of a differentiating new dyad, that of each twin and her own pony.[4] The ponies are not just abstract or condensed symbols of identity; they were also their own beings with their own realities. They offered very different challenges and opportunities to each twin.

Dona: Bobby Boy was just over eleven hands high and could jump four and one half feet. He flew around the arena and never refused or ran out. He was a remarkable pony. He could do anything but he was not an easy ride.

Dorothy: Pepper was generally considered to be the prettier pony. He was a blue roan. He had good conformation. Dorothy got the good-looking one and Dona got the better-performing one.

Although they brought new opportunities for enhanced mutuality and shared experience, the ponies stand out in our memories as our first experiences if not exactly as a non-shared world at least as mutually exclusive identity links. The ponies opened up new opportunities for positioning self and other in the twin dyad. If not exactly 'a split episode' of going our separate ways in life, each of us receiving a pony of our own marks the beginning of a transformational, pre-adolescent, individualising period of our young lives. The following statements illustrate how the physical attributes of our ponies (colouring) may continue to influence our material worlds in terms of consumption patterns, accessorising and self-styling (literally the clothes we put on our bodies today).

Dorothy: Pepper was a blue roan. Blue is my favourite colour.

Dona: Bobby Boy was a pinto [black, white and brown]. Showing Dorothy got all the flashy outfits. She wore turquoise and black. I wore brown and gold.

Dorothy: I got to wear blue and she got stuck with dull old brown or mustard yellow. Mother insisted our outfits be coordinated with our ponies. I was the big winner here since I liked blue so much.

Dona: Look in our closets today. Dona's clothes are all black and brown and Dorothy has more bright colours and pastels. Dona's hair remains dull birth brown while Dorothy is a flashy blonde.

Autobiographical memory is not simply a declaration of what we have experienced or things we have possessed; it also includes dispositions to act (Kirmayer 1996). Given the fact that we are middle-aged women, why do we feature two ponies that we were given over fifty years ago in our identity or self-styling memory narratives? Are we not, as Dorothy says, 'putting the cart before the horse'? Certainly, as we have gone our separate ways in life, our identities have taken many different and differentiating twists and turns. But ponies are an important part of our family memory stories. Although we did not realise it at the time, we were writing what Kotre (1995) calls family memory stories. In middle-class American culture, the family plays an important role in personal explanatory systems and the organisation of experience. Family memories nourish the idea that we are special and define the traits of its individual members (Kotre 1995; Bruner and Fleischer Feldman 1996).

One kind of family memory story is the origin story. In accounts of what you were like as a child, the family identifies and reinforces personality traits it sees in you today (Kotre 1995). Plomin and Daniels (1985) state that non-shared environments in a family make children from the same family different from one another. For us, beginning at age seven, our ponies became an element in a non-shared environment, but they also became a family resource for developing and dualling our distinctive identities. When Dona's husband, Richard, first met her family, he asked our older brother Barry what he (Barry) could tell him about the kid he married: his (Richard's) thirty-four-year-old wife. This is Barry's response: 'Well, you've got to understand, Richard, they had these two ponies. Dona had this hot little pony called Bobby Boy and Dorothy had this pretty pony called Pepper.' The subtext of Barry's statement is that Dorothy still needs to be pretty and Dona still needs to be reined in. Our own narratives echo these family origin themes as a strategy for presenting the past to explain more contemporary dispositions and behaviours. Dorothy (who self-styles as having put family before career) describes how Pepper made her a better mother. Dealing with a stubborn and bad-tempered pony made her patient, understanding and nurturing. Dona (who has no children, but did not mention this in the essay) is more performance oriented and refers (in response to Dorothy's mother comments) to Bobby Boy's influence on her career (Dona fell off her pony and got hurt more than Dorothy did). Comparison of the two quotes indicates sameness and difference in terms of acquisition of the same skills but of putting them to different uses.

> Dorothy: I believe that my equine experiences have made me a better mother. Learning to deal with a green animal that outweighs you by six hundred pounds, has some powerful jaws and four metal-clad hooves is excellent preparation for dealing with a human two-year-old.

> Dona: Career-wise I think the pony years gave me a sense of stick-to-it-ness and seeing it through by getting back on that pony and showing him who was the boss.

Our essays also mention how our respective ponies influenced our taste in men and our eventual spouse choices. Dorothy is divorced and Dona happily married.

> Dorothy: Dona and I have often referred to our relationships to men in pony terms. She married Bobby-Boy and I married Pepper.
> Dona: I did get the Bobby Boy. I call my [bearded] husband Fuzz Face One and my current horse Fuzz Face Two.

There are several limitations to these exercises in family memory. First of all they have little meaning as family memory stories apart from their comparison value, e.g. both are tomboys but Dona more so than Dorothy. They exaggerate our differences and distinctiveness, while overlooking our similarities. Even on our ponies we were still constantly in each other's company. Secondly, away from the barn and outside the immediate family, these stories were not shared. For example, our school friends knew we had ponies but that was pretty much it. Thirdly, many character traits we both associate with the ponies were actually recognised before we got the ponies.

> Dorothy: Actually I think our family would say Dorothy was more mothering from the get-go. Barry used to say Dorothy was the little mother and Dona the little football player.

Fourthly, we certainly recognise that our contemporary selves reflect the many different life choices we have made. There was and is a life beyond the ponies. Dorothy writes about it; Dona does not. At the end of her intensely personal pony essay that she wrote for her own children, Dorothy asks if we are putting too much emphasis on an event that happened over fifty years ago. Dona, whose essay was far less personal and is written more like a topical fieldwork report, responds, 'Maybe it's just making sense of a way of making sense.'

Before we conclude this section we would like to raise one final issue that points to both the strengths and limitations of minimalist or reflexive strategies for 'I-ing' or 'we-ing' ethnography. Person-centred ethnography is just that – person-centred. Self-involved, reflexive data can be very skewed data. The data do not encompass a very wide range of perspectives. Nor do they open the door to multiple players. In this case the family stories and opinions shared among the children of a family are not necessarily those of the parents. During the summer when we were writing our pony memories, Dona went to visit our mother and asked her how she thought our ponies had made us different. Expecting a parentally perceptive analysis of the issue, which clearly meant so much to us, Dona did not anticipate the dismissive answer Mother gave to the question.

> Mother: I used to worry about you both when you [Dona] had the good pony and Dorothy had the bad one, but then Dorothy got the better horse so you both came out equal in the end.

Mother took a long-range view and clearly was not into the details. Perhaps our father, who rode his own horse with us and who spent hours on end with us at the barn, would have a different answer, but he died even before the ponies left us. It is our siblings who currently supply the details. Our younger brother, Robert, was so touched by our essays that he put them in the family Bible. Our older brother, Barry, surrounded by children and grandchildren of his own, still tells horse show stories at family gatherings that tease us by condensing our identities to our emponyed childhood experiences.

Our ponies were real-world entities. They were also and continue to be core family symbols for defining special traits of its *individuals*. Although recognising our twinship, these family stories both document and nurture our differences, thus bringing us in line with Usan culture and its Western style of a distinctive, individuated and bounded self. Aside from Plomin and Daniels (1985), however, and their interest in how non-shared environments within a family can make children from the same family so different from one another, little attention has been paid to how nurture in the form of singleton siblings and even family pets may shape the experiential realities of twins and socialise them into wider social expectations concerning person and selfhood.

Conclusion

We began this chapter with depictions of memory as a mixture of poetic and prosaic phenomena. Identical twins, too, have their poetic and prosaic components. We have played the native card and used ourselves as data. By focusing on the dualling of twins'('s) co-biographical memories as embodied imaginaries, as collective and mutual, as material and as family self-styling stories, we have entered a territory of ethnographic investigation that lies beyond both space and time (Teski and Climo 1995: 1). Like Bloch (1995), we take issue with the assumptions of many psychologists, interested in memory in everyday life, that the relationship between actors and their external worlds are unproblematic. Through the lens of twinship and twinscapes, we have tried to explicate ways in which personal memories are culturally embedded, culturally embodied, forms of social action.

Notes

1. The term Usan culture (Boulanger 2008) refers to society and culture in the United States.
2. For example, identical twins are referred to as clones and freaks (Wright 1997); as a single unit (Segal 1999); as having mutual or symbiotic identities and diffuse ego boundaries and as inhabiting another person's being (Angle and Neimark 1997).
3. Tina and Gina's narrative comes from open-ended interviews we conducted among twenty-three sets of identical twins at the annual Twinsburg Twins Festival during the summer of 2003.
4. Autobiographical memory also includes knowledge, embodied habits and acquired skills (Kirmayer 1996). Our equine twinship memories are embodied in a co-mutuality of horses and riders as well as in the sense that our riding skills are encoded in muscle memory and remain with us today. This is a non narrative form of memory.

References

Abelson, R.P. and R.C. Schank. 1995. 'Knowledge and Memory', in R.S. Wyer (ed.), *Knowledge and Memory: The Real Story* (Advances in Social Cognition, no. 8). Hillsdale: Lawrence Erlbaum Associates, pp. 1–85.

Adler, T. 1974. 'Pinter's Night: a Stroll Down Memory Lane', *Modern Drama* 17: 461–65.

Angle, R. and J. Neimark. 1997. 'Nature's Clones', *Psychology Today* July/August: 39–69.

Antze, P. and M. Lambek. 1996. 'Introduction: Forecasting Memory', in P. Antze and M. Lambek (eds), *Tense Past: Cultural Essays in Trauma and Memory*. New York: Routledge, pp. xi–xxxviii.

Baddeley, A.D. 1992. 'Is Memory All Talk?' *The Psychologist* 5: 447–48.

Barclay, C. 1993. 'Remembering Ourselves', in G.M. Davies and R.H. Logie (eds), *Memory in Everyday Life*. Amsterdam: Elsevier Science Publishers, pp. 285–309.

Bartlett, F. C. 1932. *Remembering: A Study in Experimental and Social Psychology*. Cambridge: Cambridge University Press.

Baumeister, R.F. and L.S. Newman. 1995. 'The Primacy of Stories, the Primacy of Roles, and the Polarizing Effects of Interpretive Motives: Some Propositions about Narratives', in R.S. Wyer (ed.), *Knowledge and Memory: The Real Story* (Advances in Social Cognition no. 8). Hillsdale: Lawrence Erlbaum Associates, pp. 97–108.

Behar, R. 1996. *The Vulnerable Observer: Anthropology that Breaks your Heart*. Boston: Beacon Press.

Bloch, M.1995. 'Internal and External Memory: Different Ways of Being in History', in P. Antze and M. Lambek (eds), *Tense Past*. New York: Routledge, pp. 215–233.

Boulanger, C. 2008. 'Usans: the Real People Confront Globalization', in C. Boulanger (ed.), *Reflecting on America: Anthropological Views of U.S. Culture*. Boston: Pearson, pp. 9–11.

Boyarin, J. 1994. 'Space, Time, and the Politics of Memory', in J. Boyarin (ed.), *Remapping Memory: The Politics of Time Space*. Minneapolis: University of Minnesota Press, pp. 1–38.

Bruner, J. 1990. *Acts of Meaning*. Cambridge: Harvard University Press.

———. 1994. 'The "Remembered" Self', in U. Neisser and R. Fivush (eds), *The Remembering Self: Construction and Accuracy in the Self Narrative*. Cambridge: Cambridge University Press, pp. 41–54.

Bruner, J. and C. Fleisher Feldman. 1996. 'Group Narrative as a Cultural Context of Autobiography', in D.C. Rubin (ed.), *Remembering Our Past*. Cambridge: Cambridge University Press, pp. 291–317.

Cody, K. 2004. 'Twins Talk: a Set of Twin Anthropologists Conducting Research at the Twins Days Festival in Twinsburg Ohio', Paper presented at the Society of Anthropology in Community Colleges Annual Meeting, Montreal, April 2 2004.

Conklin, B. and L. Morgan. 1995. 'Babies, Bodies and the Production of Personhood in North American and Amazonian Society', *Ethos* 24: 557–694.

Connerton, P. 1989. *How Societies Remember*. Cambridge: Cambridge University Press.

Conway, M.A.1996. 'Autobiographical Knowledge and Autobiographical Memories', in D.C. Rubin (ed.), *Remembering Our Past*. Cambridge: Cambridge University Press, pp. 67–93.

Csordas, T.J. 1990. 'Embodiment as a Paradigm for Anthropology', *Ethos* 18: 5–47.

———. 1999. 'The Body's Career in Anthropology', in Henrietta Moore (ed.), *Anthropological Theory Today*. Cambridge: Polity Press, pp. 172–205.

Dening, G. 2001. 'Afterword: On the Befores and Afters of the Encounter', in J.M. Mageo (ed.), *Cultural Memory: Reconfiguring History and Identity in the Postcolonial Pacific*. Honolulu: University of Hawaii Press, pp. 205–16.

Fitzgerald, J.M. 1988. 'Vivid Memories and the Reminiscence Phenomenon: the Role of a Self Narrative', *Human Development* 31: 261–73.

Fivush, R., C. Haden and E. Reese.1995. 'Remembering, Recounting, and Reminiscing: the Development of Autobiographical Memory in Social Context', in D.C. Rubin (ed.), *Remembering Our Past*. Cambridge: Cambridge University Press, pp. 341–359.

Garro, L.C. 2001. 'The Remembered Past in a Culturally Meaningful Life: Remembering as Cultural, Social, and Cognitive Process', in C.C. Moore and H.F. Mathews (eds), *The Psychology of Cultural Experience*. Cambridge: Cambridge University Press, pp. 105–47.

Gergen, K. 1994. 'Mind, Text, and Society: Self-Memory in Social Context', in U. Neisser and R. Fivush (eds), *The Remembering Self*. Cambridge: Cambridge University Press, pp. 78–104.

Goffman, E. 1959. *The Presentation of Self in Everyday Life*. New York: Doubleday.

Haraway, D. 1991. *Simians, Cyborgs, and Women*. New York: Routledge.

Hirst, W. and D. Manier. 1996. 'Remembering as Communication: a Family Recounts its Past', in D.C. Rubin (ed.), *Remembering Our Past*. Cambridge: Cambridge University Press, pp. 271–90.

Hollan, D. 2001. 'Developments in Person-centered Ethnography', in C.C. Moore and H.F. Mathews (eds), *The Psychology of Cultural Experience*. Cambridge: Cambridge University Press, pp. 48–67.

Holland, D., D. Skinner, W. Lachicotte and C. Cain. 1998. *Identity and Agency in Cultural Worlds*. Cambridge: Harvard University Press.

Hudson, J. A. 1986. 'Memories are Made of This: General Event Knowledge and the Development of Autobiographic Memory', in K. Nelson (ed.) *Event Knowledge*. Hillsdale: Lawrence Erlbaum Associates, pp. 97–118.

Huyghe, P. 1985. 'Voices, Glances, Flashbacks: Our First Memories', *Psychology Today* September: 48–52.

Jackson, M. 1998. *Minima Ethnographica*. Chicago: University of Chicago Press.

Johnson, E. 2004. 'Twins Talk: an Anthropological Analysis of ESP Stories', Paper presented at the Anthropology in Community Colleges Annual Meeting, Montreal April 2 2004.

Kirmayer, Laurence J. 1996. 'Landscapes of Memory: Trauma, Narrative, and Dissociation', in P. Antze and M. Lambek (eds), *Tense Past*. New York: Routledge, pp. 173–98.

Kotre, J. 1995. *White Gloves: How We Create Ourselves Through Memory*. New York: The Free Press.

LeVine, R. A. 1982. *Culture, Behavior, and Personality: An Introduction to the Comparative Study of Psycho-Social Adaptation*. New York: Aldine.

Lowenthal, D. 1985. *The Past is a Foreign Country*. Cambridge: Cambridge University Press.

Mageo, J.M. 2001. 'On Memory Genres: Tendencies in Cultural Remembering', in J. M. Mageo (ed.), *Cultural Memory: Reconfiguring History and Identity in the Postcolonial Pacific*. Honolulu: University of Hawaii Press, pp. 11–31.

Markus, H. and P. Nurius. 1986. 'Possible Selves', *American Psychologist* 41: 954–69.

Middleton, D. and D. Edwards. 1990. 'Introduction', in D. Middleton and D. Edwards (eds), *Collective Remembering*. London: Sage Publications, pp. 1–22.

Neisser, U. 1988. 'What is Ordinary Memory the Memory of?', in U. Neisser and E. Winograd (eds), *Remembering Reconsidered: Ecological and Traditional Approaches to the Study of Memory*. Cambridge: Cambridge University Press, pp. 356–73.

Ochs, E. and L. Capps. 2001. *Living Narrative: Creating Lives in Everyday Storytelling*. Cambridge: Harvard University Press.

Plomin, R. and D. Daniels. 1985. 'Why are Children in the Same Family So Different from One Another?' *Behavioral and Brain Sciences* 10: 1–60.

Rapport, N. and J. Overing. 2000. *Social and Cultural Anthropology: Key Concepts*. London: Routledge.

Rosaldo, R. 1986. 'Ilongot Hunting as Story and Experience', in V.W. Turner and E.M. Bruner (eds), *The Anthropology of Experience*. Chicago: University of Illinios Press, pp. 97–138.

Rubin, D.C. 1986. 'Introduction', in D.C. Rubin (ed.), *Autobiographical Memory*. Cambridge: Cambridge University Press, pp. 3–16.

———. 1996. 'Introduction', in D. C. Rubin (ed.), *Remembering Our Past*. Cambridge: Cambridge University Press, pp. 1–15.

Schave, B. and J. Ciriello. 1983. *Identity and Intimacy in Twins*. New York: Praeger.

Schuchat, M. G. 1995. 'It Only Counts If You Share It', in M.C. Teski and J.J. Climo (eds), *The Labyrinth of Memory: Ethnographic Journeys*. Westport: Bergin and Garvey, pp. 129–140.

Segal, N. 1999. *Twins and What They Tell Us About Human Behavior*. New York: Palgrave Macmillan.

Singer, J.A. and P. Salovey. 1993. *The Remembered Self*. New York: The Free Press.

Teski, M. and J. Climo. 1995. 'Introduction', in M.C. Teski and J.J. Climo (eds), *The Labyrinth of Memory: Ethnographic Journeys*. Westport: Bergin and Garvey, pp. 1–12.

Tulving, E. 2002. 'Episodic Memory: From Mind to Brain', *Annual Review of Psychology* 53: 1–25.

Visweswaran, K. 1994. *Fictions of Feminist Ethnography*. Minneapolis: University of Minnesota Press.

Wright, L. 1997. *Twins and What They Tell Us about Who We Are*. New York: John Wiley & Sons.

Young, A. 1996. 'Bodily Memory and Traumatic Memory', in P. Antze and M. Lambek (eds), *Tense Past: Cultural Essays in Trauma and Memory*. New York: Routledge, pp. 89–102.

Chapter 9

REMEMBERING AND THE ETHNOGRAPHY OF CHILDREN'S SPORTS

Noel Dyck

Introduction

Positioned at the analytical intersection between childhood as a realm of socialisation and sport as a medium of physical and cultural expression, children's sports readily accommodate a premise of futurity. Games and performances conducted in the 'here and now' may be read as offering previews of the finished products – that is, the young men and women – expected to step forth in due course from these and other venues of childhood. Socialisation studies of the sort pursued within psychology tend to focus greater attention upon the definition and calibration of general stages and anticipated sequences of developmental processes than upon particular settings and differing renderings of childhood. Since anthropologists characteristically rely upon ethnographic enquiry and comparative analysis, our explorations are inclined to search out differences as well as similarities in various constructions of childhood, including those featuring complicated temporal orientations. Indeed, one of the more ticklish challenges awaiting ethnographers of childhood is that of delineating the ways in which competing versions of the future, the present and the past may collide within given contexts.

This chapter takes up these concerns through an examination of the manner in which remembering comprises a frequently encountered and yet ambiguous component of child and youth sports in contemporary Canada. In addition to identifying how varying modes of remembering operate within a social realm that is otherwise so markedly oriented towards futurity, I will consider how these practices can pose methodological problems for ethnographers working in this field. Addressing these questions requires an appreciation of the organisational features of child and youth sports and of the cultural variability of diverse forms of childhood. In tracking the experiences and beliefs of others within these environs, an ethnographer of childhood sooner or later stumbles across more or less fulsome or intense memories and personal adjudications of her or his own childhood. Was it a 'good', 'bad' or unremarkably 'normal' childhood that an individual anthropologist brings to her or his investigations of childhood? To what extent and how might fleeting memories or more finished 'accounts' of one's own childhood affect the anthropologist's perusal of the social terrain occupied by children and youth as well as by parents, coaches and other adult figures?

By the same token, many ethnographers of sport embark upon this field of study equipped with personal experience of having played one or several sports. Embodied memories of acquired physical movements and the incorporated aesthetics of particular styles of play and performance may draw one's attention to specific practices and accordingly shape the framing of analyses mounted within ethnographies of sport. In my own case, a number of dimensions of remembering have been brought into play through my return as an anthropologist to the realm of children's sports. Here I shall tackle the possibilities and implications of opting to recognise and harness memories from one's childhood as well as from other personal experiences as explicit parts of ethnographic endeavour.

In recent decades, studies of assorted aspects and applications of memory, remembering and forgetting have come to constitute a veritable growth area in the social sciences and humanities, a trend replicated within anthropology. Works by Battaglia (1993), Fabian (1996), Lambek (1996), and Werbner (1998), for example, represent merely a few of the substantive ethnographic projects pursued within this burgeoning field. Review articles by Yelvington (2002) and Berliner (2005) appraise different facets of this emerging anthropological literature and testify to its mushrooming range and scope. Especially pertinent to the questions that concern me, however, is Barrie Thorne's (1993) illuminating ethnographic reinterpretation of 'gender play' within American elementary schools.

As a teacher of university courses on childhood, Thorne recognised only too well her students' proclivities to brim over with reminiscences of their own elementary school years. Yet, upon commencing research in schoolrooms and on schoolyards, she was startled by the tugs of memory triggered by the sights, sounds and smells of children's places. Several of the children that Thorne the ethnographer encountered reminded her of some of her own classmates from decades earlier. Moreover, her field notes reflected that once again, as when she had been in the fourth and fifth grades, she was fascinated by the politics and dynamics of popularity (Thorne 1993: 24). Sensing with discomfort that she was registering and responding to the obsessions and aversions, the recollected noises and odours that linked her to her own childhood, Thorne sought inoculation through the application of prudent portions of scepticism and reflexivity. Reminding herself of the partiality and malleability of information gleaned from memories, Thorne took care to scrutinise her observations and feelings:

> I felt closer to the girls not only through memories of my own past, but also because I knew more about their gender-typed interactions. I had once played games like jump rope and status buyer, but I had never ridden a skateboard and had barely tried sports like basketball and soccer. Paradoxically, however, I sometimes felt I could see boys' interactions more clearly than those of girls: I came with fresher eyes and a more detached perspective. (Thorne 1993: 26)

Navigating her way between these not easily resolved issues, Thorne concluded that memories remain 'fragile and mysterious, continuously reconstructed by the needs of the present and by yearnings and fears of the past' (Thorne 1993: 26). In short, she found that memories can serve as sources both of insight and distortion.

But can we move any further than this in dealing with personal memories that arise involuntarily or that might otherwise be resurrected in the course of field research? Can an ethnographer's memories be advantageously 'mined' for insights that might point towards new and interesting analytical possibilities? Does the utilisation of personal memories need to be formally declared, interrogated and accounted for? Or should any use of personal memories be designated an incidental and 'backstage' aspect of the ethnographer's craft that might be – but need not necessarily be – acknowledged in passing? Alternatively, should personal memories be systematically abjured and expunged from analytical consideration if, in fact, this is possible?

A first step towards engaging these issues is to show how the making of memories may enter into child and youth sports.

Observing the Making of Memories

Formal and informal practices of remembering abound within sport. Moreover, the capacities of sport to sustain varied modes of remembering and memorialisation are drawing increased attention in the social sciences (Wieting 2001). For example, the creation of sporting records that carefully inscribe measured performances and results achieved in different places and times has been characterised as a distinctive and essential feature of modern sports:

What is a record in our modern sense? It is the marvelous abstraction that permits competition not only among those gathered together on the field of sport but also among them and others distant in time and space. Through the strange abstraction of the quantified record, the Australian can compete with the Finn who died a decade before the Australian was born. (Guttmann, 1978: 51–52)

Furthermore, the ease with which specific sporting exploits may not only be committed to memory in specific social circles but also enlisted to boost projects of nationalism has been widely reported (Archetti 1998; Cronin 1999; Mewett 1999).

The production and recitation of memories may also be observed and overheard in and around venues of child and youth sport in Canada. Imagine, for a moment, the people, places and activities that constitute this expansive field of interaction. Participants include boys and girls as athletes, their coaches, trainers, team and league officials, referees and judges, not to mention mothers, fathers, other family members and friends who may come along to a stadium, swimming pool or baseball diamond to watch or to help out with the staging of athletic competitions. These actors congregate intermittently in varying numbers and combinations at countless athletic matches, practices and training sessions, club meetings and fund-raising projects, to list only some of the more obvious events convened by community sports for children and youth. But a more comprehensive list would also include chance encounters at a local supermarket by parents who, though they may not know each other's name, nonetheless recognise one another from their shared devotion to – or hapless entanglement in – a given community sport. Choosing to acknowledge such links and to chat, even if for just a moment or two, serves to transform temporarily a grocery store aisle into an extension of the range of situations and activities constitutive of and associated with child and youth sports. What is exchanged in encounters such as these is 'small talk' that tends to be anchored in shared experiences and memories of a selected community sport scene. The recounting of 'news' and the sharing of stories about persons and happenings in the specific club or sport in which they are involved simultaneously require and augment bodies of decidedly localised knowledge. Over a period of time, it is the size of personally held stocks of such recollections that serves to distinguish parents known as community sport 'veterans' from 'newcomers'.

But the cultivation of sport-related memories can also reach much deeper than the recounting of public events that could be witnessed and commented upon by anyone who happened to have been in attendance at a particular tournament or meeting. The purposeful use of sport settings to fashion personally significant and exclusive memories can also become a valued feature of domestic life. 'Bob', for instance, refers to his early morning expeditions to drive his young sons to weekend ice hockey games with the same label that he applies to vacations and day trips taken with his wife and their boys: in his terms, these are all instances of 'making memories'. Life, explains Bob, goes by so quickly that it won't be long before his sons will have grown up and left home. The collecting of enjoyable and distinctive memories that Bob now sees himself as being engaged in through his support of his sons' sport activities is conducted in anticipation of a coming day when his sons will no longer be with him and his wife. The temporariness of this stage of family life and potentially even of a given family is succinctly expressed on a sign hanging above a suburban professional photographer's shop that reads simply, 'Keep Your Family Together Forever … In a Portrait by "Fred"'.

Parents who take photographs of their sons and daughters performing in competitions or receiving awards and ribbons may frame and display these images prominently in their homes or in carefully maintained albums or scrapbooks that include club or team photographs and reports of games or championships clipped from community newspapers. So too may frequently recited accounts of heroic or merely humorous happenings on the fields of play gradually become representations of not only particular games and seasons but also of personal character and of unfolding domestic relationships. Whether the telling of such stories and the hanging of such photographs constitute blatant parental bragging, supportive representation of a child's achievements, a preliminary instalment of the ongoing – and, perhaps, 'unauthorized' – 'account' of an individual childhood as well as of the loving parenting that went into making it possible, or, perhaps, some combination of all of the above and more besides is open to interpretation. But clearly the fabrication, assembling, current usage and stockpiling of memories for future contemplation is a pervading aspect of child and youth sports that darts between and interconnects evolving versions of the present, the future and the ever so carefully tended past.

The question that arises here concerns the extent to which the insights outlined above might have been detectable to virtually any ethnographic observer, whatever her or his prior acquaintance or lack of acquaintance with sport, whatever the nature of his or her own memories of childhood. My inclination is to proceed on the assumption that virtually any setting is open to being studied in illuminating ways by virtually any ethnographer. Yet I have several times been surprised by the insights offered by visiting anthropological colleagues who, when accompanying me to events that constituted the field sites for my study, have casually pointed out practices and phenomena that I had previously overlooked or mistakenly taken for granted. Perhaps a better way of putting the question is to ask what, if anything, the exercise of consciously reflecting upon my own memories as a one-time child and youth athlete as well as those subsequently generated through my experience as a parent and then as a coach of child athletes might have revealed to me about the complexities and workings of this field. Is there something to be learned from reviewing my practices as an ethnographer 'with memories'?

Recollecting a Life with Sport

My entry as an anthropologist into the ethnography of children's sport – which I have discussed elsewhere (Dyck 2000a) – was gradual and unintended. Nevertheless, after finally deciding to pursue formal research in this field, one of my first steps was to jot down a list of recurring memories of my own involvement as a child and as an adult in a range of sports and sports-related activities and relationships. Initially this yielded a roughly chronological account of sports and teams in which I had participated for longer or shorter periods. Touching base with my brothers and several childhood friends, I was reminded of sundry past sporting involvements and incidents that I had until then passed over.

In the midst of such protracted reminiscing it became apparent just how many of my especially prized recollections had long since become encased and polished as anecdotes or stories that might in part have been preserved through the periodic sharing of them with others. While the swapping of stories with brothers and friends who had also 'been there back then' occasionally elicited contradictory versions of my retrieved sense of certain events, what more often surfaced in our discussions were complementary accounts that narrated the matters in question from somewhat differing interactional and observational perspectives. This meandering pattern of 'telling, listening and amending', which served to interrogate as well as to elicit further memories and understandings of aspects of my own sporting past, has been replicated in subsequent deliberations, much as in the manner of the 'headnotes' that Sanjek (1990) has labelled as being inseparable companions of ethnographic endeavour. What I recall about my experiences in and around sport reflects not only a childhood imbued with sport but also a working life given over to anthropology. I cannot say precisely where the first leaves off and the second begins, but it would, I think, be reasonably correct to state that I had acquired a strong appreciation of certain properties of sport and of childhood long before I ever encountered the practice of ethnography, let alone the study of children's sports.

The infectious pleasure and excitement that playing, watching and talking about sport ignited in some, though by no means all, of the members of my family were obvious to me from an early age. My grandfather, upon his retirement from farming, spent countless hours each week reading about and listening to radio and television broadcasts of professional sports events, a luxury he had not been able to afford during his working years. Once a distance runner, he recounted in vivid detail some of his memorable races as well as semi-professional lacrosse matches that he had attended in his youth. Sharing his opinions and sport magazines with me, pointing me towards biographical sketches of athletes that he judged to be especially edifying, he nurtured a common passion that managed to bridge the more than six decades that separated us. He, along with my father, brothers and boyhood friends, effortlessly showed me just how readily and resolutely social intimacy can be constructed and enjoyed through sport.

The Sunday night 'pickup' ice hockey games staged not far from my parents' house attracted men and boys of all ages and skill levels. The unstated but, nonetheless, strictly observed rules in these rambling but enthusiastically contested matches were that everyone who turned up at the rink got to play and that stronger, faster and more skilled players were expected to 'condition' their play so that 'easy' shots on goal would always be left for and only taken by less proficient skaters, whatever their age. To create matches such as these required the inconspicuous cooperation of all involved to choreograph a single game that, nonetheless, offered graduated levels of competition to satisfy a wide range of tastes and talents. Informally managed transgenerational matches such as these not only ensured that there would always be a game but also permitted a young boy to feel very much a part of a man's world for those few hours when everyone who came to play was temporarily not a kid or a dad but just an opponent or a teammate.

Playing hockey on outdoor rinks during blistering cold spells that are an essential part of the Canadian winter also imparted stern lessons about the costs and perils of sport. The cuts, sprains and fractures – not to mention an inexorably embodied memory of exactly how it felt to be knocked off my skates and to strike the back of my head hard on the ice – went hand in hand with an introduction to the politics of organised child and youth team sports and the often iniquitous allocation of playing time. Years later, my own approach to coaching child and youth sports was determined in no small part by abiding memories of what to me, as a boy and then a man, seemed entirely unacceptable behaviour on the part of some of the individuals who coached me.

But alongside recollections such as these stand viscerally enshrined images capable of flicking on a switch to the past in exactly the same moment that they illuminate what is happening here and now. The thrill of making a perfect 'tape to tape' pass in hockey or the sounds and feelings emanating from a crushing tackle that one has delivered or received lend an aesthetic and emotional salience not only to one's own past experiences but also to the ways in which one might thereafter watch and empathise with any form of athletic performance exhibiting such attributes.

As well as playing our way through a seasonal calendar that in my youth on the Canadian prairies featured hockey in the winter, baseball (or softball) in the spring and summer and football in the autumn, my friends and I avidly read about and watched television broadcasts of the National Hockey League's Stanley Cup play-offs, Major League Baseball's World Series and the Canadian Football League's Grey Cup. But the celebrity to be gained from sport was also immediately evident in elite youth sport leagues and on neighbourhood playgrounds. One of the greatest stars of the NHL in the 1950s, Gordie Howe, had once been a student at an elementary school that I attended; during recesses my classmates and I speculated about who among us might follow in his footsteps. A few years later I took part in a citywide 'flag football' league that emulated the structure and popularity of the CFL, even to the point of having exactly the same number and names of teams as in the professional circuit. Three of the boys that I played with or against went on to have lengthy careers as professional athletes while a fourth became a sports writer and later a professional team manager. The distance between the professionals whom we watched so closely and our own exploits did not seem insurmountably wide. Indeed, having once reduced a future NHL player and coach to tears by inadvertently ripping his shirt during a flag football practice – a shirt belonging to an older brother that he had borrowed without permission – I had some sense of the ironies and illusions of celebrity, whatever the level at which it might be proclaimed.

For me and some friends who were 'jocks' as well as others who were not, the irresistible attraction of sport – whether engaged in through organised leagues, joining in impromptu 'pickup' games on the school lawn, or revelling in rambunctious and liminal family rituals built around collectively watched televised sports events – was that it enabled us to acknowledge and play with elements of life that were no less mysterious than the movement of a ball or a puck. The day that 'Norm', an enthusiastic but by no means smooth skating friend, turned up at the rink with an entirely new set of hockey equipment, including jersey, stockings and pants with the logo of a then not especially prestigious NHL team, prompted my older brother and me to look beyond the action on the ice. Norm's mother was a single parent who cleaned downtown offices at night to support her two children; she had invested what must have been a fortune for her in order to equip Norm to skate out on the ice in a way that he had never done before. Although my brother and I would never have chosen the colours of the then pitiful Red Wings, we watched with fascination as Norm proudly donned his new gear and proceeded to play the game of his life. By the time I graduated from high school, I had acquired a few injuries, a lot of memories and a decent eye for the pleasures that playing, talking and watching sport could yield, not to mention a growing appreciation of some more instrumental uses to which it might be put.

After undergraduate and MA studies, I came to anthropology and Manchester. Arriving at Gatwick, I spent a weekend in central London with the parents of an English student I had met in Canada. His father accompanied me to Stamford Bridge and my first Football League match. Chelsea FC was not then what it is now, but the chanting and singing emanating from the Shed made it a spectacle to behold. The following week I travelled north and found shared accommodation with a young Mancunian who worked in the financial district but lived for the weekend and Rugby Union. On my second weekend in England, I attended a post-match party at a rugby clubhouse, an occasion that differed in some essential respects from my Methodist grandfather's sense of what sport ought to entail. When I enquired about the 'other' game of football played in Manchester, my flatmate emphatically voiced a deep and abiding hatred of United but was willing to guide me to Maine Road, the home of Manchester City FC, Manchester United's local rivals.

By the time that the autumn term was fully under way, I had, as I was to learn, 'wrong-footed' myself in a couple of respects. First off, academics in England seemed to have little interest in and were more likely to manifest scorn for sports in general and for Association Football in particular. Certain factions of Max Gluckman's department comprised a somewhat self-conscious exception to this rule, but they tended to worship exclusively and somewhat narrow-mindedly at Old Trafford. Despite invitations to 'come over', I continued to watch the 'Blues' and then the 'Wanderers', found fellow fans and began to develop an ear for the ways in which northerners talk about and celebrate the game. Even though the names, dates, terms, expressions, rhythms and accents that I encountered were almost entirely new to me, the general tenor and artistry of such talk were familiar. An elderly Boltonian's cherished memory of the White Horse FA Cup Final that opened Wembley Stadium in 1923 took a similar rhetorical form to an uncle's accounts of journeys to Grey Cup competitions. In time, I even befriended a 'Red', who came round to mend the telephone and asked where I came from and why I was living in Manchester. Within minutes it surfaced that, yes, I had been to a football match and that he in fact had played for Manchester Schoolboys and had been an apprentice footballer with United. The following day he came by with three other telephone repairmen, and I was introduced to them as 'a Canadian who knows a bit about football'. Like a pet monkey, I performed on demand and began a friendship that has lasted for decades.

In retrospect I recognise that my first experience of fieldwork was in Manchester, albeit not at the university. Coming to terms with living in England and of later returning there at least every other year was subtly inflected by what I had discovered about sport as a child. In spite of that, an ostensible separation between anthropology proper and my sporting interests remained intact for almost the next twenty years as I concentrated my research and writing upon political relations between aboriginal peoples and governments in Canada (Dyck 1983, 1985, 1991, 1997). In practice, however, this was always a highly permeable boundary. My previous experience of listening to and seeking to comprehend my grandfather's stories as well as those of fellow aficionados of English football had whetted my appetite for narratives, thus preparing me in an unusually effective way for extended discussions with Aboriginal political leaders. Moreover, in the course of examining the ways in which the emerging politics of treaty rights were based upon carefully maintained oral traditions, I was also briefly reincarnated as an on-ice official in a nascent Indian hockey league. On several occasions I played left wing for an Indian–Métis Friendship Centre hockey team that played games against the 'non-travelling' Native Brotherhood squad in the regional penitentiary. Sport remained outside the stuff of anthropology only within the academy. Still, it puzzled me that everyday interests and activities that mattered so passionately to such a broad range of the people that I had met, lived with and worked with would continue to be dismissed with such casual but unrelenting disdain within my discipline.

Re-encountering Children's Sport

I did not return to the fields of children's play until shortly before my eldest daughter's birth, when, strolling through a park not far from the university where I had taken up a teaching post, I happened upon a girls' 'soccer' game in a local park. Community sport leagues in my hometown had catered overwhelmingly to boys, so there was a certain fascination in watching a small winger cross the ball in from near the corner flag for her striker to blast into the net. This image remained firmly planted in my consciousness during the next few years, and in due course my daughter was enrolled in soccer, becoming part of that veritable hive of bees that in those early seasons buzzed around the ball on its irregular journeys back and forth across the pitch.

Despite my familiarity with the professional version of this sport and my own past as a youth athlete, I was unprepared for several aspects of children's sports in my new place of residence. During my childhood most parents attended our scheduled games only occasionally, if at all. Dutiful and supportive parents were those who were willing and able to underwrite the cost of enrolment fees and some level of sport equipment. Having done this, they left it to their children to make the most of these opportunities and to find their own way to local sport venues. Transporting groups of players to and from 'away' games usually depended upon team coaches and managers. One father who quite regularly attended our hockey games – to shout instructions to his son and dispute a fair proportion of referees' decisions – was viewed as a bit of an oddball in the neighbourhood. In contrast, as a new 'soccer dad' in the suburbs of Vancouver, I discovered that typically at least one parent and often both will try to attend every one of their children's games or proffer an explanation of the circumstances that prevented them from doing so. The 'odd parent out' here is the father or mother who consistently does not accompany their progeny to matches and does not offer a 'good' reason for 'neglecting' to do so.

In effect, a parallel arena of action exists alongside the sidelines of children's sports. Here countless Canadian parents engage more or less energetically in performing and contesting middle-class versions of 'appropriate' and 'supportive' forms of parenting. This stands out in boldface for me because it differs so fundamentally in style and scale from the manner in which children's sports were organised in my youth. Children's sport participation outside compulsory physical education classes was once envisioned as being entirely optional and discretionary, to be pursued as long as it provided enjoyment and to be abandoned when it could no longer be afforded or had ceased to be 'fun'. Nowadays many suburban parents treat their children's participation in 'suitably' organised sport activities as being far too serious and important a factor with respect to the eventual outcome of their sons and daughters as to be governed solely in terms of such 'admirable' but 'outdated' principles (Dyck 2000b).

The physical game on the field remains a comparatively simple one that can still furnish excitement and satisfaction to those who choose to play it. A shortage of coaches declared by the local sport association prior to my younger daughter's second season of soccer prompted me to volunteer my services, thereby reconnecting me with the pleasures of practising and scrimmaging and also testing long-held convictions about what I would do if ever I was a coach. The experiences of being a parent and a coach were, of course, new ones for me. Yet in taking up these roles I was mindful of recollections of not just the ways in which my parents and different coaches had seemed to organise their deportment but also of what I had appreciated and what I had loathed about various adults' treatment of me as a kid and an athlete. In time, I also accompanied my daughters into track and field, where once again a perennial shortage of youth coaches resulted in me being pressed into service.

As a former 'jock', my re-enlistment in children's sport was, perhaps, not terribly surprising. But what also emerged out of this involvement, when at last it came into focus, blindsided me personally and professionally. My anthropological research had until that point focused upon the administration of Indian affairs in Canada. Regimes of state tutelage had been designed and implemented to 'save' aboriginal peoples by stripping them of the supposed burden and stigma of indigenous languages, cultures and practices. Residential schools and other social programmes were established to equip aboriginal children with 'appropriate' habits and beliefs that, it was claimed, would hasten their assimilation into the settler societies that engulfed them.

Consider my amazement when the existence of certain haunting structural and operational similarities between systems of state tutelage imposed upon aboriginal peoples and those contained within institutionalised sports for suburban children and youth finally dawned upon me. A set of recreational activities in which I had extensive personal experience and fond memories reaching back to my childhood and that had felt familiar and 'natural' in so many respects had quite unexpectedly been unwrapped and revealed in a rather different light. Ironically, my subsequent exploration of parents' and coaches' complicated and often contradictory modes of involvement in the social construction of children's sports (Dyck 1995, 2000b, 2002, 2003) commenced when the broader implications of, among other things, the memories that a Cree elder had shared with me about the intricate challenges of living on a reserve under the traditional form of Canadian Indian administration finally seeped into my own life.

Conclusions

The prospect of examining memory and experience as resources for doing and writing ethnography was at the outset quite appealing. After all, I had been wending my way through these matters for some time. At this point, however, I must admit that it has turned out to be a more challenging and ambivalent undertaking than I had anticipated. The difficulty has not been that of coming up with a sufficient supply of memories and experiences that might have shaped my work as an ethnographer. In truth, the number and pertinence of recollections of which I have taken note and the range of issues that these have raised came close to swamping me. I have also acquired an informed appreciation of why ethnographers might prefer to exercise a large degree of caution when pondering the option of writing about one's own memories. To do so is inevitably self-revealing and unless one is a committed exponent of the 'anthropology of me', then the risks might easily outweigh any possible benefits. Added to all of this is the lingering danger that even the briefest and most carefully edited representations of one's memories might just end up provoking responses of the sort commonly reserved for a returning holidaymaker's offer to share his or her vacation photographs with those who stayed at home. The chances of inflicting excruciating boredom increase exponentially when what is being discussed features one's past sporting exploits or one's childhood or, worst of all, one's fondly preserved memories of a sporting childhood.

But what else might this exercise have revealed? I would suggest that ethnographers can and frequently do make effective use of personal memories and experiences in our work in much the same manner that we marshal insights gleaned from reading in widely varying substantive fields for the purpose of framing ethnographic investigations and analytical comparisons. My life in sport both as a child and as an adult has contributed directly and fundamentally to my reincarnation as an anthropologist of sport and of childhood. I can well imagine, however, that other ethnographers coming to this field from quite different backgrounds might independently discover much of what I have found and more besides. I cannot, therefore, claim that I possess any particularly 'authentic' or 'native' understanding of these fields that privileges my work within them. What is more, I suspect that my brothers and childhood friends might be inclined to endorse this view. The notion of simply 'mining' one's memories for 'authentic' material might seem attractive but would be quite misleading and inappropriate if it implied that an ethnographer ought to enjoy any special form of licence or regard when engaging instrumentally in the act of recollecting.

This leads to the question of whether the use of personal memories by ethnographers ought to be formally declared, explicated and accounted for within our research and publications. I am of two minds about this. The recollections mustered for service in this chapter have – to the best of my ability – been subjected to all of the usual forms of interrogation, triangulation, and reflexivity that I endeavour to apply to any form of ethnographic data that I employ. But can a statement such as this, whether delivered in summary or extended form, ever really certify that the memories about to be presented have been 'vetted and vouched for' in a reliable manner? Would it not be preposterous to assume that we can ever isolate and link particular memories to specific insights or findings? In addition to attending football matches and talking with telephone repairmen during my years in Manchester, I also spent time in seminars, in pub discussions with my supervisor and in the library. I can't begin to sort out with any degree of exactitude which of my life experiences, including my initial and ongoing training as an ethnographer, might have been 'exclusively', 'primarily', 'secondarily' or 'sort of' responsible for my various decisions and findings as a working ethnographer. I would, in consequence, be opposed to any suggestion that anthropologists ought to consider adopting any form of 'mandatory' declaration and registration of the nature and extent of our memories as a standardised feature of our ethnographic accounts. The now thankfully receding fad within cultural studies and certain sectors of anthropology of purporting to identify in the introduction to publications 'who I am' in terms of race, gender, class and ethnicity does not need to be replaced by yet another fictitious orthodoxy.

But neither is it possible nor necessary to expunge any and all traces of ethnographers' personal memories from our work. Memories and experiences of all sorts inevitably contribute to the working knowledge that individual ethnographers bring to bear in determining where to focus their attention and how to pose the questions that serve to reveal and explain various aspects of social life. At the end of the day, what should be judged are not the earnestness of our claims about ourselves but the merits of our ethnographic accounts and the insights that these may provide.

References

Archetti, E.P. 1998. 'The Meanings of Sport in Anthropology: a View from Latin America', *European Review of Latin American and Caribbean Studies* 65: 91–103.
Battaglia, D. 1993. 'At Play in the Fields (and Borders) of the Imaginary: Melanesian Transformations of Forgetting', *Cultural Anthropology* 8(4): 430–42.
Berliner, D. 2005. 'The Abuses of Memory: Reflections on the Memory Boom in Anthropology', *Anthropological Quarterly* 78(1): 197–211.
Cronin, M. 1999. *Sport and Nationalism in Ireland: Gaelic Games, Soccer, and Irish Identity Since 1884*. Dublin, Ireland, and Portland, Oreg.: Four Courts Press.
Dyck, N. 1983. 'Representation and Leadership of a Provincial Indian Association', in A. Tanner (ed.) *The Politics of Indianness: Case Studies of Native Ethnopolitics in Canada*. St John's, Newfoundland: Institute of Social and Economic Research, Memorial University of Newfoundland, pp. 197–305.
———. (ed.). 1985. *Indigenous Peoples and the Nation-state: Fourth World Politics in Canada, Australia and Norway*. St John's, Newfoundland: Institute of Social and Economic Research, Memorial University of Newfoundland.

————. 1991. *What is the Indian 'Problem'? Tutelage and Resistance in Canadian Indian Administration.* St John's, Newfoundland: Institute of Social and Economic Research, Memorial University of Newfoundland.

————. 1995. 'Parents, Consociates and the Social Construction of Children's Athletics', *Anthropological Forum* 7(2): 215–29.

————. 1997. *Differing Visions: Administering Indian Residential Schooling in Prince Albert, 1867–1995.* Halifax, Nova Scotia, and Prince Albert, Saskatchewan: Fernwood Publishing and the Prince Albert Grand Council.

————. 2000a. 'Home Field Advantage? Exploring the Social Construction of Children's Sports', in V. Amit (ed.) *Constructing the 'Field': Ethnographic Fieldwork in the Contemporary World.* London and New York: Routledge, pp. 32–53.

————. 2000b. 'Parents, Kids and Coaches: Constructing Sport and Childhood in Canada', in N. Dyck (ed.), *Games, Sports and Cultures.* Oxford and New York: Berg, pp. 137–61.

————. 2002. '"Have You Been to Hayward Field?": Children's Sport and Construction of Community in Suburban Canada', in V. Amit (ed.), *Realizing Community: Concepts, Social Relationships and Sentiments.* London and New York: Routledge, pp. 105–23.

————. 2003. 'Embodying Success: Identity and Performance in Children's Sport', in N. Dyck and E.P. Archetti (eds), *Sport, Dance and Embodied Identities.* Oxford and New York: Berg, pp. 55–73.

Fabian, J. 1996. *Remembering the Present: Painting and Popular History in Zaire.* Berkeley, Los Angeles and London: University of California Press.

Guttmann, A. 1978. *From Ritual to Record: The Nature of Modern Sports.* New York: Columbia University Press.

Lambek, M. 1996. 'The Past Imperfect: Remembering as Moral Practice', in P. Antze and M. Lambek (eds.), *Tense Past: Cultural Essays in Trauma and Memory.* New York and London: Routledge, pp. 235–54.

Mewett, P. 1999. 'Fragments of a Composite Identity: Aspects of Australian Nationalism in a Sports Setting', *Australian Journal of Anthropology* 10(3): 357–75.

Sanjek, R. (ed.). 1990. *Fieldnotes: The Makings of Anthropology.* Ithaca: Cornell University Press.

Thorne, B. 1993. *Gender Play: Girls and Boys in School.* New Brunswick, NJ.: Rutgers University Press,

Werbner, R. (ed.). 1998. *Memory and the Postcolony: African Anthropology and the Critique of Power.* London and New York: Zed Books.

Wieting, S. (ed.). 2001. *Sport and Memory in North America.* London and Portland, Oreg.: Frank Cass.

Yelvington, K.A. 2002. 'History, Memory and Identity: a Programmatic Prolegomenon', *Critique of Anthropology* 22(3): 227–56.

Chapter 10

GARDENING IN TIME: HAPPINESS AND MEMORY IN AMERICAN HORTICULTURE

Jane Nadel-Klein

But for the professors in the academy, for the humanities generally, misery is more amenable to analysis: happiness is a harder nut to crack.

(McEwan 2005: 78)

Gardens are good to think. Equally, they are good to remember. And they are widely experienced, even among non-gardeners. Who, among the readers of this chapter, has not at some point delighted in a view of cultivated plants? But why does one person become a gardener and another, say, a chess player, a sculptor or a bingo enthusiast? And why does an anthropologist who has spent her professional life doing research among Scottish fisherfolk suddenly find herself turning to her avocation as a new ethnographic resource?

In 2003, with the appearance of my book, *Fishing For Heritage: Modernity and Loss Along the Scottish Coast* (Berg), I felt as though I had reached a turning point, in fact, a point that turned towards home. And home, for me, has always meant a garden. Ever since my undergraduate days, I have grown things. In a dark New York City apartment, that meant house plants under fluorescent lights. But not just a few philodendrons: I filled my windowsill and bought shelves. When the apartment could hold no more, I colonised the hallway windows. At this point, I was unreflectively surrounding myself with green, not thinking about the source of my desire.

When my first husband and I finally left the city and moved into a house on Cape Cod, I became pregnant with my daughter. It was a typically bleak New England winter, lots of fog and grey skies. I discovered a retail greenhouse on my way home from work at the Woods

Hole Oceanographic Institution and I stopped by at least once a week just to sit and breathe the air. Perhaps, unconsciously, I loved being in such a fecund space. My house-plant collection tripled. My daughter was born in May and I began to garden in the backyard. Ever since, the house-plants have taken a back seat, often suffering from considerable neglect, as I have moved my efforts outdoors and created bigger, more ambitious gardens. But it is only recently that I have begun to think about where my obsession comes from and what I share with others of like mind. And that has led me to think about the larger question of how we choose our field sites. I remember in graduate school hearing someone say that anthropologists have had some childhood experiences in common: either their parents took them travelling, so that they became enamoured of strange places and cultures; or they felt in some way out of place in their own settings, that their childhoods had positioned them as 'outsiders'. I have no idea whether these propositions have any statistical validity. Certainly they are not predictive, or the world would be overrun with anthropologists. But the second of these childhood experiences – that of being an outsider – certainly pertains to my own professional choices.

I wish that a garden could have helped my mother. She suffered from depression and anxiety, her agoraphobia so intense that for over thirty years, she seldom left the house. She shrouded all the rooms with curtains so that our house was always dark. During thunderstorms, she insisted that we all sit in the middle of the room, well away from her. She was convinced that lightning would try to seek her out and that, if we touched her, we would be electrocuted. Not surprisingly, I constructed myself as her opposite – I loved lightning and loved being out of doors. I spent a lot of time looking out of windows and craving colour. I wanted to believe that colour and flowers would engage her in the world and so, as a teenager, I painted her room a bright yellow and planted daffodils outside the front door. Her condition was far too complex for such simple solutions but the paint and the bulbs made me feel better. I know now that part of my love for gardening stems from my own fear of being imprisoned within dark walls. I know, also, that part of my reason for becoming an anthropologist was that it took me outside – in more than one sense. Because my mother was so phobic, not only of open spaces but of other people, my parents never socialised, never engaged with the community. As a child, I had difficulty making friends. Becoming an anthropologist also gave me a way to find those connections, to explore how other families lived and what communities meant. These questions animated my first research among Scottish fisherfolk and they underlie my fascination with what gardens do for people.

The Pursuit of Happiness

In part, of course, the question of who gardens and what they grow is a class issue. Many people simply do not have access to land or the time for work that brings in no cash income. This does not entirely answer the question, however, since many of the urban poor take part in community gardens (Warner 1987; Hynes 1996; Nadel-Klein 2002; von Hassell 2002; Klindienst 2006). And contrary to popular stereotype, many community gardeners grow flowers along with their vegetables.

There is no simple answer, of course. Along with class and location, myriad autobiographical and psychosocial factors affect what can be seen as non-utilitarian choices. In much of the world, gardening for pleasure is a very widespread activity, so widespread that it is worth asking why. In this chapter, I take an ethnographic as well as a self-reflective look at how gardeners' memories of sensory joy contribute to their decisions to devote time, energy, money and emotion into growing plants.

The pursuit of happiness, even utopia, in the garden is legendary. In the Western imagination, it begins with Eden (Brown 1999; Burrell and Dale 2002; Munro 2002). Eden was a classic Middle Eastern garden of the Biblical era, one that provided protection, 'creating privacy, intimacy and a separation from the forces that threaten from the outside' (Stein 1990: 42). Walls kept out not only the wild and the dangerous, but the ugly or unattractive. In Eden, all was perfection. It was the ultimate Durkheimian sacred space; outside, all was profane. Inside, there were no sickness, no death and no weeds.

Carolyn Merchant argues that Eden is one of Western society's most powerful tropes. She posits that Westerners engage in a 'recovery narrative' – a discourse telling us that Eden is not lost for ever. We can retrieve it; we can perfect the Earth, if we only work hard enough (Merchant 2003: 39). Merchant traces this narrative from ancient Greek and Roman ideas about the relationship of man to nature, through its various Christian interpretations and to the impact of New World discoveries upon European thinking. 'Seventeenth century botanical gardens and zoos were among the earliest efforts to reassemble the parts of the garden dispersed throughout the world after the Fall and the Flood. The scattered parts were collected and reassembled in one place to re-create the book of nature' (Merchant 2003: 59).

In this sense, modern gardeners are all engaged in recapturing Eden, if only in a limited way, and some more explicitly than others. There is no denying that gardeners share a faith in recovery – what is spring but a recovery from winter, after all? – in the power of the garden to replenish both body and soul. Inside the garden, one should feel at peace; outside, one must confront mundane problems and obligations. Inside, distinctions between past, present and future cease to weigh on us so heavily. Outside, 'the current stress on accountability and audit seems precisely to install an aesthetics that focuses each of us on delivery – *now!*' (Munro 2002: 129). Inside, the rhetoric of commodity and production fades, even if creating the garden has actually cost its owner a lot of money. The routines of tilling, weeding, planting, watering, composting and simply watching soothe away our anxieties even as they stress our lower backs.

If one succeeds in the garden, then colours harmonise, plants are carefully chosen to thrive in association with others, the rains never fail (courtesy of the garden hose) and fertility is kept in check. In fact, perfection is never reached: slugs eat the hostas, deer eat everything else; black spot afflicts the roses and the dandelions lie down with the lamb's quarters, despite the gardener's best efforts to evict them both. But the image of perfection, along with the calming rhythms of the work, keeps gardeners going. And that image comes not only from shared cultural traditions, but from childhood memories of gardens as ideal places.

Gardeners construct Edenic scenarios of beauty, simplicity, order and safety, of virtue leading to reward. Historian Jane Brown views the garden as embracing a 'duality of growing and dreaming, of digging and daydreaming, of the future's possibilities allied to the nostalgic past' (1999: 3). This alliance of future and past suggests a link between memory and a sense of moral community among gardeners. By moral community, I mean that gardeners generally assume an ethical, aesthetic and emotional commonality with other gardeners, including a fascination with plants, an ecological sensibility, a love of 'nature' and, frequently, a commitment to civic beautification and sharing botanical wealth. They also understand that other gardeners have strong attachments to what they do. This moral community is a multi-sited, 'imagined' one (Anderson 1983), in that gardeners are invested in an identity that is succoured and sustained by various popular media, including print, television and the Internet, as well as through plant shows and garden tours.

My informants are primarily suburban, middle-class, middle-aged and female, like myself. Most are politically liberal. All care about environmental issues and incline towards organic gardening practices. They own their own homes and cultivate spaces that range from a few hundred square feet to an acre or more. They read the national American magazines – particularly the upmarket ones like *Fine Gardening* and *Horticulture*. They also belong to garden clubs and drive long distances to buy plants from specialised nurseries. For them, gardening is a serious avocation.

Since I, too, am such a gardener, we speak with ease. We share local knowledge, admissions of failure and triumph at success. But, because of this intense degree of sharing, I cannot pretend to have much distance from my informants. I am, in short, a native and therefore a highly subjective ethnographer. As many ethnographers 'at home' have noted, this has its complications (Myerhoff 1978; Norman 2000). When the gap between observer and observed is small, it is easy to miss significant details. Moreover, the researcher's identity occupies a shifting platform: from insider to outsider and back again (Reed-Danahay 1997). This may be particularly true when memories are in play. When someone tells me about learning to plant from her grandmother, I identify. In the instant of hearing her story, I 'see' the grandmother, the garden, the child. Since I am not telepathic, my visions are coming from my own memory banks, my own imagination, inspired by her words. Whose memories are they, then? In such a context, telling and hearing become a joint enterprise in memory-mining, a process that must, inevitably, shape my interpretation.

When I contemplate my own garden memories, I find them filled with leaf and bloom, their colour, scent and detail amplified by the enlarging perspective of a child's imagination and interwoven over the years with layers of reinterpretation and analysis. They are also filled with emotion. For me, those memories are inextricably linked with a deep need for safety and warmth. My childhood was not a happy one – my mother was a reclusive, drug-addicted invalid, my father very distant. My younger sister and I were largely left to fend for ourselves and our house was dark, silent and hopelessly cluttered. Even the small backyard was dark and damp, overshadowed by tall pines and a brown wooden fence. The one bright spot was the lilac, which became my own micro-garden. No one tended it, but lilacs are hardy souls, often thriving around abandoned New England doorways for generations. I attached myself to that shrub, checking its buds every day in spring as I came home from school.

I had another, more important refuge, however. On his twenty acres outside Hartford, Connecticut, my father's father had a small farm. He sold his produce at a little roadside stand. Every Sunday, my father drove me out there to spend the day, chasing chickens and barnyard cats and following my grandfather around the fields. I have vivid recollections of flowers and the fruit trees, with their clouds of white and pink blossom, strawberries and maize that towered above my head. It was an impossibly beautiful, limitless place, where I could play freely. Alas, when I was six, my grandparents sold the farm, joining the Jewish retirement exodus to Florida. I was desolated but quickly learned to look for gardens everywhere I could find them: at the houses of other relatives, in the local park, and even in the cow pasture across the road.

But nothing compared with the farm. On Saturdays, I went to an aunt's house. Tina's idea of gardening was very different from my grandfather's. She believed in order. In her backyard, vegetables and marigolds marched along straight lines laid out with string. I could play there, but not explore. The yard was one big open space where you could see – and monitor – everything at once.

My mother's mother had a garden that I remember less well because I spent little time there, but I know it had a very different feel. I think it must have been a more artistic place, a more 'designed' garden, with subtle interplays of foliage and curves. It unfolded gradually; sinuous paths led through trellised arbours to mysterious, unseen destinations. But it was Elizabeth Park, a few short blocks from my primary school, that offered me my first glimpse of truly formal, 'English'-style gardening. It had, and has, a world-class rose garden, along with perennial beds, rock gardens, paths, ponds and imposing trees. As soon as I was old enough to walk there by myself, I made it my own. In sum, like my informants, I have vivid garden memories.

Memory, Emotion and Refuge

Most ethnographic discussion of memory, both personal and collective, deals with 'big' issues: tragedy and loss, victimisation and powerlessness. This focus reflects a disciplinary commitment to the oppressed and the vulnerable that continually immerses us in contexts of inequity and conflict. Narratives of war, poverty, disease, displacement from home and struggles for cultural survival are tales that reach beyond the individual, as the teller links personal experience to change so sweeping that his or her life is transformed for ever (Brody 1981; Shostak 1983; Murphy 1990; Karakasidou 1997). In listening to them, we become aware of how global forces impinge on individual lives and how those lives can educate us about the cost in pain and suffering of human failure or natural disaster. Implicitly, they sustain our conviction that only social problems are important and revelatory, and that we, as ethnographers, are uniquely well placed to chronicle and analyse them (Scheper-Hughes 1992; Kulick 2006).

From this perspective, the decorative arts – especially as practiced by the middle class – hardly seem worthy of our attention: 'In its ineffectiveness, architecture shares in the bathos of gardening: an interest in door handles or ceiling mouldings can seem no less worthy of mockery than a concern for the progress of rose or lavender bushes. It is forgivable to conclude that there must be grander causes to which human beings might devote themselves' (de Botton 2006: 20). I concur with Herzfeld in his praise of 'mereness' in the scope of human activity: pleasure is a topic worthy of our attention (2001: 313). Thus, I take my cue from the famed English gardener, Vita Sackville-West, who said, 'Small pleasure must correct great tragedies' (2004 [1946]). When I read Sackville-West's words, I am reminded of my father, who repeatedly told me – in part because he was unwilling to make changes that would have improved life at home more substantially – that one must take satisfaction in life's tiniest joys: the smell of a flower, the warmth of sunshine, a good book.

Many would argue that the pleasure of gardens is not that small, particularly in distressing contexts. For example, one of my neighbours, a woman of Japanese descent, recalls the internment camp where she and her mother spent the years of the Second World War. 'My mother always had a garden. When they had to leave their home (in California) to live in the camp, I remember how she begged marigold seeds from one of the guards. It helped her get through it.' The daughter, now a comfortably middle-aged, married woman, gardens with her husband in Connecticut. Together, they cultivate a hidden garden. Passing by the small, Cape-style house, no one would know that behind their wooden fence sits an ordered tapestry of trees, paths and perennials. Their garden, and their perspective on it, is entirely interior. But I saw no marigolds. Not all gardens are meant to be recapitulated.

Gardens in internment camps exemplify what Helphand calls 'defiant gardens'. These 'flourish in seemingly improbable sites, like deserts, prisons, hospitals, highway medians, vacant lots, refugee camps, dumps, wastelands, cracks in the sidewalk' (Helphand 2006: 1). Such gardens shake a fist, so to speak, at misery. In such places, 'Gardens promise beauty where there is none, hope over despair, optimism over pessimism and finally life in the face of death' (Helphand 2006: 7). I have heard, anecdotally, that some two thousand school gardens were planted throughout the United States following the traumatic shootings of children at Columbine High School in Colorado (J. Dodson, personal communication). While one cannot prove that these plantings were all explicit responses to Columbine, there is no doubt that gardens are commonly viewed as places of recuperation and that they are frequently created as commemorations.

Healing, sanctuary and therapy are common themes when gardeners discuss their motivations. The American Horticultural Therapy Association (n.d.) cites on its website that 'In the nineteenth century, Dr. Benjamin Rush, a signer of the Declaration of Independence and considered to be the "father of American Psychiatry", reported that garden settings held curative properties for people with mental illness.'

Not only may gardening sustain the elderly, the disabled and the depressed, but it may rehabilitate in other ways as well (Lewis 1995). Some members of the Connecticut Herb Society help tend a garden at a women's prison.

> We quickly learned it didn't matter much what we were doing with the prisoners; we could be making balls out of scraps of string as long as we were visiting and talking to them like human beings. The care of an herb garden is an especially good venture to do with disenfranchised people because the plants are relatively easy to care for, they grow fast, and change is evident. They also evoke memories, have long and colorful histories that can be shared and they smell and taste good. (Van Nes 2006: 15)

We expect gardens to heal us, whether by producing plants that have direct somatic effect or by simply providing an atmosphere of respite, of sanctuary. Text after text offers versions of the same refrain: 'Gardens are refuges. In search of replenishment we retreat to them as to a safe haven' (Osler 1997: 5).

Novelists frequently deploy gardens' symbolic power. In an icon of children's literature, we find the archetypal healing garden. This is, of course, Frances Hodgson Burnett's *The Secret Garden* (1994 [1911]), where the children who discover it find their minds and bodies transformed. As they restore the hidden, walled garden to life, their own lives take on colour and vitality. They discover strength, friendship and happiness. In a more recent novel, written for adults, an emotionally starved young woman finds new life in another secret garden (Humphreys 2002). It is 1941, and she has been sent as a representative of the Royal Horticultural Society to an old Devonshire estate. Her task is to direct a unit of the Women's Land Army in planting potatoes for the war effort. She accomplishes this easily (potatoes will grow pretty much anywhere) and soon begins to explore the estate. When she finds a garden that has been cleverly concealed, it becomes a nearly magical place. There, she confronts memories of trauma and lost love and comes to terms with the war.

Without those memories, the hidden garden would merely be an unexpected, pretty place. So it is to memories that we must turn in order to understand the full import of gardens for gardeners, bearing in mind that 'memory is an abstract painting – it does not present things as they are, but rather as they *feel*' (Collier 2001: 97).

The memories I log here are clearly of the personal and individual variety, but they are guided by the idea of what Connerton calls social memory (1999), a larger, collective discourse about the past – memory whose meaning is inscribed in the present through practice, response and interaction. In conversations with each other, in the horticultural histories and illustrations that tell us what a good garden should be, and in the very acts of planting and weeding, gardeners preserve and renew aesthetic ideologies. A good garden is determined in part by its form and its contents, its references to important – that is, recognised – gardens of the past, to legendary designers and their styles: Gertrude Jekyll, for example, with her path-breaking use of colour, or Vita-Sackville West, famed for her white garden at Sissinghurst in Kent.

Thus a gardener must always mediate between personal and social memory. The latter encodes 'taste' and the conventions of style (Bourdieu 1984). The former, while constructed within a cultural framework, is also fraught with emotional associations. In other words, a personal memory of a garden with bright annual plants – marigolds and petunias – may be the site of a particular fount of happiness, but contemporary, class-inflected garden ideology stresses texture and form over colour, perennials and trees over annuals (see Nadel-Klein 2010). Similarly, personal memories may bias gardeners against plants they associate with sadness (as was the case for my Japanese-American informant who eschews marigolds). Many gardeners feel they must 'live up' to standards imposed by the arbiters of 'good' gardening to be found in magazines or garden shows, not to mention the neighbours.

Making Sense

Gardeners must be receptive to the senses, and, indeed, their memories are highly sensual. Sight, smell, touch, taste and sound – these echo and repeat as narrators evoke magically contented days spent with fathers, mothers, aunts, grandparents tending cultivated spaces. Consider the words of Janice Bowers:

> The first garden I remember, my paternal grandmother's, smelled like citrus blossoms, too. It seems that I can recall her garden in every detail until I try to grasp it. Then it fades into tantalizing shapes and colours and the hugeness of the spaces that a child sees. Mostly I remember row upon row of flowers, an immense expanse of blossoms, it seemed then – dahlias, cosmos, roses, stocks, marigolds, marguerites, hollyhocks, phlox...Now I would love to be lost in such a garden. (1999: 5)

For Bowers, as well as for others, gardening is the ultimate, embodied experience of place. Recalling the sight of marigolds in her hometown, Eugenia Collier connects this sense of place explicitly to her personal development: 'Whenever the memory of those marigolds flashes across my mind ... I feel again the chaotic emotions of adolescence, illusive as smoke, yet as real as the potted geranium before me now. Joy and rage and wild animal gladness and shame become tangled together in the multicolored skein of fourteen-going on fifteen' (2001: 98).

Clearly, gardens can be a source of powerful feelings that are lodged and reproduced in memory. They engage our senses and so concentrate our emotions. Gardeners recapture this by constructing havens that replicate in some fashion the feelings they had as children. Garden designer Penelope Hobhouse claims this explicitly. Writing about her grandmother's garden, she says that 'What I discovered then was a great joy in its beauty. It also fulfilled my need for a feeling of seclusion, for solitude, and for somewhere to escape from the real world. I like to think that the experience shaped my own design work, in which I try to implement this desire for a refuge, a place apart' (Hobhouse 2002: ix).

To comprehend such feelings, any analysis of gardening must pay attention to the wide variety of sensory inputs that helped create them. Stoller (1989, 1997) and Seremetakis (1996) each argue that Westerners concentrate so intently upon the visual that we ignore information coming to us from other sources. We should know better: that memories may be evoked by the taste of a madeleine dipped in tea has become a cultural cliché (Proust 2002). For Seremetakis, recalling the taste of a peach crystallises the losses of exile (1996: 1–18). It would be impossible to understand a garden's impact from sight alone, since the memories located there are not restricted to images of flowers but include sound, scent, texture and often flavour as well.

Brown attributes the pleasure we take in gardens directly to our very earliest sensory experiences:

> When washed and swaddled and laid in our mother's arms, these familiars – huge coloured blossoms as big as our own heads – arrive as votive offerings at the bedside ... the equation of flowers and pleasure is confirmed: the pungency of daffodils, of the heady sweetness of lilies, passes into infant sensory memory as good, synonymous with well-being and happiness. From the very beginning the fortunate child (and would it were the birthright of all children) put out to doze beneath the blossom trees, becomes quite naturally a creature of the flower world, a child of the garden. (1999: 28–29)

Brown's account is very English: we can envision the baby in its pram, safely ensconced in the back garden or, perhaps, under a tree in the park with its nanny. But the idea that garden memories imprint themselves favourably from the very beginning is one that transcends narrow cultural boundaries.

An African-American woman rhapsodised to me about the pleasures of dirt. She compared them to the joy of good food: 'You have to know the taste of good dirt – not the gravelly, gritty stuff, or the clay, but the good dirt – you can smell it. I ate dirt when I was a child.' Her sensitivity enables her to be a better gardener, even a plant rescuer. Her words suggest that she associates plants with offspring. 'I can take a plant – you think that it's dead, but I just wash off the roots with room-temperature water – you have to feel it on your wrist, like the milk for a baby's bottle – and replant it and it grows.' I knew what she meant about the smell of dirt – though I have never actually eaten it. Good, warm earth is a promise of fertility.

One does not have to be a gardener to have memories of gardens from childhood. Over the years, in teaching a course called 'Gardens and Communities' to first-year students, I have asked them to recall their earliest memories of being in a garden. Of the forty some essays I have collected, not one associated gardens with anything but pleasure. Students describe gardens as 'vibrant', 'serene', 'uplifting', and – my favourite – 'like Narnia'. Their accounts are filled with colour and fantasy. Not surprisingly, their gardens were populated not just with flowers but with family: chiefly parents, siblings and grandparents. At the end of the term, I asked them to imagine their ideal gardens, free of any normal constraints, like time and money. Some 'built' extravagant confections with fountains and statuary. Others envisioned picturesque expanses of lawn leading to lakes or rivers. But one young man kept it simple: a hillside, a swing hanging from a tree and some vaguely colourful shrubs in the background. He was clearly recapitulating a memory of his younger days, playing idly in a safe, enchanted spot.

An adult informant, a man who regularly contributes to garden magazines, expressed his thoughts similarly:

> A garden is a sensory place, not a garden so much as an environment, a fantasy rainforest, idealised nature, a different place. It is engaging and enrapturing. As a little kid, I'd run to the woods. Today, my garden is a retreat. I'm a real grunt labour kind of person. I find the work therapeutic. It connects me to the natural world, what the deer, hawk and owl do. I know where the wet spots are. It's a microcosm. It's my own country.

His garden today is surrounded by forest. The woods encroach at every turn and from every angle.

Making Connections

Memories do more than embrace the senses. They relay social networks that run like vast root systems through gardeners' lives. If gardens are refuges, they also provide places where social connections may flourish. Consider these comments from community gardeners in California: 'You come here to forget all your problems and to be with other gardeners,' says one. 'We've had people meet here and get married.' Says another, 'It's my gym and my church' (Singer 2005).

Garden clubs also provide vital links for people – most often for women. Many of the twenty-five members of my garden club have attended its monthly meetings faithfully for years. Not all of us have gardens any longer. Not only do we know each other's gardens, but we know our family histories. We expect to see pictures of children's weddings and children's children. We have made memories in the garden club, in part by sharing a common obligation to maintain two small public gardens for the town where most of us live.

When walking through an informant's garden, I often hear a recitation of people and plants past: 'I tried this plant here but it died so I've planted this instead'; 'I got this cutting from an old friend of my mother's back in Georgia'; 'I'm growing some castor bean plants. You've heard of castor bean? My relatives in the Caribbean grow it.' Plants and planting tips are a prized medium of exchange, vehicles for reciprocity that keep gardeners linked in their imagined, moral community.

These exchanges happen frequently. Rarely does one tour a garden without being offered plants or cuttings. My own garden contains many plants that came from others' generosity. So often, a gardener tells me, 'If you need some of this ground cover, don't go and buy it. I'll give you all you need.' Sometimes I will take a plant and then fail to get it into the ground before it withers. When this happens, I feel quite guilty, as if I have failed not just the plant, but the giver. In this open-ended *kula* ring of plant exchange, I am incorporated into the garden and vice versa, as the garden's very substance is transmitted through the gift. If possible, I find a plant I think my donor might like, and give it to her.

Reciprocity and redistribution are important mechanisms for establishing sociality in the world of gardeners. Gifts that come from others' gardens have a different valence from those purchased at a plant centre or nursery. In Seremetakis's terms, personal (as opposed to formal) garden tours are commensal events, 'devoted to the consumption, distribution, sharing and exchange of substances ... usually seen as performances and protocols whose synchronic rules and structure are kept in people's heads like a pre-programmed game plan' (1996: 11). The gardener expects to give, the visitor to receive, both plants and memories. They are linked in a chain of hyper-extended reciprocity. That is, the recipient may or may not give anything back to the giver; it is enough that he or she pass on a plant to someone else.

Not only do shared plants create offspring, the shared children and grandchildren of their planters, as it were, but they symbolise the links between gardeners of different generations. They make connections through both time and space. Many gardeners present themselves as descending, both literally and figuratively, from ancestral gardeners. One of my informants, now a professional garden designer, recalled:

My parents always gardened, especially my mom. She had a big vegetable garden with morning glories (which I can't grow because it's too shady). We moved a lot: Illinois, Indiana, Michigan, Arizona (where we grew tangerines, avocados, pears), San Diego, Pittsburgh. My dad was an artist and interior designer ... My grandfather in Wisconsin was an awesome gardener: he won prizes for dahlias and snapdragons.

Her own garden recapitulates her father's design sensibilities. It is filled with found objects, artfully placed along paths that wind through dense arrangements of unusual plants. Her house conveys the same impression of serendipity, adventure and curiosity.

Another informant, also a professional garden designer, proffers her gardening matrilineage:

There's no question, it's in the genes. Every woman in my family was a gardener. As a small child, I remember getting up in the morning, really early, and seeing my mother out in the garden. When I was little I didn't help in the garden, but I loved watching her work. Mother taught me to make cuttings. She still grows stuff in Florida. I want to grow my own food. I want to eat what I've grown. My sister lives in Maine and is an unbelievable gardener. She even has a cranberry bog. That's what we loved doing. It was all women. My father mowed the lawn.

Ancestors, of course, imply the idea of an ancestral home. A garden, whether remembered or actual, is such a home. It is home to the gardener, as well as to the plants that grow there. In the act of nurturing, the plants themselves may become proxies for a kind of extended family and provide opportunities to tell the stories that keep families – and gardens – alive. Lee May, an African-American writer, reveals in *In My Father's Garden* (1995) that he can only garden when his family relationships are in order. In Dominique Browning's collection, *Paths of Desire*, tales of family twine through the essays like the wisteria that devours her trellis. Her garden, she says, 'has been marked and shaped by my young married life, by my life as the mother of two boys, by my life as a woman at the end of her marriage' (Browning 2004: 2).

The plethora and popularity of published garden memoirs tell us that gardeners cherish not only their own memories but also those of others. By memoirs, I mean books that primarily reflect upon the roles that gardens have played in the authors' lives, rather than works that emphasise the technicalities of gardening itself. On my shelves alone I count at least a dozen such memoirs and memoir anthologies (MacVicar 1985; May 1995; Fleischman 1997; Kincaid 1999; Dean and Wachsburger 2001; Capek 2002 [1929]; Fish 2002; Warner 2002; White 2002; Wilson 2002; Browning 2004; Lane 2004; Kunitz 2005).

Conclusion

In thinking about my role in this investigation – my status as an empathetic insider, as well as the memories that impel me to be both gardener and anthropologist – I find myself pondering what this study would look like if done by someone with no familiarity with the world of horticulture. This is, of course, a more typical position for ethnographers and one that I occupied in my earlier work in Scotland. To this day I still get very confused by the technicalities of boats, fish and EU regulations. I will always wonder about the extent to which I 'got it right' as I interpreted the fisherfolk's response to tourism and the vicissitudes of the heritage industry. Undertaking this new study, where I am positioned entirely differently, has raised this question even more sharply – because I now have a greatly enhanced appreciation for just what goes into a 'thick description' (Geertz 1973). Take, for example, the basic question of how gardeners respond to each others' gardens.

While garden magazines contain a great deal of information, they seldom voice a word of criticism. Gardens are frequently referred to as works of art, but no one says – in print, anyway – that a garden is rubbish. Other forms of landscape design – notably golf courses – are scathingly evaluated (see Klein 2006). There seems to be some tacit understanding that in gardens viewers should tread carefully, that to denigrate a gardener's efforts openly would be a form of moral trespass.

This is not to say that gardeners are saints, or that they lack a critical faculty. Certainly, garden competitions provide opportunity for explicit commentary. The professionally staged landscape designs on view at flower shows, such as Philadelphia or Chelsea, may be rigorously examined for flaws. And I have been on many garden tours, both in the United States and in the United Kingdom, where I have heard (and voiced) many a snide comment about the arrangement of plants, the overall design or the choice of garden ornaments.

Certainly, gardeners have strong opinions about garden taste. Garden gnomes and pink, plastic flamingos are a running joke. The point is that, while these concerns may be addressed in general, or in venues explicitly dedicated to competition, they are not applied directly to individuals. Gardeners try very hard not to offend each other, particularly when the gardens are attached to domestic settings and even when the gardens have been opened to public view, as in the open days around the United States or the United Kingdom's National Garden Scheme. Both of these raise money for charity or for garden preservation. It is understood that an attitude of careful respect is mandatory.

Writers judge and evaluate commercial enterprises and works of art that are presented for consumption. Why not gardens? I would argue that the answer lies in the idea of moral community that I raised earlier. A garden stands in close proximity to its producer. Apart from estate gardens, which are professionally maintained, a garden is generally understood to be the work of an individual, perhaps a couple, who pour great love, as well as sweat, into its creation. Those who visit see it empathetically. They know that plants are temperamental, effects are ephemeral, time and money are short and egos are fragile. They nearly always give it 'A' for effort, even if they are privately unimpressed with the results. In the garden, good intentions count.

The question of garden evaluation and public criticism brings us back to memory. I suggest that the wealth of emotion tied up in gardeners' efforts, emotion that is closely tied to gardeners' remembrances of Edens past, unites them in feeling that they share a common ethos, a shared sensibility too precious to subject to evaluation. Above all, they want to feel *good* in the garden. Gardens are social and domestic places: we invite people in, the way we do to our homes. And just as no one would dream of openly sneering at another's wallpaper, no one would dream of running down another's garden design or plantings.

My combined position as gardener and ethnographer allows me to appreciate this aspect about the nature – and internal limits – of garden criticism. An outside observer is less likely to grasp this aspect of garden culture, as is the gardener herself. I have made this observation to many people and consistently get a surprised reaction. It is one of those taken-for-granted aspects of culture that 'natives' don't see or think about.

The insider perspective has also been invaluable in navigating a multi-sited ethnographic context. This is a 'tribe' with roots everywhere. Yet, instead of feeling a little lost at sea, I feel very much at home. There's no need to apologise for the resonance with the subject matter. By the same token, I undoubtedly have to keep asking myself if I'm missing things that might strike an outsider as important. The nature of ethnography, as theorists of anthropology's reflexive turn have noted, is that we are imperfect, partial observers, no matter what our connection to the field (Marcus and Fischer 1986; Clifford 1988). Simply put, we bring ourselves, our strengths and our limitations to the field and try to do the best we can. But caring for the subject matter and being able to recognise the craftwork that sustains a moral community have been, for me, distinct assets.

References

American Horticultural Therapy Association, (n.d.). www.ahta.org/information/; accessed February 2007.

Anderson, B. 1983. *Imagined Communities*. London: Verso.

Bowers, J. 1999. 'A Garden Is Like a Life', in J. Garmey (ed.), *The Writer in the Garden*. Chapel Hill: Algonquin, pp. 3–9.

Brody, H. 1981. *Maps and Dreams*. New York: Pantheon.

Brown, J. 1999. *The Pursuit of Paradise*. London: HarperCollins.

Browning, D. 2004. *Paths of Desire*. New York: Scribner.

Bourdieu, P. 1984. *Distinction: A Social Critique of the Judgement of Taste*. Harvard: Harvard University Press.

Burnett, F.H. 1994 [1911]. *The Secret Garden*. London: Puffin.

Burrell, G. and K. Dale. 2002. 'Utopiary: Utopias, Gardens and Organization', in M. Parker (ed.), *Utopia and Organization*. Oxford: Blackwell, pp. 106–27.

Capek, K. 2002 [1929]. *The Gardener's Year*. New York: Modern Library.

Clifford, J. 1988. *The Predicament of Culture*. Cambridge: Harvard University Press.

Collier, E. 2001. 'Marigolds', in C. Dean and C. Wachsberger (eds), *Of Leaf and Flower*. New York: Persea, pp. 97–111.

Connerton, P. 1999. *How Societies Remember*. Cambridge: Cambridge University Press.

Dean, C. and Wachsburger, C. (eds). 2001. *Of Leaf and Flower*. New York: Persea.

De Botton, A. 2006. *The Architecture of Happiness*. New York: Pantheon.

Fish, M. 2002. *We Made a Garden*. New York: Modern Library.

Fleischman, P. 1997. *Seedfolks*. New York: Harper Trophy.

Geertz, C. 1973. *The Interpretation of Cultures*. New York: Basic Books.

Helphand, K. 2006. *Defiant Gardens*. San Antonio: Trinity University Press.

Herzfeld, M. 2001. *Anthropology*. Oxford: Blackwell.

Hobhouse, P. 2002. *The Story of Gardening*. London: Dorling Kindersely.

Humphreys, H. 2002. *The Lost Garden*. New York: Norton.

Hynes, H.P. 1996. *A Patch of Eden*. White River Junction: Chelsea Green.

Karakasidou, A. 1997. *Fields of Wheat, Hills of Blood*. Chicago: University of Chicago Press.

Kincaid, J. 1999. *My Garden (Book)*. New York: Farrar, Straus and Giroux.

Klein, B.S. 2006. *Rough Meditations*. Hoboken: Wiley.

Klindienst, P. 2006. *The Earth Knows My Name*. Boston: Beacon.

Kulick, D. 2006 'Theory in Furs: Masochist Anthropology', in *Current Anthropology* 47(6): 933–52.

Kunitz, S. 2005. *The Wild Braid*. New York: Norton.

Lane, P. 2004. *There is a Season*. Toronto: McClelland and Stewart.

Lewis, C. 1995 'Gardening as Healing Process', in M. Francis and R. Hester (eds), *The Meaning of Gardens*. Cambridge, Mass: MIT Press, pp. 244–51.

MacVicar, A. 1985. *Gremlins in My Garden*. London: Arrow.

Marcus, G. and M. Fischer. 1986. *Anthropology as Cultural Critique*. Chicago: University of Chicago Press.

May, L. 1995. *In My Father's Garden*. Tuscaloosa: University of Alabama Press.

McEwan, I. 2005. *Saturday*. New York: Doubleday.

Merchant, C. 2003. *Reinventing Eden*. New York: Routledge.

Munro, R. 2002. 'The Consumption of Time and Space: Utopias and the English Romantic Garden', in M. Parker (ed.), *Utopia and Organization*. Oxford: Blackwell, pp. 128–54.

Murphy, R. 1990. *The Body Silent*. New York: Norton.

Myerhoff, B. 1978. *Number Our Days*. New York: Simon and Schuster.

Nadel-Klein, J. 2002. 'Growing Pains: Ideology and Politics in the American Community Gardening Movement', Conference paper, American Anthropological Association. New Orleans.

———. 2010. forthcoming. 'Cultivating Taste and Class in the Garden', in A.S. Gronseth and D.L. Davis (ed), *Making Sense*. New York: Berghahn.

Norman, K. 2000. 'Phoning the Field' in V. Amit (ed.), *Constructing the Field*. London: Routledge, pp. 120–46.

Osler, M. 1997. *A Breath From Elsewhere*. London: Bloomsbury.

Proust, M. 2002. *Swann's Way*, transl. L. Davis. New York: Penguin.

Reed-Danahay, D. (ed.). 1997. *Auto/Ethnography*. Oxford: Berg.

Sackville-West, V. 2006 [1946]. *The Garden*. London: Francis Lincoln.

Scheper-Hughes, N. 1992. *Death Without Weeping*. Berkeley: University of California Press.

Seremetakis, C.N. 1996. 'The Memory of the Senses, Part I: Marks of the Transitory', in C.N. Seremetakis (ed.), *The Senses Still*. Chicago: University of Chicago Press, pp. 1–18.

Shostak, M. 1983. *Nisa. The Life and Words of a !Kung Woman*. New York: Vintage.

Singer, L. 2005. 'The California Garden', *The Times*, 3 March.

Stein, A. 1990. 'Thoughts Occasioned by the Old Testament', in M. Francis and R. Hester (eds), *The Meaning of Gardens*. Cambridge, Mass.: MIT, pp. 38–45.

Stoller, P. 1989. *The Taste of Ethnographic Things*. Philadelphia: University of Pennsylvania.

———. 1997. *Sensuous Scholarship*. Philadelphia: University of Pennsylvania.

Van Nes, C. 2006. 'Herbs Heal in Women's Prison', in *The Herbarist* 2006: 14–16.

von Hassell, M. 2002. *The Struggle for Eden*. Westport: Bergin and Garvey.

Warner, C.D. 2002. *My Summer in a Garden*. New York: Modern Library.

Warner, S.B., Jr. 1987. *To Dwell is to Garden*. Boston: Northeastern University Press.

White, K. 2002. *Onward and Upward in the Garden*. Boston: Beacon.

Wilson, E. (ed.). 2002. *Two Gardeners: A Friendship in Letters*. Boston: Beacon.

PART III

ETHNOGRAPHIC SELVES
THROUGH TIME

Chapter 11

THE ROLE OF SERENDIPITY AND MEMORY IN EXPERIENCING FIELDS

Tamara Kohn

> A person must make a self, and a life, from obdurate materials – the
> conditions of one's birth and the vicissitudes of one's journey through the world.
> (Linger 2005: 180–81)

In this chapter, I shall examine how personal accidents and emotion-laden incidents generate lasting but changing memories or reflections – they can quite literally be where 'shit happens' (as we shall shortly see), but, through the passage of time and space and the maturation of memory, they may come to be recognised as productive sites of anthropological and self-'knowledge'. In our attempts to demonstrate proficiency, fluency and purpose in our studies of others, particularly in our writing and even when we are at our most reflexive, we have tended to let those moments go – to erase them from the serious work of our trade – to label them as incidental or anecdotal or even see them as trivial embarrassments to be swept away, at least from the academy's eyes and ears. Edwin Ardener always implored his students to search out the 'unexpected missing' that he said would be found hiding in 'the social space' (personal communication). So here the unexpected missing is to be found very close to the heart – where we are most vulnerable, most human, least distanced – where our own accidents and illnesses and misinterpretations are deeply felt and then managed through our reflexive mobility over time and through different life encounters.

I would like to suggest that to consider the anthropologist as an ethnographic resource is to provide her with agency and the freedom to celebrate the unexpected, reflect on pasts and futures, acknowledge the personal in flux. It moves us one step beyond the relatively static rendering of 'reflexivity' that simply sees the anthropologist as a filter (engendering ethnicity, sexual orientation, politics, education, etc.) through which the 'other', at home or away, is observed, interacted with and described. Even more sophisticated analyses of reflexive fieldwork, positioned in an understanding of shifting subjectivity, the poetics of exposing the interior self to other selves (Rose 1983; Prattis 1997), the identities and solidarities created through processes of mimesis and alterity (Taussig 1993), etc., fail to fully recognise the freedom that is afforded to the anthropologist who moves and thinks and writes and feels and remembers in a mobile world.

A Mobile Reflexivity

We experience our social lives through constant reference to memories near and far, experienced and borrowed, etched in ink or narrated in fluid and ever-changing tales. We study other lives through our social engagement with those 'others', the selective recordings we make on paper and tape of their voices and actions (and our own) at specific moments in time, and the timeless yet ever repositioned tales that we tell ourselves and our colleagues, students and friends about our remembered experiences.

Remembering has long been described as a dynamic and constructive process related to established interests (Bartlett 1961: 312). But memory's ability to construct emerges from the individual's contact with other people and places and events. As Certeau writes, 'Memory is a sense of the other. Hence it develops along with relationships – in "traditional" societies as in love … It responds more than it records' (1984: 87–88). One must ask: What does it respond to? Where does it reside? Students learning about the hallmark of participant observation in anthropological research imagine that memory responds to things said and acts performed that are recorded on paper and translated into ethnographic texts, but I'd venture to say that often it's the least recorded, most unexpected personal moment or accident that becomes most viscerally remembered and then in the most unlikely places afterwards, the anthropologist's memory is refigured. Certeau adds: 'Like those birds that lay their eggs only in other species' nests, memory produces in a place that does not belong to 'it … it is outside of itself, it moves things about' (1984: 86–87).

If memory itself moves things about, and serendipitous moments in the life course move the anthropologist and her subjects about through time within and between places, then the study of anthropology is always the study of movement. This is as true for the fieldworker who devotes a whole career to fieldwork in one small village, as it is for one who studies transnational migrants or tourism or one who has worked in a number of different field sites. My own career and life so far have spanned a number of continents – from growing up in the US to marrying in the UK, fieldwork in the Scottish Hebrides to fieldwork in East Nepal, jobs in Oxford and then Durham, multi-sited fieldwork of a leisure practice in the US and Europe, and finally my recent migration to a job in Melbourne, Australia. The spark that stimulated the movement from one place or condition to the next was never designed, but arose out of often unexpected and serendipitous moments. Across all these places and times I've carried my past, present and future into every social encounter as well as through a private consciousness that I would suggest is enlivened through its emotional engagement with the world.

I'll now share a few personal stories in order to illustrate the potential of paying attention to accidents, but more importantly the generative potential of a very mobile reflexivity – a reflexivity to be found in the journey rather than the moment.

Isle of Siall, Inner Hebrides of Scotland, 1984–87

The Isle of Siall, where I conducted my first fieldwork in the mid-1980s, was home to a small intimate community of approximately 150 incomers and islanders. Half a mile down the road from my house on the north end of the island was a farmhouse where nine-year-old Hazel[1] lived with her elderly parents. Hazel treated me like an older sister and used to come to visit nearly every day. After my first year on the island I travelled to Oxford for several weeks at a time to conduct library work in preparation for my D.Phil. study of incomers. Before I left for the first time, I made a special gift for Hazel – a little black and white sheep made from 'Fimo' moulding clay you can bake hard in the oven. I put it on a little silver chain that I had had since I was a girl and when I gave the gift to Hazel she was totally ecstatic and had to run home to show her family the 'wee sheep'. A number of weeks later I returned to the island from Oxford and Hazel came running over to visit as soon as I got back. I noticed she wasn't wearing the sheep, so at some point in our chat I asked, 'So, Hazel, where's your little sheep necklace?' 'Em … not here,' she replied awkwardly. 'Did you break it?' I asked gently. 'No.' 'Did you lose it?' 'No …' 'Well, then, what happened to it?' I asked. She hesitated a moment, obviously wondering how I'd react to her answer, but then her face lit up with a hugely pleased smile as she told me in a rush, 'I took it to the gift shop and it got sold!'

When she said this, I was inwardly horrified and frankly quite hurt, although one isn't supposed to take children's actions too seriously … I thought of the hours I'd spent crafting the sheep, and the little silver necklace that I had had for many years – all for naught! Maybe I'm not all that special to Hazel, I moped inwardly. But then my mind wandered to the thought of the silly English tourist in the tiny island gift shop, buying a 'local Scottish Island product' made by an American anthropologist for the opportunistic daughter of a pair of English incomers, and I started to smile.

I have told this tale many times in very different contexts over the past twenty years, and the story is kept alive but fluid in association, detail and meaning through the retelling. It's a very funny story when told anywhere but on the island where it happened because the listener is shocked and then humoured by the way a meaningful gift is suddenly turned into a commodity. The first time I told the story was to Edwin Ardener, my supervisor at St John's College, Oxford. He roared with laughter. It evoked a story he then told about a time he was visiting a Bakweri chief in Camaroon whose daughter had a rat in a cage that she liked to play with. Edwin was enamoured by this apparent and unexpected evidence of pet-keeping, but then one day the cage was empty: 'Where is your little rat?' said Edwin to the girl. 'I ate it!' she replied! So then Edwin and I both laughed. One parallel is obvious. In both examples, the child's actions caught the anthropologist slipping into his or her own cultural expectations about conventions of gift-giving or pet-keeping. We laughed together at mistakes we anthropologists sometimes make as interpreters of culture. But, in the case of the sheep necklace, my feelings were wrapped up in a close and daily reinforced relationship that I had developed with young Hazel over more than a year. My laughter then was bittersweet because the interpretive lesson was only the intellectual part of the message in the action. Back on the island a few weeks later, I told the story to a close adult friend and islander, and she began to chuckle but then stopped as the idea of the tourist buying the silly American sheep gave way to something else. My reported story became hijacked by another story wrapped up in local knowledge about Hazel's home life and how her very loving English incomer parents were dreadful alcoholics who spent most of what they earned on whisky. One local told me, 'You know they went to the shop to buy Hazel a birthday box of chocolates and decided they would get a bottle of Bells instead so they could *all* celebrate her birthday – just think how that poor child *feels* – on the mainland this would never happen – she'd be removed from them and taken into care!' Aha. So it wasn't me after all – poor Hazel was just following her parent's example – making money even at the expense of a loved one's feelings.

Many years have passed. I've only returned to the island a few times since 1988 and Hazel's long grown up and moved away. I did learn with horror, however, that only a few years ago, one of the two shepherd tenants who lived at her house throughout her childhood had been accused and convicted of paedophile offences that were taking place during much of Hazel's youth. My heart weeps for Hazel as I wonder what I could have done to prevent this. Even the lasting humour of the sheep necklace's sale is underpinned now for me with yet another layer of gloomy reflection. And yet I can still laugh as loudly as the next person when I now find the basic tale very useful pedagogically – I tell it in introductory lectures on gift exchange to provide a lovely personal example of Maussian social reciprocity gone awry, or to demonstrate the distinction between a gift and a commodity.

Excavating Meaning from the Reflexive Anthropological Self

Pels has suggested that 'in its most elementary form, reflexivity presupposes that, while saying something about the "real world" one is simultaneously disclosing something about oneself' (2000: 2), but what Hazel and the sheep necklace teach me goes beyond this to demonstrate how active reflection on a personal interactive moment may carry on for years, in and out of the 'field', and may reveal the fresh worlds of meaning and emotion that Hazel's sale of my gift evokes. Revealing the anthropologist's subjective and reflexive 'self' (and that self's changing consciousness of 'other') is thus an ethnographic tool that carries on excavating significance through time and space as the tale is remembered, told and re-remembered. The 'self' in this context is revealed to be a consciousness of one's embodied actions and understandings of interactions as it reacts to movement through social time and space.

The 'self' only exists as a construction or illusion experienced through a consciousness that society, culture (Holland and Quinn 1987), language, metaphor (Ewing 1990), experience, action and practice (Bourdieu 1977) provide – it is feeling-based rather than an object or 'thing' (deMunck 2000: 39). Ethnographers who have tried to understand subjects' notions of selfhood in various cultural contexts often effectively demonstrate the way in which people's ideas and bodily reactions are felt to shift and adapt to changing circumstances (see Kondo's book *Crafting Selves* (1990),which explores particularly social and relational aspects of the Japanese 'self'). However, the ethnographer's *own* self remains curiously static in many reflexive renderings, which tend to centre around issues of method, authenticity and acknowledged bias. One example might include Hortense Powdermaker's seminal reflexive ethnography, *Stranger and Friend: the Way of an Anthropologist* (1967), which muses on her position with the Lesu of Melanesia as a white person and as a woman, as well as discussing problems about 'going native'. Another example, by Murphy, based on fieldwork in Italy, focuses on the problem of handling one's presumed political persuasion in a politically divided community, aptly entitled, 'On Jogging with Fascists and Strolling with Reds' (1992). Rabinow's *Reflections on Fieldwork in Morocco* (1977) illustrates how the particular friendship one might have with a particular person in the field context shapes the field experience. And yet all these reflexive texts are about particular moments in time and any notion of 'self' identity is fairly static in nature (e.g. around gender, politics, ethnicity/race, etc.). What I believe is less often examined or even acknowledged is the way in which the anthropologist's self matures and changes in subtle ways through its movements and new encounters in life, and how this change may then be applied to rethinking events and stories of self, other and field.[2]

It's not just that one continues to learn new details about one's subjects as time passes long after fieldwork, and that events richly described in due course become stories that are continually reworked into many different versions (Jackson 2005: 11), but that the anthropologist's capacity to make sense of stories that she tells herself about those remembered events will continue to be affected by her own changing experiences in the world. The next sections will attempt to demonstrate this, with reference to my fieldwork in Nepal.

East Nepal, 1989–90

Shit 1

The first year that Andrew[3] and I lived with the Yakha[4] in the Sankhuwasabha district of East Nepal, we stayed with the *Pradhan Panch* (a village headman, whom we called Appa, the Yakha term for father) and his wife (Ama) and daughter (whom I will call Baini here, meaning 'little sister'). We were very generously welcomed into their home; we were given a tiny room that was part of a wooden extension built along the side of the house, with a tiny open window looking towards the magnificent mountains of the Kanchanjunga (Everest) Range. It took many months to learn our way around the community, speak Nepali and a smattering of Yakha well enough to converse comfortably and start to feel at ease. About once a week, Baini would *lipnu* the floor of the dark kitchen and the front porch, where visitors sat to talk business with Appa or bring news from other areas. To *lipnu* is to take a fresh cow or buffalo patty of manure, mix it with water and massage it by hand into a smooth watery paste before smearing and rubbing it onto the floor. Another paste of red clay is then made to provide a colourful contrast part way up the side of the wall. This 'cleans' as well as decorates the house very effectively – it works like a fresh layer of plaster, filling holes and cracks that appear in the mud floor, which dries out and gets dusty as it is continuously trodden upon. Baini told us that she enjoys *lipnu*(ing) best of all household tasks – it is a purifying task due to the sacred nature of the cow that produced the dung.

During our second year in Sankhuwasabha, we moved to our own little house, which had been abandoned because it had been hit by lightning... twice. When we had cleaned it out and painted the woodwork in 'traditional' Yakha style, I asked a neighbour to teach me how to *lipnu* the floor. I somatically remember how I felt the first time. The smell, the texture, the thought of where that stuff had been gave me a feeling of overwhelming disgust, which I desperately tried to hide with a smile. The revulsion was only tempered by a self-conscious indulgent thought that this was the 'stuff' of bona fide fieldwork. But then I also remember admiring my handiwork afterwards – feeling the good housekeeper glow just like I used to for at least an hour after a rigorous house-cleaning at home in England. 'I keep looking at my handiwork with pride,' I wrote in my journal. With time I remember thinking that to *lipnu* wasn't so bad.

Shit 2

Months later, not long before we were going to leave the village, I went to the *charpi* (our long-drop latrine, surrounded by a little fence with a gate). As I squatted there, contemplating how the 'long drop' had become rather too 'short' after a year of use and how perfect the timing of our departure was on that front, the wooden board supporting my left foot snapped and I screamed as my foot and leg went plunging deep into the shit. Hugely embarrassed, I was pulled out of the latrine by Andrew, assisted by an English male visitor (also an anthropologist in Nepal), and later I spent hours scrubbing my running shoes and body at the spring. The accident was only funny in retrospect; at the time it was absolutely disgusting and embarrassing. This is one story that has not been recalled very often, certainly not for teaching, publishing, or conference papers – but it is told here because it helps shape the third and final story of shit.

Shit Illuminated

Six years later, I returned to Nepal for several weeks during a research leave period when our son Ben was five years old – he managed the long trek into Sankhuwasabha, where all our Yakha friends and 'family' fussed over him. Little Ben and elderly Appa went off for walks to tend the animals, having long 'conversations' – each speaking different languages. But then Ben got sick with the most violent stomach virus. One night we rushed to the *charpi* (the one that Appa had built for us when we first came to his house years before) to hold our crying, vomiting and diarrhoeal Ben over the hole. The large flashlight somehow slipped from grip in the chaos and fell down into the disgusting waste below. Later, when Ben was asleep, we explained to Baini what had happened and that she and her parents shouldn't be shocked if they go to the *charpi* and find it illuminated from within!

Early the next morning Baini called us into the kitchen to eat an early morning snack of fried rice, and there on the wooden rack directly above the pan of food in the hearth hung our totally dissected flashlight, drying out in the heat! I said in Nepali, 'Wow – is that what I think it is?' as the thought of her fishing the thing out of the *charpi* through that small and smelly hole in the very early dawn flashed though my mind. She replied, 'It should be ready for you to use later today.' In one voice we insisted that she should keep it or give it to someone else, and that we had another flashlight to use.

I remember thinking at the time that her action poignantly demonstrated the huge disparity in our cultural assessments of value, and that, for even a relatively wealthy Yakha and landowner in the community, a flashlight is not easily dispensed with, even if it's buried in excrement. Waste not, want not, even in waste! I wondered to myself what I'd do if a valuable diamond ring heirloom slipped from my finger and got buried deep in the *charpi*. Would I try to fish it out? Of course I would ... in my own shit, and of course my son's. But then that intellectual bit of my reasoning became overpowered by a deeply visceral recollection of my own body plunging into the last *charpi* I'd encountered in the same village years before. And that was mostly my own shit! 'Not for all the tea in China!' I mused.

A few years later I came across my notes from my early *lipnu*ing experience as well as a picture of me crouched on the floor of my Yakha home, wearing a lungi and smiling while smearing on the cow shit. I revisited my memory of the flashlight and began to wonder if Baini had been un-phased by the human faeces since faeces is just faeces and digging around in it may not be pleasant but is certainly not an issue. 'Shit happens', and through time it comes to take on a different quality of meaning and bodily association. I ambled slowly away from the field to a point years removed where I could come to slightly revised conclusions about my own judgements. The events themselves had not changed: only my interpretations and feelings had altered.

Serendipity 'is the interactive outcome of unique and contingent "mixes" of insight coupled with chance', according to Fine and Deegan (1996: 434). There's an assumption in most renderings of 'serendipity' that the event or accidental 'discovery' is fairly immediately cognised by the researcher. The happy 'Aha' moment of realisation is often thought to be 'coupled' with particular events or actions, which are then labelled serendipitous. But this is surely inadequate. One can hardly imagine that the moment of falling into a pit latrine could ever be called serendipitous, The event wasn't serendipitous, but the stuff of life that over the longer term made me think differently of those many 'shitty' moments was, indeed, full of many happy discoveries. If, as Rapport (1997) tells us, the self-conscious individual engages in multiple social and cultural environments, and if her memories are active cumulative experiences born out of a lifetime of intersecting and transforming reflections, then serendipity, like reflexivity, should be considered as a journey rather than a destination.

The Ethics of Shifting Recall

I have suggested that it is essential for our understandings of selves and others to accommodate change and re-evaluation that serendipitous journeys reveal, but to do this will clearly require a significant revamping of accepted notions of research process and ethics in the social study of human subjects. What we have always called 'field data' are traditionally assumed to reside in notes and documents that are relatively fixed in time and place. Sometimes one of those variables is challenged. For example, with regard to time, anthropologists often physically revisit their 'field site(s)' (as the Nepal example demonstrates) and the new observations and interviews justified by explicit research aims and objectives produce further notes and documents, which contribute to a growing corpus of material. Such ethnographic data may be perceived as a living and growing beast that travels the globe and is reframed, retamed, reanalysed within the researcher's shifting consciousness that a growing maturity and changing relationship to 'the field' afford.

Yet several problems of method still remain. If we accept that such a mobile and maturing reflexivity is particularly useful or revealing, then we need to find ways to incorporate it into our discipline's discourse through teaching and the writing of ethnographic texts. This is far from simple. If texts continue to report events, discussions and meanings as social facts fixed in time and space and hence only momentarily placed within a reflexive context, one could easily see how a later reworking of these in terms of present understandings and moralities would demonstrate presentist or

Whiggish scholarship. But, if one understands how events, discussions and meanings are located in the ethnographer's changing awareness of self as being-in-the-world, then any resultant ethnographic writing becomes free of such charges of presentism as it incorporates such change.

And yet one might also ask what the position of such data is in a research culture that has designed its ethical guidelines based around a scientific lab-based model. An anthropologist's 'lab' would presumably equate to a community in a particular village, town or city at a given period of time, or even to the mobile worlds of Traveller Gypsies or dancers on tour. The spaces between and beyond the controlled environment of a 'field', often well out of reach (in space and time) of consent forms, are fertile sources of reflexive understanding, which we as sensitive informed researchers should be able to harvest, but current institutional guidelines on ethical research practice determine that we shouldn't do this.

Let me illustrate. I lived on Siall for three years as a resident and a researcher, and in East Nepal for two years and, during those years, in the mid- to late 1980s, I spoke to local people at appropriate moments about my research interests and objectives, but I gave them no written statements of purpose and have no consent forms from them, as this was an era that pre-dated the institution of informed consent forms and ethical clearance panels for qualitative fieldwork.[5] But let us imagine for a moment that I had followed what is now considered current research protocol and Hazel and her family and neighbours in Scotland and Baini and her family in Nepal had signed University of Oxford-endorsed forms that spelled out their rights and my intentions (at the time), which would cover my time in the Siall and Sankhuwasabha 'labs'. And let us imagine further that years after the field research was completed and after the places of those two villages receded into my memory, my understandings of particular people, events and meanings there were to become deeply affected by new serendipitous contacts and reflections. How might I write about these people and my own shifting understandings and feelings? Or to come to the point, have I, in the previous section, committed ethical offences by revealing the multiple layers of meaning that Hazel's sheep necklace sale and Baini's flashlight washing revealed long after those events might have disappeared from the protagonists' own memories? I would hope that researchers who understand the position of the reflexive and maturing researcher in the data would say I haven't. One such anthropologist would be Pat Caplan. Caplan's reflexive chapter on fieldwork in Tanzania over a twenty-year span demonstrates how she discovered her gendered self over the years and learned that 'being an ethnographer means studying the self as well as the other... while at the same time, the other, because of familiarity, and a different approach to fieldwork, becomes part of the self' (1993: 180).

And yet in her study, the field place remains static and her revelations of self are all in relation to that Tanzanian life. The picture becomes more complicated, I would suggest, when multiple field sites speak to one another through the embodied life experiences of the anthropologist over time, and the next section demonstrates this to show the way ideas may be reframed through travel in, between and out of 'fields'.

Illness and Memory

In December 1989, after a bout of asthma and a very long trek back to our house in East Nepal, I felt unwell, and within hours I was sure I was having a heart attack – I could hardly breathe for the pain in my chest. I became very sick and couldn't keep food or liquids down as my temperature rose. I self-medicated on antibiotics, which did nothing, but I hoped they would work, and I also felt we might as well make use of this illness and called the local shaman to come, positioning a tape recorder by the bed. He never arrived, and as I became delirious I remember begging Andrew to phone for a helicopter (a fantasy, as the nearest phone was many hours' walk away).

Then our Yakha family and many neighbours came to visit my bedside. As I lay on my bed struggling to breathe and unable to sit up, I thought about how strange the scene was to me, for none of the visitors seemed even to notice I was there! They chattered and laughed and talked to each other about recent events in the village – none of the hushed concern and fussing and hand-holding I imagined I would receive at home in a hospital. I wondered why they were doing this – I wondered if I might die like this. Eventually, the shaman did arrive, only to act as a porter and carry me out of the village in a cut-out seat made from a carrying basket – he performed some magic with my sleeping bag in order, he said, to protect me from the dangers of the hospital. Barefoot, for seven hours, up 3,000 feet and with only a ten minute rest, he carried me up the mountain. As we passed people I knew in the village, they looked concerned and asked what was wrong, but then, as we entered terrain where we were just white strangers, children pointed and laughed at the funny vision. Then we took a long drive with some Peace Corps volunteers to the Terai and the ex-Gurkha military hospital in Biratnagar, where doctors admitted me with double pneumonia – I had very nearly died.

I revisit this memory often, and not just as a hero's tale of fieldwork. As I have grown and changed, so too has the memory – not substantively, but emotionally and cognitively. In 2001, after a very long illness, my mother lay on her deathbed, which was positioned in the living room of her California home. I flew from Durham and arrived with my heart bursting from grief. For nearly four weeks she held on to life, slipping slowly into silence, and we carried on living, cooking, talking and eating around her as various family and friends came to visit. She was the centre of attention and also very much peripheral to it. One day I snapped when a visitor made loud comments about my mother's imminent death (based on a medical observation the hospice nurse had made). I took his wife outside and demanded she tell him to stop it – to tell him that my mother could hear everything we said and still feels deeply, even if her eyes are closed.

I experienced my mother's death through my memories, not only of my life with her, but of my fieldwork lives far from 'home'. I imagined her thoughts and feelings on that bed through my referential knowledge of similar social scenarios in the past in entirely different cultural settings. But I have also refigured my memory of my near-death experience in Sankhuwasabha eleven years before, through the emotional growth that attending my mother's death revealed. While I can speak from my old notes of how I felt on my village bed in Nepal in 1989, when I think back now to my close relationship to many of the people sitting around me, I can only imagine that their own remembered experiences of sickness, death and loss comprised a background consciousness to their happy chatter at my bedside – of course they were worried for me! It has taken me many years to figure this out.

Years of living and moving can offer perspective, depth and a new (if never 'real') purchase on a lived and remembered sense of 'truth' and meaning. This implies that we should, I believe, feel impelled to openly share our shifting revelations – to use ourselves as authoritative (as any other) resources – and write again and again as our reflexive knowledge evolves. The saddest irony is that the greatest amount of time that most academics have free for in-depth, long-term field research is in pursuit of a Ph.D., generally conducted in their twenties. These researchers examine other people's traversing of a life course before they've progressed very far through their own. They describe informants' experiences of childbirth long before they have experienced the pain of childbirth for themselves, or publish symbolic studies of illness and death ritual before they've experienced loss. There are, no doubt, many notable exceptions, such as Rosaldo's oft-cited reflexive article (1984) on his wife's death and the resultant increased empathetic understanding of how Ilongot headhunting could be inspired by overwhelming rage. Rosaldo's revelations, however, took place as a result of a sudden and tragic accident in the field and he could write up his results with the authority of the ethnographic present. In the examples I have provided so far from my own experience, the self as ethnographic resource travels long distances and through many life changes to become a particularly useful tool. Our findings are not just added to with time (e.g. from our future visits and other people's work) but they are often dismantled or at least reframed by our own developing sensitivities and interactions with other people and other 'fields'. I believe we must think of ways to incorporate this knowledge into our teaching and writing.

So this chapter hopefully leaves the reader with more than just a few evocative tales of mishap and woe from one person's ethnographic journey. It should make one reassess the locations and sometimes mutually constituted constructions of 'knowledge', 'culture', 'self' and 'other'. Events are not just variously interpreted, but they are multiply remembered against very different personal and deeply emotional associations, which change through time. We think and feel through our memories, and, as we travel through time around the world, the memories grow with us. I agree with Tonkin that 'memory is a part of cognitive empowering and a means to being' (1992: 112), but I'd add that this empowerment is realised through the ethnographer's altering emotional connections to memory and flexibility in allowing for a changed understanding of self. Truly memorable experiences are ones that slap us in the face with personal embodied senses of pain, grief, hilarity, disgust, etc., and then, instead of crumbling away until only remnants remain, the memories become reworked due to the continually extended dialogic relationship the ethnographer has with her maturing self through her experiences with others. To recognise these subtle changes and allow for these altered framings to feature in our teaching and writing and 'knowing' is to revel in the *processes* of serendipity and reflexivity and to celebrate the often surprising nature of human interaction. It allows us to recognise the anthropological 'self' as a rich ethnographic resource.

Notes

This chapter was based on a paper given at the 2006 EASA conference in Bristol, and I am grateful to the University of Melbourne for funding that trip. I would also like to thank Anselma Gallinat, Peter Collins, Vered Amit, Mary Patterson, Alan Thorold, Yoko Demelius and Michael Hartfeld for their comments and suggestions on earlier drafts of the paper.

1. Note that I have altered names of people and places to preserve anonymity.
2. One fine exception is found in an article by Caplan (1993) that reflects on her changing experiences over twenty years in Tanzania, and I introduce it later in this chapter.
3. Andrew Russell was my husband at the time, and a fellow anthropologist, and after I completed my D.Phil. in Oxford based on work in the Scottish Hebrides, we moved to Nepal. The 'serendipitous' opportunity I had to work

in Nepal was a result of my desire to accompany Andrew to his chosen field site rather than from any research-driven motivation. However, my research interests did shape what I saw and experienced, as well as what I wrote about the community there.

4. The 'Yakha' who reside in Sankhuwasabha are an ethnic group belonging to a larger group of Tibeto-Burman origin called the Kiranti and closely related to other Kiranti groups such as the Limbu and the Rai.

5. The circumstances of my research and hence the methodologies used in Scotland and Nepal were quite different, so these 'appropriate moments' were quite different as well. In Scotland I was already living in the community as an incomer amongst incomers and I was interested in the way people naturally expressed their identities in action and interaction with others (see Kohn 2002), so I explained my research aims only when I very occasionally conducted formal interviews, or when I needed access to historical records. In Nepal, my presence as an obvious stranger in a village far from the tourist trail required formal and informal explanation whenever new people were encountered.

References

Bartlett, F. 1961. *Remembering: A Study in Experimental and Social Psychology*. Cambridge: Cambridge University Press.

Bourdieu, P. 1977. *Outline of a Theory of Practice*. Cambridge: Cambridge University Press.

Caplan, P. 1993. 'Learning Gender: Fieldwork in a Tanzanian Coastal Village, 1965–85', in D. Bell, W. Caplan, W.J. Karim (eds), *Gendered Fields: Women, Men and Ethnography*. London: Routledge, pp. 168–81.

Certeau, M. de. 1984. *The Practice of Everyday Life*. Berkeley: University of California Press.

deMunck, V.C. 2000. *Culture, Self, and Meaning*. Prospect Heights, Ill.: Waveland Press.

Ewing, K.P. 1990. 'The Illusion of Wholeness: "Culture", "Self", and the Experience of Inconsistency', *Ethos* 8: 251–78.

Fine, G. and J. Deegan 1996. 'Three Principles of Serendip: The Role of Chance in Ethnographic Research', *Qualitative Studies in Education* 9: 434–47.

Holland, D. and N. Quinn. 1987. *Cultural Models in Language and Thought*. Cambridge: Cambridge University Press.

Jackson, M. 2005. *Existential Anthropology: Events Exigencies and Effects*. Oxford: Berghahn.

Kohn, T. 2002. 'Becoming an Islander Through Action in the Scottish Hebrides', *Journal of the Royal Anthropological Institute* 8(1): 143–58.

Kondo, D. 1990. *Crafting Selves: Power, Gender, and Discourses of Identity in a Japanese Workplace*. Chicago: University of Chicago Press.

Linger, D.T. 2005. *Anthropology Through a Double Lens: Public and Personal Worlds in Human Theory*. Philadelphia: University of Pennsylvania Press.

Murphy, M.D. 1992. 'On Jogging with Fascists and Strolling with Reds: Ethnoethnography and Political Polarization in an Andalusian Town', in P. DeVita (ed.), *The Naked Anthropologist*. Belmont, Calif.: Wadsworth Publishing, pp. 173–83.

Pels, D. 2000. 'Reflexivity: One Step Up', *Theory, Culture and Society* 17(3): 1–25.

Powdermaker, H. 1967. *Stranger and Friend: The Way of an Anthropologist*. London: Secker and Warburg.

Prattis, J.I. 1997. *Anthropology at the Edge: Essays on Culture, Symbol, and Consciousness*. Lanham: University Press of America.

Rabinow, P. 1977. *Reflections on Fieldwork in Morocco*. Berkeley: University of California Press.

Rapport, N. 1997. *Transcendent Individual: Towards a Literary and Liberal Anthropology*. London: Routledge.

Rosaldo, R.I. 1984. 'Grief and a Headhunter's Rage: On the Cultural Force of Emotions', in E.M. Bruner (ed.), *Text, Play and Story: The Construction and Recontruction of Self and Society*. Washington: American Anthropological Association, pp. 178–95.

Rose, D. 1983. 'In Search of Experience: The Anthropological Poetics of Stanley Diamond', *American Anthropologist* (NS) l85(2): 345–55.

Taussig, M. 1993. *Mimesis and Alterity*. New York: Routledge.

Tonkin, E. 1992. *Narrating Our Pasts: The Social Construction of Oral History*. Cambridge: Cambridge University Press.

Chapter 12

SERENDIPITIES, UNCERTAINTIES AND IMPROVISATIONS IN MOVEMENT AND MIGRATION

Vered Amit

I live in a country with one of the coldest climates in the world. In February, when the snow has been piling up on the ground for months, ice coats the sidewalks in treacherous sheets or hangs in icicles from roofs, nights are cold and long and even sunlamps don't seem able to keep SAD (seasonal affective disorder) at bay, I have been known to ruefully note that I ended up 'here' because my father was looking for a place 'without sunshine'. Of course this comment exaggerates and simplifies even if it does capture some of the more ironic elements of my trajectory into, out of and now across Canada. As a young child, my family's migration to Canada was initially prompted by my father's experience of melanoma in Israel, the country of my birth. Although he was successfully treated for this disease, his doctors advised him that a prolonged respite from the intense sun of Israel – in a period before the development of effective topical sunscreens – could substantially assist his recovery. So we sought out a cold climate for what was originally planned as a temporary stay abroad in Montreal. That was the first of several long-distance moves that have since punctuated my life. Two subsequent moves back to Israel, as a child and then as an adolescent, were still dependent on my parents' situation and decisions. As an adult, I undertook other journeys of my own volition that took me elsewhere in Canada, then abroad to several different locales for a number of years and eventually back to Montreal. So, in truth, I 'ended up' in Montreal as much because of my own choices and circumstances as my parents'. But it is also true that the paths, resources, outlooks and recognised possibilities that shaped my movements had been set in train by my father's initial, unexpected experience of a devastating illness.

In this chapter, I want to consider some possible articulations between, on the one hand, my own (and by extension my family's) intimate experiences of the serendipities and happenstances sometimes shaping movement, and on the other, the situations of intra- and trans-statal mobilities on which most of my research career has focused. I will argue that these articulations underline the importance of sensitivity to the ragged and unpredictable nature of human experience but they do not resolve the dilemmas of abstraction that are at the heart of the anthropological enterprise.

Is it Serendipitous?

Much of the scholarly interrogation of serendipity has concerned its status in the research process itself, particularly the role of chance or accident in unanticipated or unsought findings. A key question within this long-running debate has concerned whether it is possible to observe productively a surprising fact or relationship without a prior predisposition towards noticing the anomalous; hence Pasteur's famous observation that 'chance favours only prepared minds' (Pasteur as cited in Van Andel 1994: 635). Without this kind of open-minded orientation, what Van Andel has termed the art of 'loose blinders' (Van Andel 1994: 645), the surprising occurrence might not be noticed at all, or, if noticed, not acted upon. Thus, in his survey of one thousand examples of serendipity in science, technology and art Pek Van Andel concluded that '[s]erendipity does exist' (1994: 644): 'It is arrogant to think that "God's will", an (un)-conscious mind, a plan, strategy, ideology, research-proposal or -project, (computer) program or expert system can intentionally anticipate unknown, unforeseeable, unpredictable, contra-intuitive, surprising facts or relations' (ibid.). However, he also argued that '[s]erendipity plays a supporting but essential role' (ibid.) in the process of discovery. The unforeseen occurrence needs the purposeful engagement of a curious and perceptive observer to render it a 'finding'. Van Andel's observations have implications for anthropological research as for any form of formal enquiry, but here I am especially interested in its utility for the way in which we more generally conceptualise the role of creativity and improvisation in social action. Furthermore, while a dialectic between serendipity and improvisation is hardly particular to the kind of mobility choices and pathways with which I am concerned in this chapter, this is a field of activities that can especially highlight this dynamic because so very often it involves personal engagements with the unfamiliar and the unknown.

Like the unforeseen in scientific discovery, the illness that so radically changed my father's life and, through him, mine was not really new.

Today, watching out for indicators of and being checked regularly for skin cancer have become a faithfully observed element of his regular routine. But at only twenty-six years old, in a period during the 1960s when there was relatively little public awareness of skin cancer, my father was unprepared for the possibility that his life would be so endangered or that a short while later he would leave Israel as a result. The fairly radical implications of this unforeseen event were not, however, simply or even primarily a consequence of the illness itself but of the way in which my father responded to it. After a few years working in Canada, he decided to use the opportunity to pursue a university education, a decision that at the time was regarded by many of his consociates and relatives as an unusual course of action for a thirty-year-old man with three dependent children. That decision in turn led to a new career as a scientist and university professor in Montreal, a fairly significant change from his pre-migration livelihood as a dairy farmer on a kibbutz. It was a course of decisions that led him to Wales, Israel and eventually back to Montreal. Would he have embarked on this path even if his illness had not occurred? He might have gone back to school, but it is unlikely that this would have happened in quite this way, with the same journeys, in the same places or with the same people. On the other hand, someone else faced with a similarly fateful illness might have refused to leave Israel in spite of the risks or, alternatively, might have left the country only for a few years and then returned to take up as much of their former life and routines as possible.

Years later, I travelled to Iran as a junior member of a joint Canadian/UK university archaeological team. I was supposed to stay there for only a few months but when I met the man who would become my first partner I stayed on for ten months, witnessed the remarkable events of the first phases of the Iranian revolution, changed my academic métier, returned briefly to Canada and then on to the UK where we were both able to pursue our doctoral educations and where I eventually worked for a time. It was a much less consequential interlude for the other members of the team with whom I arrived in Iran. Years later, when I considered myself settled back in Montreal, I met and married my present husband. That marriage led to a dramatic reconfiguration of my annual routines around an ongoing schedule of long-distance movement criss-crossing the second largest country in the world. I now regularly travel between Montreal, where I work, and the Lower Mainland of British Columbia, where my partner works.

The 'choices' I have briefly detailed above, my father's and later my own, while idiosyncratic, were also crucially shaped by much larger systemic factors: immigration and border policies in Canada, Iran and the UK during this period; diplomatic relations between the countries through which we were respectively moving; job markets in all these countries; and university entrance requirements, funding sources in Canada and the UK and so on. They were also enabled by more specific aspects of our respective circumstances and backgrounds, particularly the kind of financial resources, personal networks, organisational links or humanistic values that we could respectively draw on in working out our responses to events and persons.

Hence, to the interaction between serendipity and the willing agent that Van Andel highlighted as essential aspects of discovery we can also add the broader structural context and the more specific social background and circumstances of this observer as crucial influences on her possible responses to the unforeseen event or relation. But one of the key ongoing dilemmas for social analysis is the weight that should be accorded to the systemic and collective as opposed to the role of uncertainty and personal agency.

Keith[1] was a hydroelectric engineering consultant whom I interviewed in 2002 as part of a larger study of travelling professionals who specialised in international projects (see Amit 2006; Amit 2007). I interviewed Keith in Greater Montreal, where he had been based since 1975, but he was originally from Melbourne, Australia. He had always been interested in travel, he said, but he had not initially planned a career involving international work: 'When I was working in Australia, I was working mostly on jobs in Australia so my work there was primarily travelling within Australia. It was only when I came to Canada in '76 that I actually started travelling on the job'. He had started working in the hydroelectricity sector in Australia, but in 1975 he was offered a job by a Canadian consulting group:

> to come to Montreal, where I've been ever since. And I worked for them for twenty years and almost immediately, once I started working for them, they started sending me off on international projects. And I enjoyed it, I think I was good at it. I didn't set out to get into the international field, but once I was working in it, I was very happy doing that.

For Keith, international work turned out to be more exciting and challenging than the humdrum 'nine-to-five' routine of domestically based work:

> The first time I went overseas for [Waterworks Engineering][2] was not long after we'd moved here. I think that was probably the hardest for my wife and kids. I went to Iran for four months, two months before Christmas and two months after Christmas. It was their first Canadian winter and so that was probably the most difficult. I don't think any of us realised at that stage

what it was going to be like. But in the end, we adjusted and we've gone from there.

His assignment in Iran was originally supposed to last only six weeks but stretched instead to four months, a feature of instability that often characterised his subsequent international work. But after the experience of this first project and while his children were still young, Keith had been determined to ensure that he would not be gone again for longer than a month at any one time, although sometimes this meant more time spent travelling back and forth. In the 1980s, however, Keith accepted a longer-term assignment in Peru, which lasted four years:

> I've worked a lot in Latin America. I've always been interested in Latin America and that particular job, I had gotten a site visit for a proposal, and prepared the proposal, and negotiated the contract. It was sort of like it was my job. And that was a [requirement]: if we got the job, we'd [Keith's family] all be going down there together.

But despite this plan, Keith's family was only able to stay with him for three of the four years during which he resided in Peru. When the political situation in Peru became tense and a number of foreigners had been kidnapped, Keith's wife and two children returned to Montreal and he stayed on by himself an additional year: 'In the mid-1990s, the children had already left home or were about to leave home and that's when I went to Vancouver for a year on a job. I was partly commuting back here and my wife was coming out there every two or three months on the frequent-flyer points and so on. So that was relatively easy.'

But the experience in Vancouver, which came on the heels of a second corporate merger involving the consulting company with which he had started off in Montreal, suggested to Keith that it was time he went 'out on my own' as an independent consultant. He didn't like the changed atmosphere in the newly merged company and he realised that he was pocketing only a small fraction of the fees that his employer was charging for his services in Vancouver. During the six years before my meeting with him, a period in which Keith had been working as an independent consultant, the pattern of his working travels had changed, and he now felt able to accept many more assignments that took him away for months at a time. Indeed, from a professional point of view, he much preferred the longer-term assignments, since they allowed for a deeper involvement.

> The longer assignments have been more so in the last six years since I've been out on my own. The kids have left home, my wife has a job three times a week and she's busy. She's involved in three choirs and so on so she keeps

very busy and in fact, she doesn't even notice half the time that I'm gone [laughs]. So once the kids have left home or once they're adults or late teens...

Keith worked on projects for many different companies, both Canadian- and foreign-owned but he still often worked with the firm that had originally employed him in Australia. One of his children was now living in Australia, while the other still resided in Montreal. He and his wife tried to visit Australia every second year, although the unpredictable scheduling of some of his projects sometimes disrupted these vacation plans. They were happy with their home and friendship networks in Montreal and had no plans to relocate elsewhere.

Keith's career, migration and travelling experiences had thus been a combination of planning and ad hoc responses to opportunities and events as they had happened: a job offer, a first 'international' assignment, the unexpected political shifts affecting a long-term stay abroad, a company takeover and so on. On the whole, Keith felt that his career and way of life, while often developing in directions he had not initially planned or expected, developments that had required 'adjustments' on his own part and his family's, had worked out happily enough. Keith's background had provided him with assets that had to an important extent influenced both the opportunities that became available to him as well as his room for manoeuvre in responding to them. Not only did he hold specialised credentials in civil engineering, but he had acquired them at a major Australian university that was well respected and recognised in Canada. A Canadian company viewed his initial Australian-based professional experience in hydroelectric development as sufficiently relevant to their own work to recruit him actively. And he and his family were able to gain immigration status as permanent residents in Canada. Many more recent immigrants to Canada from southern hemisphere locations in Asia or Africa have found Canadian companies much less willing to recognise their foreign educational credentials or work experience and/or have also experienced significant difficulties in sponsoring their dependents for immigration. But Keith's professional credentials and origins are not the whole tale.

Marina, whom I interviewed in 2002 as well, had also worked for 'Waterworks Engineering'. Like Keith, she was a civil engineer with a specialisation in hydraulics. She had been born and raised in Montreal and was hired within three weeks of finishing her engineering degree at a local university for what was originally supposed to be just a temporary job. Unlike Keith, 'working overseas' was a personal ambition from the outset of her career:

I just happened to know an acquaintance who called me and said, 'Can you work three weeks for us?' and it turned into a permanent job for [Waterworks]. And I was really keen on working overseas and I guess I went around talking to a lot of people about the possibilities. And at the time, I was very young and there was a lot of – not opposition, but I think they realised or felt that I was too young. And people who went overseas were really people with a lot of expertise … and not necessarily people like me who were just right out of school. But I guess I had some computer programming background that nobody else had and I ended up being able to go to Africa. And, after spending a bit of time in Africa, that really created the base upon which I could then say, 'Well you know, I have this background and I can go and do X, Y, Z.' And so I think I was probably one of the first people, women, one of the first women to go long-term overseas for [Waterworks].

But you need to be careful about what you wish for. Marina's travelling career took off with a vengeance. After an initial six months' assignment in Cameroon, she went back to Montreal for a year and then, 'craving another overseas experience', she was sent to Indonesia, first on a long-term contract of two years and then on and off for another three years. In between her trips to Indonesia, she went back to Africa, worked in Vietnam, India and Bangkok. She had just started another long-term contract of two years in India when she was asked by 'Waterworks' to carry out a dam inspection in Vancouver. It was supposed to be just a temporary visit:

So I really came out here [Vancouver] … it was only supposed to be temporary and I didn't want to be here. I wanted to be either in India or at home in Montreal. I had bought a condo in Montreal which I never got to live in because I bought it in '89? Well, when I got back from Africa, so '89, '90. And I travelled after that so much that I never got to live in it and I more or less came out here thinking it would be temporary and it turned out to be permanent. Six weeks into my contract here, into the job that was supposed to be three months, they asked me if I would move here permanently. And at that point, I had been overseas for about six years and I was very fed up …

She 'felt the need to settle down'. 'So I was thirty-four, going on thirty-five, and I felt the need to settle down. Through all of this I had had long-distance relationships and those were tremendously difficult to maintain, being overseas. And I felt I wanted to have a family and to settle down.'

When a British Columbia utility company asked 'Waterworks' to second Marina to them, she accepted on condition she wouldn't have to travel any more. But, having worked hard to establish a reputation as a specialist in international projects, Marina found it difficult to rejig her career around domestic work. After a year and a half, although still based in Vancouver, 'Waterworks' started to send her on overseas assignments again. So, when the opportunity arose to work for another Vancouver based company specialising in environmental matters, she accepted. But, because her curriculum vitae featured so much international work, she found herself yet again travelling, this time to Honduras, Guatemala and Peru: 'And by that time I was thirty-eight, thirty-nine and I really felt like my life hadn't settled down.' So she left consulting and took a stationary job at the local utility company in Vancouver for whom she had initially worked on secondment from 'Waterworks':

> And I had contacts at _____ and I was offered a job at _____. And I thought that was an opportunity to kind of change my life. I'd had enough of travelling. There was a time in India when I would sit up and stare at these ceilings of these incredibly ornamental hotels with gilded ceilings and did a little bit of that in Peru as well. Stared up at the ceiling and wondered if this was what I wanted for the rest of my life, to be working overseas. And so I accepted a job from _____ and decided not to travel any more. Now I don't know how long that's going to last because _____ is restructuring and they'll probably sell off the engineering portion of their assets and then I'll probably end up travelling overseas again. But it did give me an opportunity to settle down.

For both Keith and Marina, secondment to a Vancouver project by their Montreal-based company became a turning point in their careers and employment. Marina had planned for and successfully achieved a career involving international travel, but eventually felt entrapped by the expectation that she would continue to be an international specialist. Vancouver offered an escape, if an uncertain and episodic one, from a life in motion. But Keith, who had not planned to travel, found himself with opportunities to do so and spent much of the subsequent three decades of his career working on international projects for longer and shorter stints. A year in Vancouver only convinced him it was time to work independently as a travelling consultant. Beyond their credentials and their experience of overseas projects, there were of course, other more specific features of their respective situations that shaped Keith and Marina's different responses to work, travel and migration opportunities as these arose. Keith had already established a family before starting out on a peripatetic career and his wife was willing, for the most part, to accommodate his job changes, mobility and frequent absences and was available to care for their children when he was away. Marina was a young, single woman when she embarked on international consulting. Her itinerancy had interrupted and disrupted her capacity to develop romantic relationships and start a family.

But, if I reduced Keith and Marina's experiences of and reactions to unexpected opportunities, plans made and remade, settling and travelling, to their professional credentials, passports, gender and age, I would be imparting to their lives a predictability that stands in sharp contrast to their own sense of repeated uncertainties and improvisation. My father didn't expect to leave Israel, to settle for a time in Montreal or to live today in a 300-year-old house in Nova Scotia. I didn't expect that my short stay in Iran would plunge me into the maelstrom of revolution or would by and by lead me to a six-year stay in Britain or that I would end up shuttling across thousands of kilometres to a part of Canada I had barely known before. And, if my national or ethnic background, education or gender had a factor in what it was possible for me to do, I cannot believe that they made the various courses of my life necessarily predictable or even likely. So why should I smooth out the uncertainties and happenstance of Keith and Marina's lifestyle any more than I would my own or my father's? But what, then, is the more general significance of Keith and Marina's peripatetic careers and lives which, after all, my fieldwork sought to comprehend?

Creativity and Context

Anthropologists and their associates in sister social science disciplines are long used to taking account of the structures and social situations that frame the actions of particular people although the scope of that contextualisation has been repeatedly revised, deepened and complicated. Nowhere is this effort more evident, and inescapable, than in the diverse interdisciplinary examination of population movements, both within and especially across state borders. Indeed this kind of movement increasingly tends to be framed within the very broad rubric of globalisation, as one amongst a set of 'social, economic, cultural and demographic processes that take place within nations but also transcend them, such that attention limited to local processes, identities, and units of analysis yields incomplete understanding of the local' (Kearney 1995: 548). This shift in the scope of contextualisation is highlighted by the shift in emphasis occurring in the titles of two literature overviews on population mobility, which were published by Michael Kearney in the *Annual Review of Anthropology*. Thus Kearney's 1986 review of migration was entitled: 'From the Invisible Hand to Visible Feet: Anthropological Studies of Migration and Development'. But his 1995 review appeared under the title of 'The Local and the Global: the Anthropology of Globalization and Transnationalism' and linked trans-statal movements of population to global and transnational flows of information, symbols, capital and commodities.

This kind of reframing is by no means restricted to scholarly analyses but is also reflected in political ventures such as the Global Commission on International Migration (GCIM) whose 'mandate was to provide the framework within which a "coherent, comprehensive and global" response to the issue of international migration could be developed' (Grant 2006: 13). While the GCIM's 2005 report still links migration principally to development and recognises states as the principal arbiters of their own national policy, it also calls for the establishment of an Interagency Global Migration Facility and examines the flow and impact of remittances and investments between receiving and sending countries as well as the role of international law and human rights agreements (Martin and Martin 2006).

But, as has often been noted (Smart 1999; Graeber 2002; Amit 2007), efforts to relate to globalisation – whether as a phenomenon for study or as a context for the phenomena and processes being studied – poses special challenges for a discipline such as anthropology, which has traditionally focused on small-scale face-to-face relationships and systems. The temptation, Graeber argues, has been to respond to this dilemma by concentrating on the responses of particular peoples, usually non-elites, to larger influences imposed on them 'from above', giving anthropologists the niche role of 'reminding everyone that the little guys still exist' (2002: 1223). Graeber is worried that this small-scale orientation could leave anthropologists out of important conversations about the nature of global capitalism and even mask some of its harshest effects. Equally, however, this emphasis on the local as *responding* to the global risks overly condensing the circumstances and scales in which people are making decisions. In this framework, migrants are thus viewed as reacting to a variety of large-scale structures and processes: global economic restructuring, the flows of information, media and communication possibilities unleashed by new forms of technology, ethnic and regional conflicts, trade agreements and so on. By virtue of their scale, these kinds of forces appear systematic, predictable and generalisable. Why, then, does the experience of mobility so often feel surprising, piecemeal and ad hoc?

Mascia-Lees and Himpele have recently argued that this scalar and hence spatial approach to globality distorts the multiplicity, simultaneity and contradictory nature of movement and experience (2006: 9). To remedy the distortions introduced by our over-dependence on spatial metaphors, Mascia-Lees and Himpele suggest that we turn to theoretical physics' 'anthropic principle', which posits that 'electrons exist in either of two states at the same time', as a potentially useful metaphor for also rethinking the local and the global as simultaneous (2006: 11). They also note the:

central place given to observation in representations of the universe in contemporary 'anthropic theory'... Bohr, Heisenberg and others revealed a probabilistic universe dominated by chance and complexity, one comprehensible only through overlapping, and sometimes even contradictory descriptions, since the very act of observation could be shown to constitute and change the object of analysis, ideas that clearly found their counterpart in the contemporaneous cinematic work of Eisenstein and later worked their way into anthropology. (Ibid.)

Mascia-Lees and Himpele's anthropic principle could certainly be applied to my own as well as Keith and Marina's experiences, in terms of both the sense of 'chance and complexity', the observational positioning and the simultaneity of different temporal and spatial dimensions: intimate relationships converging with revolutions, civil tensions, transnational and global development banks, national and transnational consulting companies, movement, friendship, domesticity. But haven't we been here before? How is the emphasis on the act of observation as constituting and changing the object of analysis markedly different from constructionism? And isn't the 'uncertainty principle which depends on an accumulation of experiments/observations to approach what can never be seen from a singular fixed position' (Mascia-Lees and Himpele 2006: 11) rather similar to the generation of generalisations through cumulative ethnographic comparisons that has been the hallmark of anthropology as an empirically grounded discipline since the early twentieth century?

Virtually from anthropology's disciplinary start, its practitioners have reflected on and debated the levels and limits of their analysis, the role of individual creativity versus collective social reproduction, change and continuity. Over the last thirty years especially, various analysts have repeatedly anguished over the distortions that enter into our representations as we move from fieldwork to analysis and text. Our notions of *their* culture versus *our* psychology (Rosaldo 1989), exoticism and boundedness (Clifford and Marcus 1986), the reifications and distortions vested in the culture concept itself (Abu-Lughod 1991), the erroneous temporalities and mis-historicisation of the ethnographic present (Fabian 1983), privileging collective identity at the expense of individuality (Cohen, 1994; Rapport, 1997), our failure to take account of transnational connections (Basch et al. 1994), and of globality (Tsing 2000) are just some of the insufficiencies that have been correctly noted without readily resolving the gaps in our analyses. Over the history of our discipline, as we've expanded the repertoire of situations we subject to investigation, we have also repeatedly interrogated and questioned the modalities of our fieldwork practice: the boundaries of the 'field' in urban, national and transnational contexts (Epstein 1964; Marcus 1995); our notions of immersion (Amit 2000); the 'where' of electronically mediated relationships (Miller and Slater 2000); and so on.

Unni Wikan's observation, some fifteen years ago, that in our pursuit of abstract, generalised knowledge, we smooth out, at some cost, 'messy inchoate experience, dismissing things as insignificant when they do not fit' (1991: 288) and her calls for an 'experience-near' anthropology, one that comprehends emotion, ambiguity, uncertainty, contesting visions and 'the disorder and unpredictability of much of everyday life' (1991: 289) are echoed in my own preoccupation with the serendipities and improvisations highlighted by mobility or Mascia-Lees and Himpele's search for new models with which to better apprehend simultaneity, multiplicity, contradiction and co-presence. And we are hardly alone. These are calls that have been and are likely to continue to be revisited so long as we remain a grounded discipline because they identify a key dilemma of our enterprise that is not easily resolved and in some senses shouldn't be.

Experience, including both that accumulated willy-nilly in our personal histories and that which we encounter and participate in through our fieldwork, is muddled and uncertain, calling as much, if not more, for creative improvisation as for routine practice. That kind of unpredictability is an inherent part of our research modalities as, to a greater and lesser degree, it is for any form of enquiry. But the uncertainties of our field experiences merge with and resonate with the inchoate volatilities of all our other life situations more thoroughly than in the more tightly circumscribed laboratory sciences or in the more textually oriented philosophical pursuits. In that sense our memories and field experiences are inseparable. I cannot become someone else in order to live for weeks or months somewhere else in the 'field', let alone around the street corner, as is the case for so many of our current studies. It would take a kind of schizophrenic distantiation to dismiss the messiness of the experiences we seek to study while otherwise living this untidiness day by day.

But, if I want to move from these particular life experiences to more general insights, then I must inevitably distil and select as I move from the particular to the more general. And the simplifications and distortions inhering in that process of abstraction are the same whether I apply them to my personal memories or the situations I've 'studied'. Indeed memory, be it mine, Keith's or Marina's, is itself constituted and rendered meaningful through a mode of selectiveness and abstraction. As Debbora Battaglia (1993) has noted, forgetting is critically a part of remembering. There is no model, whether anthropic, rhizomic or experience-near, that can resolve the inevitable simplifications of abstraction. But that process of abstraction is key to the process of discovery. It is what makes a surprising or unexpected occurrence a finding, rather than an oddity easily forgotten among the detritus of our memories or field notes. So we smooth out the ragged, untidy edges of experience as we move ever further away from the event and the memory of it to the cumulative generalities it may yield through comparison: 'in noting that the unexpected fact must be strategic, i.e., that it must permit of implications which bear upon generalized theory, we are, of course, referring rather to what the observer brings to the datum than to the datum itself. For it obviously requires a theoretically sensitized observer to detect the universal in the particular' (Merton as cited in Van Andel 1994: 635).

If anthropologists are more likely to search for the general than the universal, we cannot nor should we seek to avoid the dilemmas attendant on the strategic observation that is also the hallmark of our own research and analysis. Without it, we could not participate in the kind of conversations about globalisation to which Graeber is calling us to contribute potentially important insights (2002: 1223) or in conversations about any other important general social phenomenon. But at the same time, our strength as a discipline grounded in the depth of particular lives and situations means that we are constantly bumping up against the limitations and reifications of our generalised abstractions. So the anguished critiques of Wikan, Lees and Himpele and a host of other anthropological interrogators are crucial to reminding us to keep our feet on the ground. The strength and the irresolvable dilemma of anthropological enquiry is our Sisyphean oscillation between the messy uncertainties of experience on the one hand and the necessarily tidied general abstractions we derive from them.

Acknowledgements

I would like to thank Anselma Gallinat and Peter Collins for inviting me to consider the role of memory and experience in my fieldwork. I would also like to thank Noel Dyck for his thoughtful and insightful comments on drafts of this chapter although responsibility for any sins of omission or commission remains my own.

Notes

1. This study was made possible by a standard research grant from the Social Sciences and Humanities Research Council of Canada. In order to protect the confidentiality of people interviewed for this project I have used aliases in place of their real names.
2. I have used an alias for this organisation.

References

Abu-Lughod, L. 1991. 'Writing Against Culture', in R.G. Fox (ed.), *Recapturing Anthropology: Working in the Present*. Santa Fe, N.Mex.: School of American Research Press, pp. 137–62.

Amit, V. 2000. 'Introduction: Constructing the Field', in V. Amit (ed.), *Constructing the Field: Ethnographic Fieldwork in the Contemporary World*. London and New York: Routledge, pp. 1–18.

———. 2006. 'Claiming Individuality through "Flexibility": Career Choices and Constraints among Traveling Consultants', in V. Amit and N. Dyck (eds), *Claiming Individuality: The Cultural Politics of Distinction*. London: Pluto Press, pp. 90–109.

———. 2007. 'Globalization through "Weak Ties": A Study of Transnational Networks among Global Professionals', in V. Amit (ed.), *Going First Class? New Approaches to Privileged Movement and Travel*. Oxford and New York: Berghahn Books, pp. 53–71.

Basch, L., N. Glick Schiller and C.S. Blanc. 1994. *Nations Unbound: Transnational Projects, Postcolonial Predicaments, and Deterritorialized Nation-States*. Basel, Switzerland: Gordon and Breach Science Publishers.

Battaglia, D. 1993. 'At Play in the Fields (and Borders) of the Imaginary: Melanesian Transformations of Forgetting', *Cultural Anthropology* 8(4): 430–42.

Clifford, J. and G.E. Marcus (eds). 1986. *Writing Culture: The Poetics and Politics of Ethnography*. London, Berkeley and Los Angeles, Calif.: University of California Press.

Cohen, A.P. 1994. *Self Consciousness: An Alternative Anthropology of Identity*. London and New York: Routledge.

Epstein, A.L. 1964. 'Urban Communities in Africa', in M. Gluckman (ed.) *Closed Systems and Open Minds: The Limits of Naivety in Social Anthropology*. Chicago: Aldine, pp. 83–102.

Fabian. J. 1983. *Time and the Other*. New York: Columbia University Press.

Graeber, D. 2002. 'The Anthropology of Globalization (with Notes on Neomedievalism, and the End of the Chinese Model of the Nation-State)', *American Anthropologist* 104(4): 1222–27.

Grant, S. 2006. 'GCIM Report: Defining an "Ethical Compass" for International Migration Policy', *International Migration* 44(1): 13–19.

Kearney, M. 1986. 'From the Invisible Hand to Visible Feet: Anthropological Studies of Migration and Development', *Annual Review of Anthropology* 15: 331–61.

———. 1995. 'The Local and the Global: the Anthropology of Globalization and Transnationalism', *Annual Review of Anthropology* 24: 547–65.

Marcus, G.E. 1995. 'Ethnography in/of the World System: the Emergence of Multi-Sited Ethnography', *Annual Review of Anthropology* 24: 95–117.

Martin, P. and S. Martin. 2006. 'GCIM: a New Global Migration Facility', *International Migration* 44(1): 5–12.

Mascia-Lees, F. and J. Himpele. 2006. 'Reimaging Globality: Toward an Anthropological Physics', *Anthropology News* May: 9, 11.

Miller, D. and D. Slater. 2000. *The Internet: An Ethnographic Approach*. Oxford and New York: Berg.

Rapport, N. 1997. *Transcendent Individual: Towards a Literary and Liberal Anthropology*. London and New York: Routledge.

Rosaldo, R. 1989. *Culture and Truth: The Remaking of Social Analysis*. Boston: Beacon Press.

Smart, A. 1999. 'Participating in the Global: Transnational Social Networks and Urban Anthropology', *City and Society* 11(1–2): 59–77.

Tsing, A. 2000. 'The Global Situation', *Cultural Anthropology* 15(3): 327–60.

Van Andel, P. 1994. 'Anatomy of the Unsought Finding, Serendipity: Origin, History, Domains, Traditions, Appearances, Patterns and Programmability', *The British Journal for the Philosophy of Science* 45(2): 631–48.

Wikan, U. 1991. 'Toward an Experience-near Anthropology', *Cultural Anthropology* 6(3): 285–305.

Chapter 13

ON REMEMBERING AND FORGETTING IN WRITING AND FIELDWORK

Simon Coleman

Some twenty years ago David Lowenthal (1985) famously quoted the opening lines of L.P. Hartley's novel *The Go-Between* (1953) in telling us that 'The past is a foreign country.' But it might equally be said that, for many anthropologists, a 'foreign country' – or at least a field site, wherever it happens to be – represents a very particular kind of past, constituted by field notes and other, less tangible but often powerful kinds of memory. L.P. Hartley's image uses a spatial metaphor to indicate the distance of the past from us, its irretrievability from the perspective of the present – the full quote is: 'The past is a foreign country: they do things differently there.' But the anthropologist as author is concerned rather to bring the field site back to life and into comprehension – if not into a spurious ethnographic present (Davis 1992), then into an ethnographically faithful and theoretically fertile representation of past experiences that are assumed to be retrievable because of their direct relationship to the author as fieldworker.

So, while Clifford Geertz (1988) has famously argued that anthropologists have often been concerned with how to translate an 'authentic' sense of 'being there' to the reader, we can add that ethnographies also contain tensions linked to how 'being *then*' can be worked into a text that may be written many years later. Or, as Johannes Fabian has put it (2004; see also 2001),[1] we need to understand what the grounds of such ethnographic 'being' consist of once we have left the field. Indeed, does the passage of time do more than simply turn an autobiographically proximate 'there' into a more distant 'then'? By showing how remembrance seeps into ethnography's manifold forms of representation, Fabian uses the complexities and treacheries of memory to question what is actually meant by 'presence' 'in' the field. In doing so he is also revealing a temporal ambiguity contained in the very word 'ethnography': after all, in common anthropological parlance it is both a method for conducting fieldwork in the present and a means of subsequently writing about the field (see also Reed-Danahay 1997).

In the following I am interested, along with other contributors to this book, in the importance of memory (and, therefore, also the importance of forgetting) in practising fieldwork and writing ethnography. But I also want to invoke some of the more general social scientific research on memory to explore what is going on when we attempt to 'recall' the field. Unsurprisingly, we find that the single word 'memory' masks many different kinds of recall, and moreover that the unreliability of memory poses questions concerning authorial control and consciousness in the production of ethnography.[2] Fabian (2004) shows how the involuntary nature of individual memorising means that one part of ethnographic enquiry is, as he puts it, '*out* of control': positivism, one might say, roundly defeated by Proust. Along similar lines, Judith Okely[3] has previously argued that the most fruitful approaches in fieldwork are those that let the fieldworker follow what beckons, rather than adhering to some preordained positivist agenda, but she also notes that free association may continue when accumulated field experience is reinterpreted and analysed through writing up. And writing up itself is for Okely more than pure cerebration, since (1992: 16) examining field notes can trigger bodily and other hitherto subconscious memories, themselves relics from a research methodology that is so markedly embodied.

We see how recalling the field, and not just fieldwork itself, involves a combination of the serendipitous and the structured. The mediations of memory can act as ghosts in the ethnographic machine, and these can affect both ethnography as data-gathering process ('writing down') and ethnography as authorship ('writing up') (see Okely 1992). I think they also add another dimension to an argument Peter Collins and I have made elsewhere about how a metaphor of performance can be deployed to describe the ethnographic constitution of the field. We argue (Coleman and Collins 2006) that fields are constructed through plays of social relationships established among ethnographers, informants and others that may extend across physical sites, comprehending embodied as well as visual and verbal interactions. Our argument therefore has resonances with Clifford's (1997: 199) depiction of the field as a habitus rather than a place. However, 'performance' in our sense not only suggests ongoing, material, mutual[4] implication in constructing the field, but also contains a performative element (see also Dilley 1999), a sense that ethnography is being pieced together out of the circumstances of the present as well as the observations of the past. So if fields (and associated relevant 'contexts') are created anew each time the ethnographer, with or without informants being physically present, invokes the field in the process of research or writing, then memory is a key constituent in seeing the field as ongoing event, as constantly in a process of becoming. In this latter respect, we agree with Tammy Kohn's opposition to assumptions of a static reflexive self in the contemplation of the field (expressed elsewhere in this volume). The changing authorial 'self' may spend many years reworking the memory of an original, serendipitous moment of insight or experience.[5]

These debates reveal a particular kind of tension inherent in the post-fieldwork experience for anthropologists. On the one hand, one might argue that temporal distance provides a valuable form of detachment, the kind of cartographic sensibility that allows us to place data into theoretical categories or comparative schemas.[6] On the other, we need to appreciate that the objectivist assumptions behind such an argument bring their own problems. Hastrup (1992: 117ff.), for instance, argues that distinctions between subjects and objects are themselves modernist artefacts. It might be the case that 'fieldwork experience has become memory before it becomes text; the relics are embellished to pass for ethnography' (ibid.: 127), but it is also evident that the dramas and dialogues, the tensions over reality and representation, that are inherent in fieldwork continue long after the return home. In expressing her worries over bogus forms of realism, Hastrup chimes with Susan Radstone's (2000: 10) discussion of recent attempts to eschew crude binaries between 'the happened' and 'the imagined'. Memories in these terms become texts to be deciphered rather than lost realities to be rediscovered, or (ibid.: 11) 'complex productions shaped by diverse narratives and genres and replete with absences, silences, condensations and displacements that [are] related, in complex ways, to the dialogic moment of their telling'.

We need not go so far as to see memory as mere fabrication in order to appreciate the politics of its production in the (ever-shifting) present, or to understand the need for an examination of the cultural, social and intellectual influences on its expression. Maurice Bloch (1998: 114ff.), for instance, argues that recall in the present might conflate stories heard with events actually experienced, as an inferential fleshing out of narratives occurs. Or a speaker might be recalling not an event itself but rather the last time he or she recounted the story of that event.[7] As anthropologists we need, as far as possible, to use our memory knowingly, with an appreciation of its internal heterogeneity and dynamic qualities.

But can we then say something more about what might trigger useful or at least salient memories within the ethnographer? I shall be exploring various such triggers but I am particularly interested here in what one might call the total fieldworking career of the anthropologist. After all, we probably visit a number of sites over the course of our careers,[8] and spatial journeys also involve movement between memories, prompting us to ask how memories of fieldwork experiences may gradually leach into each other. By using the term 'ethnographer' rather than 'fieldworker', I am consciously conflating the state of being in the field with that of writing about it, since over the course of a career one may at times be reacting as much to what one has previously written about a place as to one's memories of having been there; but I am also interested in whether there might be a conflation at the level of memory between different sites. By this I do not mean that we inadvertently mix up memories of what happened to us in site X as opposed to site Y, but rather that experience (or recall) of one site can trigger particular kinds of memories of another. How, then, might we consider in more detail what Parkin (2000: 93) calls the biography of remembered ethnographic events, how they fare in the long passage from initial experience to theoretical – and, one might add, textual – placement?

These are themes that I shall be investigating in the following, and a particular dimension of my exploration will be a concern with how different examples of recall reveal different levels of conscious control over memory. However, before I do so I want very briefly to say something about the social scientific study of memory. After all, it is worth using our own discourses to work *at* memory even as we attempt to understand what happens when we work *through* it.

Conceptualising Memory

Tulving's influential distinction between 'semantic' and 'episodic' memory (e.g. 1983; see also Lowenthal 1985: 201) suggests that the semantic type governs our knowledge of events occurring independently of our own experience of ourselves; it is learned from others, recalled through symbols and ordered as networks of factual concepts, such as lists of monarchs or lines of verse.[9] Episodic, autobiographical memory, on the other hand, underlies our subjective sense of identity and invokes personal experience. In similar fashion, Connerton (1989) distinguishes between cognitive memory claims, where knowledge of the context of learning is irrelevant, and personal, experiential memory claims, which take as their object one's life history. To these, Connerton adds a third type: habit memory, or the embodied capacity to reproduce performances, such as riding a bicycle.

Maurice Bloch (1998: 115) has argued that the distance between autobiographical and more semantic forms of memory may not always be that great, but he also makes an important distinction (ibid.: 118), which is more immediately relevant at this point, between conscious 'recalling' and less controllable 'remembering'.[10] For Bloch, individuals may not be fully aware at any given moment of what they might remember, so that certain memories that appeared to be totally lost can be retrieved when the person concerned re-enters the emotional state they were in when the original event occurred. The past is therefore an ever-changing resource according to situations or moods in which persons find themselves, just as – following Halbwachs[11] – topography can also be seen as infused with history, mnemonically facilitating a re-experiencing of the past.

These general points about memory clearly link with some of the remarks from ethnographers that I mentioned earlier. In both we have the emphasis on some kinds of memory as being embodied; we have questions around the relationship between performance and memory; and also there is some agreement on the unpredictability of memory and its triggers, often centring on distinctions between conscious, intended recall and less controllable remembrance. If previous commentary on ethnography has frequently worried about the agency of informants, here we have a particular query about the agentive powers of authors. But how can thinking about memory itself act as a tool in both doing and writing ethnography? How can we understand its mediations not only as a potential hindrance but also in a positive light? I do not pretend to provide a comprehensive answer in what follows, but I do hope to make some suggestions that may resonate with the experiences of other ethnographers.

The Shock of the Old

My first point of exploration refers to ethnography as fieldwork practice rather than as process of inscription. I have been conducting fieldwork for some twenty years now – off and on – with a Swedish charismatic ministry called the Word of Life (*Livets Ord*) (e.g. Coleman 2000). Of course, the group itself has changed over that time, but what interests me here is one particular recurrent feature of my revisits. Every time I go back I experience the same fleeting but visceral sensation as I enter one of the Word of Life services for the first time in a given visit. It is best described as a momentarily experienced and ritually prompted raising of the hair on the back of the head, before I fall fairly easily into the patterns of the service.

Now services at the Word of Life are usually dramatic affairs, and are indeed meant to be, often involving large numbers of people, speaking in tongues and body movements as well as video images of the service played back to the congregation as it worships. The excitements of the present are invoked precisely to ensure that participants experience the power of present spiritual experience, and not merely a comforting invocation of past ritual tradition. But my question is what to make ethnographically of this moment of initial but very fleeting shock, experienced as if I were diving into a cold swimming pool on a hot day. I want to suggest that what is happening is an adjustment of, or better perhaps a reinvocation of, an embodied memory, a movement from a kind of external to internal habitus – a kind of 'click', if you will, into ethnographic place, as initial surprise is followed by bodily recognition. The Word of Life itself is still characterised by a fairly strong contrast between the relatively everyday character of what its members do away from the group and the charismatically extreme (extreme at least in the Swedish context) nature of what goes on behind closed doors, and so it is not surprising that the adjustment is not necessary until I go to a service.

From a fieldwork perspective I think I may be experiencing a personally located, microscopic replay of the numerous tensions that the group has experienced with other Christians and social commentators in Sweden: what has appeared as manifestations of the bizarre to outsiders – variously described as madness, uncontrolled shamanism, brainwashing – is experienced as relatively routine on the inside. Re-entry into the field therefore implies a movement across this threshold from outsider's to insider's view as memory of past involvement is engaged, and this movement is itself instructive in trying to understand the different ideological worlds with which believers contend. So this is a memory that I can contemplate in theory, but which can only be realised in practice through participation. In a sense, it provides me with another dimension of what 'performing' the field might mean: in this case recall of the specific habitus of a fieldwork situation, made possible by return to that situation.[12] The ethnographic 'self' is once again revealed to be unstable, or at least made vulnerable to context. This example also has a curious if suggestive parallel to Word of Life ways of describing proper participation in worship: only believers are said to have the 'spiritual eyes and ears' to see and hear worship properly, in the right spirit. Perhaps what is seen as an entailment of belief for congregation members looks to me – the unsaved but returning anthropologist – like an entailment of a certain kind of memory. To that extent, reflections on memory may bring me a little closer to comprehending a dimension of religious commitment.

Missing Memory

An alternative way of viewing the Word of Life example described above is to see my experience as involving a kind of embodied forgetting, prior to recognition: the sense of being 'at home' within such charismatic ritual lies latent until being reinvoked, with a jolt, by re-entry into the field.

Other forms of forgetting also permeate our understandings of the field, of course. I imagine that many ethnographers have shared my experience of being convinced that a particular incident in the field had occurred in a certain way, only to discover that one's field notes stubbornly tell another story. In many such cases, I suspect, memory has been affected by the development of certain 'dispositions' in the use and analysis of field data, which have prompted well-worn but not always reliable tropes of thinking about one's field.

The very lack of anthropological interlocutors inherent in much of the data gathering that we do – our love of so-called 'lone' fieldwork[13] – may encourage this type of misremembering, and so it might be argued that collective research could help to mitigate the problem. However, in this section I want to explore an example of research that can illustrate the significance of a lack of memory in writing up fieldwork carried out by a group. The problem here is less one of forgetting, and more of never having had the original experience that can form the basis of memory.

Some of my more recent fieldwork has been done as part of a research team, including Peter Collins[14] as a fellow ethnographer but also some other researchers who are not anthropologists, in tracing the impact on staff and patients of transformations in hospital spaces in the north-east of England. In a way, the project is itself about transformations of memory, as we have been trying to see how people adjust to a new hospital landscape that has actively involved the erasure of the old. Fieldwork consisted of conducting interviews, administering questionnaires and doing a certain amount of 'hanging around' in key parts of a newly expanded hospital in Middlesbrough, and we split up such work variously amongst members of the research team. Fieldwork was followed by discussion of experiences and results, and we are now in the stage of moving from writing down to writing up (Macnaughton et al. 2005).

What is significant here and what I want to emphasise is the way a project that is about memory has had to deal with a particular problem of recall built into its own methodology. Given the divisions of labour involved in data-gathering, no single person can be said to 'own' the embodied memory of the project. What we have been dealing with here is less multi-sited ethnography and more a site co-constructed by multiple ethnographers. The diffusion of what one might call autobiographical investment in the data that have been gathered has made the process of reconstructing the ethnography as a totality particularly challenging. How easy, after all, is it to 'write up' data that one has not originally 'written down'?[15] And what does the nature of such research gathering mean for issues of ethnographic control, before we even enter the realm of dealing with the unreliability of memory itself? One analogy here is surely with the distinction between semantic and episodic memory: for much of the time the episodic memory of one researcher is only 'semantically' appropriated by other members of the team, as post-fieldwork discussions take place in which experiences are compared. Another analogy is with the classical distinction precisely between anthropology and history, the use of the archive as opposed to the experience that contributes to the field note.

As a project team, we have deployed various means to create a joint narrative out of the separate fieldwork experiences that we have had: group meetings to discuss the data we have gathered; the construction and monitoring over time of mutually agreed, emergent themes for questioning and analysis; in some cases the carrying out of some pieces of fieldwork with another person. Such techniques have helped to shape a project that all can recognise, if not 'own' in the same way that we might construct a relationship with a project carried out alone. At times, they might be said to have created a situation where a researcher in one context (at the hospital) becomes a kind of informant in another (in reporting experiences to others in the research team). But need we always set up apparently rigid distinctions between the individual and the visceral on the one hand, and the relatively fragmented and the diffuse on the other? In response, I want briefly in the next section to suggest the sometimes generative character of what I call memory as 'lateral recall'.

Lateral Recall

In explaining what I mean by this term let me briefly discuss an ethnographic observation. In an article contained in Deborah Reed-Danahay's volume on *Auto/Ethnography*, Michael Herzfeld (1997) discusses how he deals with developing an understanding, a 'knowledge', of nationalism, despite his general lack of sympathy with its politics. As an anthropologist he 'knows' that nationalism is not 'natural' (ibid.: 182), and yet he is still moved by a memory of a Florentine night in 1961 when at the age of fourteen he was overwhelmed by a performance of Verdi's Nabucco. Herzfeld draws on this experience to give him some kind of empathy with the sometimes strident patriotism of those he has met in his fieldwork in the Mediterranean. What one might call 'ethnography by experiential analogy' is in this case a juxtaposition of powerful autobiographical memory with what is for the anthropologist a problematic aspect of ethnography. Herzfeld's strategy has some similarities with Bloch's idea of how autobiographical and narrative knowledge can be combined, at least in the sense that an 'inferential fleshing out' of one cultural context through the tool of another is occurring. Of course there are considerable epistemological issues to be considered here. Meanings may not be shared in any simple sense (Reed-Danahay 1997: 15), but at least in the context of European ethnology a degree of cultural terrain is hesitantly – subjunctively – traversed.

What I want to take from this example is Herzfeld's use of memory of one relatively unfamiliar cultural landscape in prompting interpretation of another. A version of such ethnography by analogy has also worked between field sites in my own career, though in my case the prompting has involved opening up fields of observation and questioning as much as it has suggestions for analysis. My original fieldwork on the Word of Life was followed by work on English pilgrims to the shrine of Walsingham in eastern England, a project that is also ongoing. The two sites – Swedish and English – both invoke Christianity but from very different theological positions (expressed not least in different attitudes to both memory and materiality). Word of Life self-understanding (as noted above) contains much of a charismatic rhetoric of worshipping in the moment, the focusing on experience of the now, combined with a partial mistrust of overtly religious images in prompting worship. Walsingham pilgrims, on the other hand, are often concerned precisely with using images drawn from the past of an ancient site to attempt to reinhabit history, providing the skeletal – semantic – historical narratives represented by the site with both ritualised and autobiographical flesh. Using images derived from informants' own words, one might say that my fieldwork trajectory has juxtaposed a charismatic emphasis on the 'Spirit' (at the Word of Life) with a more Catholic concern (among Walsingham pilgrims) with spectres of the past, sometimes embodied in a belief in ghosts that haunt the pilgrimage shrines.

The relevant issue here is that I am intrigued by the way my work at Walsingham has encouraged a kind of re-reading and re-membering of fieldwork carried out at the Word of Life. My growing interest in the aesthetics of charismatic commitment – looking at how Swedish believers incorporate a very powerful if usually implicit visual aesthetic in their daily and worship lives – has emerged in part as a result of subsequent fieldwork in the very different Christian arena of a pilgrimage site. The point is not at all to say that British Roman and Anglo-Catholic pilgrims have the same attitudes to the materiality of religion as Swedish charismatics, or that I can simply transfer my understandings of Walsingham spirituality to Sweden; rather, it is to say that fieldwork on pilgrimage has expanded my fieldwork habitus, and that the embodied memory of analysing one form of worship has leached into a different kind of sensibility in approaching and interpreting another. My experience of fieldwork in Sweden has been different post-Walsingham to that carried out pre-Walsingham.

This discussion of the 'leaching' of ethnographic sensibilities has certain parallels with examinations of the role of voicing and intertextuality in discursive formations. Thus, for instance, Bakhtin's examination of the tensions between monological and heteroglossic perspectives (see for example Silverstein and Urban 1996: 4) tells us how a single narrative voice can conceal other voices, despite their implicit presence through imitation, opposition or quotation. I am trying to capture here the sense in which the supposed uniqueness of an ethnographic site – the Word of Life as opposed to Walsingham, for instance – is itself challenged by the ways in which apparently disparate sites may be constructed through the mutually implicated memories and experiences of a given ethnographer. Of course, the sites and the ethnographer are themselves always changing, but we need also to appreciate the methodological, theoretical and biographical links that may be evident between such fields. In Bakhtinian terms, a previously explored field site becomes a kind of ethnographic 'voice' inherent in the sensibility of the researcher entering a new site.

Concluding Remarks

In this chapter I have explored three ways of thinking about the relationship between ethnography and memory. Each has emerged from my own fieldwork, and each might be thought of as exploring a shifting metaphor of a bridge between 'field' and ethnographer. In talking of 'the shock of the old', I referred to the almost involuntary sense of shifting from one habitus to another in re-experiencing charismatic worship. Such an example illustrates the contextual basis of some forms of memory, but also implies that the 'dialogic' nature of constructing memory can transcend the linguistic level that such a term implies and enter a more embodied realm. The idea of 'missing memory' was to look at how constructing bridges of memory becomes complicated when the experiential relationship to an ethnographic event cannot be drawn upon. I therefore referred to some of the ways in which a research team (as opposed to a 'lone ethnographer) attempted to create – confabulate, though not in a negative sense – a common narrative out of an ethnographic project. Finally, in discussing 'lateral recall', I mentioned the sometimes strategic use of experience in one ethnographic realm to establish a connection with another, apparently separate, context of research. While the idea of bridging refers to each of these examples, it is not meant to imply that a simple method of getting at 'what really happened' is ever possible – after all, it is not as if that can be achieved even while a given event is occurring in 'real' time.

Anthony Cohen (1992: 226) has talked of 'self-conscious anthropology' as involving an exploitation of the intrusive self as an ethnographic resource rather than an enduring of it as a methodological hindrance. In Cohen's case, the task is to use the complexity of understandings of the self as a way of challenging the anthropological temptation to simplify others. Here, I have been concerned to see memory as posing significant questions as we carry out and interpret our research: asking what it means to re-enter a field that one has known before, or indeed to re-read a field afresh in the light of another site, or to ask what kind of work is necessary to convert a partial, fragmented, autobiographical knowledge of a given site into something that can be worked into a collectively crafted ethnography. If constructing the field is both a performance and a performative act, it involves seeing fieldwork sites as theatres for the playing out of different kinds of memory (Samuel 1994), and moreover theatres whose temporal as well as spatial boundaries cannot easily be separated either from each other or from the everyday life of the ethnographer.[16] Samuel (1994: 27) calls for 'a historiography that [is] alert to memory's shadows – those sleeping images which spring to life unbidden, and serve as ghostly sentinels of our thought – [and which] might give at least as much attention to pictures as to manuscripts or print'. My call, meanwhile, is for an anthropology that appreciates the importance of differentiated processes of memory in the construction of ethnographic 'presence', and which sees such processes as relying on written words (e.g. field notes) but also other catalysts for memory, including serendipity, embodied experience, dialogue and even fieldwork in other sites.

Notes

1. Remarks to 2004 EASA Meeting in Vienna.
2. An interesting early 'worry' about the relationship between authorial authority and memory came with the publication of Edmund Leach's magisterial *Political Systems of Highland Burma: A Study of Kachin Social Structure* (1954). Leach had lost his fieldwork notes during the Second World War, but was careful to note in an appendix that he was confident that his recall had been enhanced by the writing of an earlier manuscript before embarking on the work that would become the present volume.
3. Remarks made to 2004 EASA Meeting in Vienna: 'Fieldwork as Free Association and Free Passage'.
4. Albeit often hierarchical.
5. Compare Okely and Callaway's argument (1992) that ethnography can involve many refractions of self: as resource for making sense of others; through plural identities; via gendered awareness; involving ageing and transitions evident when returning at later dates to the same place and people, and so on. Furthermore, multiple selves are complemented by multiple texts (ibid.: xii) – diaries; field notes; journals of informants; letters to and from the field; autobiographies and novels by individuals; local histories; indigenous forms of social science.

6. Such a view of fieldwork memory sees it as almost akin to classic ethnographic descriptions of the movement of elders into ancestorhood, as idiosyncratic details become a little hazy even as the social and political worth of invoking the past is increased.

7. Compare Stromberg (1993) on the power of narratives to reinvoke an autobiographical connection with a 'past' event.

8. As we in effect become 'multi-sited ethnographers' over time (Coleman 2006).

9. Bloch's piece (1998) challenges this distinction to some extent, suggesting that the two may sometimes be closer than the model allows, as narratives about a past event combine with inferences about the experiencing of that event.

10. In some ways this distinction reminds me of the contrast made by language teachers between 'active' and 'passive' vocabularies.

11. Halbwachs's (1992) basic Durkheimian point is that a society needs to find its landmarks, and that divinely charged spaces can act as bearers of memory.

12. This is not to imply that the Word of Life itself has remained static over time, but certainly the main elements of its worship services have remained broadly stable.

13. Despite the fact that we are of course surrounded by informants.

14. One of the editors of this book.

15. Such a situation may of course be created by the use of research assistants.

16. In her discussant remarks on the conference presentations that formed part of this volume, Vered Amit noted that ethnography has shifted some of its focus from examining self-consciously identified peoples towards the investigation of sometimes tenuously linked sites and networks. Such 'multi-sited ethnography' may be created through the strategic movements of the ethnographer, but, as Amit noted, memory itself can act to draw connections between apparently discontinuous events, and even between consciously articulated fieldwork experiences and more overtly 'everyday', non-fieldwork experiences.

References

Bloch, M. 1998. *How We Think They Think: Anthropological Approaches to Cognition, Memory, and Literacy* Boulder, Colo.: Westview.

Clifford, J. 1997. 'Spatial Practices: Fieldwork, Travel, and the Disciplining of Anthropology', in A. Gupta and J. Ferguson (eds), *Anthropological Locations: Boundaries and Grounds of a Field Science*. Berkeley: University of California Press, pp. 185–222.

Cohen, A. P. 1992. 'Self-conscious Anthropology', in J. Okely and H. Callaway (eds), *Anthropology and Autobiography*. London: Routledge, pp. 221–41.

Coleman, S. 2000. *The Globalisation of Charismatic Christianity: Spreading the Gospel of Prosperity*. Cambridge: Cambridge University Press.

———. 2006. 'The Multi—Sited Ethnographer', in M. Unnithan and G. de Neve (eds), *Critical Journeys: The Making of Anthropologists*. Aldershot: Ashgate, pp. 31–46.

Coleman, S. and Collins, P. (eds.) 2006. *Locating the Field*. Oxford: Berg.

Connerton, P. 1989. *How Societies Remember.* Cambridge: Cambridge University Press.

Davis, J. 1992. 'Tense in Anthropology: Some Practical Considerations', in J. Okely and H. Callaway (eds), *Anthropology and Autobiography.* London: Routledge, pp. 205–20.

Dilley, R. (ed.). 1999. *The Problem of Context.* Oxford: Berghahn.

Fabian, J. 2001. 'Remembering the Other: Knowledge and Recognition', in J. Fabian (ed.), *Anthropology with an Attitude: Critical Essays.* Stanford: Stanford University Press, pp. 158–78.

Geertz, C. 1988. *Works and Lives: The Anthropologist as Author.* Cambridge: Polity. Press.

Halbwachs, M. 1992. *On Collective Memory,* ed. L. Coser. Chicago: University of Chicago Press.

Hastrup, K. 1992. 'Writing Ethnography: State of the Art', in J. Okely and H. Callaway (eds), *Anthropology and Autobiography.* London: Routledge, pp. 116–33.

Herzfeld, M. 1997. 'The Taming of the Revolution: Intense Paradoxes of the Self', in D. Reed-Danahay (ed.), *Auto/Ethnography: Rewriting the Self and the Social.* Oxford: Berg, pp. 169–94.

Leach, E. 1954. *Political Systems of Highland Burma: A Study of Kachin Social Structure.* London: Bell.

Lowenthal, D. 1985. *The Past is a Foreign Country.* Cambridge: Cambridge University Press.

Macnaughton, J., P. Collins, P. Kellett, G. Purves, A. Suokas, M. White and K. Taylor 2005. *Designing for Health: Architecture, Art and Design at the James Cook University Hospital.* London: NHS Estates.

Okely, J. 1992. 'Anthropology and Autobiography: Participatory Experience and Embodied Knowledge' in J. Okely and H. Callaway (eds), *Anthropology and Autobiography.* London: Routledge, pp. 1–28.

Okely, J. and Callaway, H. 1992. 'Preface', in J. Okely and H. Callaway (eds), *Anthropology and Autobiography.* London: Routledge, pp. xi–xiv.

Parkin, D. 2000. 'Templates, Evocations and the Long-Term Fieldwork', in P. Dresch, W. James and D. Parkin (eds), *Anthropologists in a Wider World: Essays on Field Research.* Oxford: Berghahn, pp. 91–107.

Radstone, S. (ed.). 2000. *Memory and Methodology.* Oxford: Berg.

Reed-Danahay, D. 1997. 'Introduction', in D. Reed-Danahay (ed.), *Auto/Ethnography: Rewriting the Self and the Social.* Oxford: Berg, pp. 1–17.

Samuel, R. 1994. *Theatres of Memory: Past and Present in Contemporary Culture.* London: Verso.

Silverstein, M. and G. Urban1996. 'The Natural History of Discourse', in M. Silverstein and G. Urban (eds), *Natural Histories of Discourse.* Chicago: University of Chicago Press, pp. 1–17.

Stromberg, P. 1993. *Language and Self-transformation: A Study of the Christian Conversion Narrative.* Cambridge: Cambridge University Press.

Tulving, E. 1983. *Elements of Episodic Memory.* Oxford: Oxford University Press.

Chapter 14

THE ETHNOGRAPHIC SELF AS RESOURCE?

Peter Collins

Introduction

This chapter is about the ethnographic self. I will argue that the ethnographic self is the self, no more, no less. I will argue, further, that the self is maintained and sustained through narrative and that this is the case whether or not a person is engaged in ethnography. The self and narrative are mediated by memory: one is constantly recalling narratives in the process of engaging with others and making sense of the world. So, I aver, as the self is a resource in life, so must it be during the doing of ethnography. There are two preliminary points that I want to make explicit. First, while I shall address the important contribution that reflexivity can make to this discussion, reflexivity is not my major focus in this chapter. Secondly, I shall not take the definition of 'self' as given, so that when we use the term 'the ethnographic *self* as resource' (as in the title of this book), we shall have a clearer understanding of the complexity of that term.

There are at least three preconditions for the operation of a resourceful self in ethnography: the practice of reflexivity, the centrality of the narrative self and finally a commitment to a dialogic methodology. After briefly outlining these mutually dependent preconditions I will go on to show that the use of one's self as an ethnographic resource becomes not only possible but unavoidable. But let us begin with a brief consideration of the term 'ethnography'.

Ethnography

It has been a common assumption that the definition of ethnography as a means of data collection is more or less synonymous with participant observation. However, this is to oversimplify what is for most of us a far more diverse and complex practice. And although anthropologists might fail to agree entirely on what ethnography consists of they most certainly would concur that ethnography is far from being an uncomplicated activity. There are a variety of methods used in collecting 'ethnographic data': participant and direct observation, interviews – from the most to the least 'formal', mapping, diaries, various quantitative strategies from the measurement of blood pressure to the logging of household accounts, the collection of visual material through digital devices, as well as drawings, plans and diagrams made by both fieldworker and research participants, the learning of 'native skills' whether that is fishing or farming, biochemical analysis or bee-keeping. The competent use of such data collection methods is, of course, just a part of the story. On top of this is the challenge of just getting by from day to day – of getting on with people and keeping company, of dealing with minor and sometimes major crises in both one's own life and the lives of one's research participants, some of whom will probably become friends, perhaps lovers. There is the effort expended in trying to sustain, simultaneously, the roles of 'insider' and 'outsider', to be sympathetic and at the same time alert to the opportunity for further data collection. However, while this is complicated enough, we have yet to mention all of those sensual experiences we participate in, sometimes without knowing: the sights of the city, the sounds of the desert, the aromas of the village – spices, sewage, smoke; then there is an awareness of the feel of things – of great practical significance for the ethnographer who is, for example, working as a carpenter's assistant. And taste? Taste enters our experience of fieldwork in critical ways, in how we perceive a meal, a drink, a drug and how these perceptions are perceived by our hosts. We can easily underestimate such sensual experiences, and may be surprised when they come back to haunt after we have 'left the field' (see Coleman's chapter in this volume for an evocative account of such recovered 'feelings').[1] Just as important are those emotional responses to life in the field; one's feel for a place will determine the extent to which the anthropologist is accepted and acceptable. These are 'data' that are often not recorded on paper or digitally, but become instead a part of our selves and may reoccur in memories, whether or not that is our intention.

Obviously, in purely practical terms, each of these methods is likely to offer a wide variety of opportunities (and also obstacles) for the use of the self as a resource. For example, when I began participant observation among British Quakers I was already a Quaker, though to think of myself as 'an insider' would have been and is simplistic, naive even (see Gallinat in this volume; also Collins 2002a). However, as a member of the group, I came to the field with relevant knowledge and skills: I already had an understanding of the way in which business meetings 'worked', I knew something of the history of the movement, I was a meeting house warden and therefore knew something of the way Quakerism was perceived by others – and so on. These are more or less context-specific ways in which I might draw on myself as a resource; rather like other members of the Quaker meeting I had sat through long hours of conducting Quaker business – there were 'in' jokes which I didn't have to worry about 'not getting' – I could even joke knowingly and therefore confidently about such experiences myself and raise a smile, perhaps a laugh. But what other less 'context-specific' skills, experiences and memories did I take into the field? Here is a key question in relation to the central aims of this book and it is difficult, maybe even impossible to answer, at least comprehensively. Most people could see that I am male, white, middle-aged, of relatively small build – I could spill a quantity of ink noting my more obvious physical features. After ten minutes' interaction, others would probably recognise me as a British, middle-class academic. These qualities might well have helped me in establishing a rapport with a research participant, or perhaps even with a group of them. Equally, it is not difficult to imagine a situation in which the same attributes would be or could become an obstacle in forming relationships with others. Then there are qualities that further contribute to what makes me 'me', which are generally hidden from others and possibly even from myself. It might well be true to say that only during interaction with others do such qualities emerge – and only with their emergence might it become clear that I might draw on them as a resource in some way. However, although I have tried to make it clear that we collect different kinds of data during ethnographic research, it remains true to say that ethnography primarily involves us in conversation and, while I appreciate that to focus on talk will limit my account, it is a warrantable limit in this context. Let us now turn to consider four such 'ethnographic' conversations taken more or less at random.

Storied Conversations

In this section I draw on ethnographic research undertaken among British Quakers during the early 1990s.[2] Quakers comprise a religious group that grew out of the social, political and religious turmoil of mid-seventeenth-century England. Quakerism is creedless and has a very simple liturgy. Members of the group are probably best known for their energetic involvement in social movements and in particular prison reform and pacifism. Quakers in Britain meet for worship on a Sunday morning in a building owned by the local meeting (congregation). Typically, meeting for worship will start at 11 a.m. and end at 12 noon. Friends arrive at the meeting house, gathering in small knots, talking about this and that. Worship itself is mostly silent. Friends sit in a circle or hollow square and every now and then, a participant might stand and offer vocal ministry – that is, say a few words – in the form of a prayer, a short reading, a comment or reflection on a recent news item. Following worship, Friends will again meet and talk, generally over tea and coffee. Indeed, it is almost as if the dam of silence breaks and a torrent of words follows.[3] This is the context in which the following conversations took place between myself and other Friends in a Quaker meeting house in 1992.

Conversation A

Joe: It is true that extraordinary things can happen in meeting.

Peter: Yes.

Joe: Although it's more than 30 years ago I remember my first meeting for worship as though it was yesterday.

Peter: Why, what happened?

Joe: I'm not really sure, everything just felt so right. It was like coming home.

Peter: I know what you mean. It wasn't that long ago but I remember feeling much the same. There was a lot of silence, then a chap stood up and talked at length about his experiences in Ghana.

Joe: Oh yes.

Peter: Yeah. Well, it just so happened that my wife, sitting next to me, had just returned from two years in Ghana – there was a strong resonance.

Joe: Resonance, hmm, yes, it's not always that powerful, but sometimes, it is!

I imagine that most if not all anthropologists will have noted conversations like this: unplanned, opportunistic, serendipitous, the kind of conversation that one might well have at any time and in any walk of life. No matter how many specialised data collection techniques we might employ, it is talk that constitutes the ethnographic air we breathe during fieldwork.

Talking relationships, as Rapport (1987, 1993) calls these interactions, develop in all kinds of places in all kinds of circumstances – maybe during a formal interview, perhaps standing at a bus stop or during the course of a ritual. Sometimes something is said that elicits a complementary experience – as in this instance. I should further add that my contribution to this conversation necessarily depends on my powers of recall, that is, on memory. I discuss this important subject at some length later on in the chapter, but what is clear is that my self functions as a resource in this moment of ethnographic fieldwork

Such talk can and often does help establish rapport, generate new talking relationships, open up novel lines of enquiry, save time, facilitate triangulation, increase one's legitimacy/authenticity as a 'participant' – and so on (Berger 2001). In this chapter I am primarily interested not so much in these 'benefits' or 'advantages' but rather in the preconditions necessary for establishing the self as an ethnographic resource; and, secondarily, in the impact this might have on one's understanding of what it is to do anthropology. Here are extracts from three further conversations, each of which took place in the meeting house.

Conversation extract B

Anna: Well [looking out onto the meeting garden], it's a wonderful year for roses – mine have never looked better.

Peter: You're right there, it's great to see them looking so well.

Anna: Just when the summer is coming to an end ...

Peter: Yes, my mother used to say the same – they cheer you up just when the weather starts getting miserable.

Anna is a serious gardener and likes to talk flowers and vegetables. Our conversations generally revolved around the subject of growing things – but what may appear to be a narrow subject turns out not to be and our talk ranges across all manner of topics – generally returning, however, to gardening – the hub, if you like, about which our talking relationship turns.

Conversation extract C

Peter: Bad result yesterday [referring to the local football team].

Brian: Yes, very depressing [shakes head dolefully]. Terrible performance.

Peter: Well, I don't know if you'll agree but football, well y'know, that's what football is like! One minute you're up, next you're down. I've always supported Cardiff City, so I should know.

Brian: [laughs].

Brian and I regularly chatted about the performance and fortunes of the local football team. As in each of these cases, our talk gravitated towards a shared interest and these conversations comprised a long and coherent narrative. He had supported several different teams before moving to Bolton – as I had done. Although we talked about plenty of other things we would eventually drift towards sport and inevitably, before long, to football. These short extracts are indicative of the casual way we all (ethnographer included) tend to fall into sharing stories with those among whom we live regardless of whether we meet in the street, the church, the village square, on the railway platform. To be in a talking relationship with someone implies that we have a story for every occasion. Our memory will generally come up with a relevant script but this obviously becomes a greater challenge during utterly novel experiences. Having said that, the facility of the memory to provide a relevant reference makes it difficult to imagine what an 'utterly novel experience' might be! What remains true is that during our meeting with others we draw on our memories to provide the requisite narrative, and this is to draw on our selves as a resource. Why should this not be the case in doing ethnography?

Conversation extract D (Mark and Serena are talking about Mark's recent move to Bristol with his family when Peter joins them)

Mark: … we're glad that we have finally found a place; it's just a matter of settling in now.

Serena: We've moved so often we're just glad to be settled in one place for a bit.

Mark: The new house is OK, its new and really just a box.

Peter: Yes. A few years ago we moved into a small Georgian place a few years back, lovely little place. Exposed beams, tiny fireplace, odd-shaped cupboards – you know the kind of thing. The problem was that the longer we stayed there the more impractical it became. Now I think we'd prefer boxes!

My experiences of moving regularly from one place to another formed a large resource upon which I regularly drew during fieldwork, only partly consciously, in order to signal empathy with the other. Empathy, or the ability to achieve rapport with others in the field is much vaunted – one of the 'secret ingredients' of successful fieldwork (Berger 2001). Rapport is an awareness of the meeting of selves, of engagement. Often, individuals meet in disharmony – there is misunderstanding, frustration, bewilderment, suspicion – and, although I have in mind the meeting between anthropologist and research participant, this is true of social interaction more generally. Sometimes, individuals meet in harmony – there is a common sense, at least, of shared meaning, of empathy, of rapport. Occasionally, rapport is more or less instantaneous; sometimes we 'get off on the wrong foot' but go on to become friends, or at least to meet in mutual toleration. The nature of this process lends empirical support to the argument that 'we contain multitudes'. Further proof, though less obviously empirical, is provided by our own occasional ambivalence: surely, we are all caught, sometimes, on the horns of a dilemma: 'Could I ...?' 'Should I ...?' 'What if I ...?' At such times, we experience, perhaps painfully, an internal dialogue, which may continue for minutes or months, even years. Indeed, one could argue that our internal life is best characterised as one of interminable dialogue.

A Very Short, Though Necessary, Note on Reflexivity

Despite the editors' assertion that the focus of this volume is not reflexivity, I shall argue here that reflexivity is the first precondition for an anthropology in which the self can be considered a resource.[4] Reflexivity is both central and peripheral to my concerns here. It is central in so far as no contemporary anthropologist cannot be reflexive in their ethnographic labours, if by 'reflexivity' we mean an awareness on the part of the anthropologist that they are implicated in or more or less a part of 'the field'. So the practice of reflexivity facilitates an exploration of the ways in which our various involvements in the field inform and transform our fieldwork and, inevitably, our ethnographic accounts of that fieldwork. Given that I am, here, interrogating the idea that the self can be called on as a resource in ethnographic research, this chapter (like all the contributions to this volume) is reflexive – but it is not, let me repeat, *about* reflexivity. In published ethnographic accounts, an awareness of such matters is nowadays sufficient and it is an awareness that, where present, will be manifest in our ethnographic accounts.

Although there may be exceptions, the time has passed where we, as anthropologists, need to preface every account we write with an explanation of our existential position vis-à-vis the field. Surely, no contemporary anthropologist believes that they are detached and separate from 'the field' in the way that natural and physical scientists have generally thought of themselves (as external to the world of bacteria and butterflies)? Indeed, it has long been claimed that good anthropology involves 'getting close' to others, establishing a rapport, developing an empathy, getting inside their skins, seeing the world as others see it. This is a process which, although I am not entirely sure how, transcends dichotomies such as objectivity/subjectivity, emic/etic and insider/

outsider.[5] The possibilities that each and every conversation indicates demand that we seriously question 'distancing techniques' of whatever pedigree – not only the objectifying strategies of earlier structural functionalist thinking but more recent and subtle efforts, such as Bourdieu's 'participant objectivation' (Bourdieu 2003) – in so far as it is patently feasible to be simultaneously both subject and object. If anthropology is partially grounded in reflexivity then the self, as the engine of the reflexive, must be an equally integral part of doing anthropology.

The Self

What, then, of 'the self'? Given the exponential increase in publications discussing the self, there is no doubt that here is a social phenomenon whose time has come. Holstein and Gubrium brilliantly summarise a century of writing on the self in two sentences:

> The story of the social self has come a long way in a short hundred years. Building on countless narratives and reflecting myriad institutional developments, the self is now distinctly appropriated and developed virtually everywhere. Far from being a grand narrative settled at or near the center of personal experience, the self now materializes in myriad nooks and crannies of everyday life, reflecting one sense of who we are in one site, turning a second option for personal definition in another one. (2000: 215)

For several decades anthropology presented itself as a generalising science. We focused on the attributes which, for us at least, characterised those others which comprised our field. Unfortunately, shared characteristics too easily became stereotypes in which the individuality of others is lost; we have indeed presented others as 'cultural dopes', as ciphers, as mere tokens consisting of grossly simplified roles and statuses. If our aim is to capture, in our ethnography, the similarities of those who comprise the field, then differences will become blurred and will eventually become entirely invisible. If we conceive the other to be homogeneous, then it seems likely that we shall understand the self in the same way. More recently, anthropologists have attempted to know others as individuals, with unique stories, which can be compared and contrasted with the stories of others – and not only of others but also of ourselves.

And, while it has long been argued that we sustain different roles (it's trite to point out that one may be, simultaneously, mother, British Asian, friend, neighbour, consumer, amputee etc.), the term 'role' has too often been characterised in simplistic and deterministic terms: 'role' is largely socially determined, it is entrenched, static, limiting. To accept that one is a mother is not merely to accept a role as generally defined, but is actively to co-construct a self.[6] The point is that we are simultaneously members of many worlds, some overlapping in a simple sociological sense, others separate – unless, of course, we are active in bridging the distance between them. This 'bridging' is made possible by the narrative proclivity of the self, by our extraordinary facility for trading stories.[7]

Although this is not the place to become embroiled in a lengthy discussion on the nature of the self, it is worth pausing for a moment to consider what conversations such as those extracted above suggest. The very question posed in the heading of this section suggests a single, homogeneous entity, a coherent and bounded 'thing' that endures. Is this the case? Gubrium and Holstein would appear to agree with Bruner (1990: 107), who suggests that there is something worthwhile in the idea of a 'distributed self'. Dennett argues that the self is a necessary fiction and goes on to paraphrase Gilbert Ryle thus: 'there is no conscious self that is unproblematically in command of the mind's resources. Rather, we are somewhat disunified. Our component modules have to act in opportunistic but amazingly resourceful ways to produce a modicum of behavioural unity, which is then enhanced by an illusion of greater unity' (Dennett 1992).

The question of whether the self is a unity or to some extent multiple remains the source of much debate and the question need not detain us here.[8] All are agreed, in any case, that the self, whether it is single or in some way multiple, is a social construction and that it is constructed during interaction with others. My contention is that any theory of the self needs to pay due attention to the process of narrative in its construction and continuity. Dennett believes, and I concur, that this amazing resourcefulness hinges on our ability to create narratives – to tell stories. The argument for the centrality of narrating in self-construction is not new, but it has gathered strength in recent years. Jerome Bruner has consistently argued this line for more than two decades and has been particularly influential in the process. He writes, in *Acts of Meaning*:

> Freed of the shackles of ontological realism, a new set of concerns about the nature of the Self began to emerge, rather more 'transactional' concerns. Is not Self a transactional relationship between a speaker and an Other ... Is it not a way of framing one's consciousness, one's position, one's identity, one's commitment with respect to another? Self in this dispensation, becomes 'dialogue dependent', designed as much for the recipient of our discourse as for intrapsychic purposes. (1990: 101)

It is these 'transactional concerns' that are of central import here. Many others, apart from Bruner, have come to emphasise the centrality of storytelling in our lives, but it is in the work of Roger Schank (1990) that we find the most concerted attempt to link narrative and memory.[9] During interaction with others, we clearly rely on memory in order to retrieve and narrate those experiences which seem somehow to 'mesh' with the story or stories we are hearing. Schank argues that the process of remembering is done most successfully through the generation of narratives.

Narrative Memory

Schank (1990: *passim*) argues that narrative is central to our ability to remember, suggesting that memory is largely a matter of being able to tell the right story at the right time. The ability to remember the gist of a story, to index and reference a multitude of stories (they are reduced in complexity by being woven into threads) – by both self and other (in this case, the anthropologist) – is engaged in the same project; to be able to articulate them is an important and useful act of intelligence.

In experiencing the world we construct stories and in doing so, make sense of it. Schank suggests that, when someone experiences something in the world, she has a set of scripts (developed over the years) that she uses as general reference points, e.g. attending a church service, going to a football match, singing in a choir. A script is 'a set of expectations about what will happen next in a well-understood situation' (Shank 1990: 7). We have these general scripts which function as aides-memoires for all kinds of activities in our lives.[10] Scripts enable us to run, as it were, on autopilot, they obviate the need for much thought in familiar situations. Without such scripts, every experience would be entirely new every time, making everyday life impossibly challenging. Scripts are used like a set of expectations about how certain familiar situations will play out. We often seem to act out a role both in private and in public. These scripts through which we understand and represent our experiences are adaptable to new information that comes to us – life is easier if our scripts are flexible.

Along with the creation of a catalogue of stories, we construct an indexing and referencing system. It is Schank's contention that our understanding of an experience is that which is relevant to my expressing the essence of what happened. The form and content of my telling can vary; the range of my tellings will be unique and, in detail at least, different from those presented by all others. A story is a more efficient and effective way of capturing the gist of an event than simply relating a chronology of things that happened or registering a set of beliefs or attitudes. If my story is good enough, the point of the story, along with my beliefs, should be obvious.

Apart from being an effective means of communication, stories help us to form memories of particular events. An important means of organising all of the incoming information is what Schank calls a 'memory organisation package' (MOP). A MOP covers a context-dependent aspect of memory. Memories are partially based on scripts, but, as we recall events later, we remember how the event perhaps varied from a script, or we remember how a particular event happened within a particular context. A MOP might be singing in a choir, attending Quaker business meetings or going to a football match. Any MOP is made up of a set of scenes that are imaginable and easily recalled within the framework of the MOP. Episodes that occur are stored in terms of their circumstances and may be connected to the larger context by reconstruction. This is true even of novel or shocking experiences.

Our knowledge amounts largely to experiences that become established through the stories we tell of those experiences (both to ourselves and to others). This explains the apparently compulsive drive to tell stories – as apparent in the short extracts taken from conversations around the meeting house. Also, we remember our experiences through stories because another's story will facilitate recall of stories of our own. Schank argues that, typically, we are better at indexing and recalling stories than we are at presenting propositional beliefs or attitudes because stories are easier to remember and catalogue. What we communicate to others are often stories or fragments of stories. In this model, knowledge is experiences remembered as stories. Intelligence is the ability to tell the right story at the right time.

If we agree that the story I tell about an event is bound (because of our inherently different perspective) to be completely different from others, the reality of the situation is that we often choose to tell what we want to tell and thereby manipulate our own experience according to our needs. Galen Strawson (2004) reminds us that 'revision' is likely to be present in narrative accounts – though he and Schank suggest that this is most often an imaginative, creative process rather than simply lying. Indeed, it is in such cases that one's imagination shifts, as it were, into a higher gear. Generally, we tell stories to certain people, in certain ways, in order to give them a certain sense of the way we wish them to perceive us. What we keep in memory is the skeleton of a story, which we can tell in different ways – depending, for example, on the circumstances and the impression we hope to create.

The conversations with Quakers suggested a concatenation of themes, the most prominent being 'participants in meeting', 'friends and family', 'Quaker business' and 'leisure pursuits'. Schank suggests that our stories are always set in context, in both time and place, and can only be understood in these terms. When a Quaker has sat, for the first time, through a four-hour business meeting and has become increasingly frustrated, she becomes aware of these kinds of frustrations suffered by others – more so than she had before. She will, as a result, go on to talk about the prevalence of such frustrations to others in meeting. One might think of this process as both centripetal and centrifugal – the result is a narrative thread that conjoins individual, local and canonic (or 'official') discourse (Collins 2003) – and which the ethnographer cannot help but become more or less involved in. Certainly, the discourse becomes prominent in one's memory. In future, others' stories of other frustrations are likely to prompt her to revisit and retell her frustration story.

The generation of narrative is a memory-creating experience in itself. A memory is born when a story is told, and will contain the gist of the story that we remember. Although Schank (1990) – rather like Bruner – typically overemphasises language, arguing that *talking* is memory creation, he is correct, I believe, in arguing that, if one has an experience that is never narrated, it is unlikely that the experience will generate a long-lasting memory. Repeated narration, on the other hand, is likely to ensure that the experience is prevalent as a memory. This explains much of the redundancy of talk in the meeting house. On the other hand, Schank, like Bruner and others, believes that narrative is a process involving the reconstitution of reality. All we have are the perspectives and stories that we tell, constructed through the lenses of the other experiences we have had and the beliefs and attitudes that we have about the world. It is quite likely the case that the process of reconstitution involves us in producing memories that others might agree do not constitute 'facts'; however, that does not therefore mean that our stories are entirely fiction. And, although those fictions or 'imaginings' are constructed through the medium of narrative, we should not conclude that they did not happen or that they are based on anything at all – only that they are necessarily perspectival.

Schank's model assumes that narrative, memory and the imagination are intimately related. Given what we know of narrative and narrative enquiry Schank's model of memory makes sense. Both 'self' and 'memory' require a process that is at least something like the one he proposes. It is not just that we, as human beings, are inclined to tell stories, but that we are compulsive story-makers: we act as if our lives depended upon it. We reconstitute experience as story, which the memory compresses and catalogues as script. Social interaction, including that which is involved in conducting ethnographic fieldwork, is unimaginable without memory.

During the course of the Quaker fieldwork I became increasingly conscious of what I saw as a moral obligation to 'equalise' or 'balance' the relationship between myself and research participants – regardless of the context. I became increasingly aware of opportunities to encourage, particularly through conversation, the generation of narrative. My response to the talk of others was increasingly couched in narratives drawn from my own experience. A tendency that was previously largely unconscious became, over the course of several years, a conscious strategy.[11] However, it would be wrong (and indeed ridiculous) to suggest that I consciously prepared each response as an act of narrative engagement before speaking. Rather, it was the case that the longer I spent in Friends' company the more our narratives became conjoined. As time went on, it became less and less feasible to talk with Quakers without co-constructing stories. Regular meetings provided an accumulation of shared experiences, which both anthropologist and research participants might draw on. Conversations noted in the field regularly begin:

> You remember that I told you about …
>
> That reminds me of what you said about …
>
> Yes, I understand, I had a similar problem myself …
>
> Of course, I remember it well, I was about twenty-three at the time …
>
> As far as I can recall, we felt the same at the time …
>
> Etc.

And, as Schank points out (1990: 17) 'Conversation is reminding.' Not all conversation is public, of course, and several prominent theorists (including Vygotsky 1962, Bakhtin 1981 and more recently Rom Harre 1994) present a strong argument for the social significance of private or inward dialogue: we perpetually talk to – or with – ourselves. To return to a point touched on above, storied conversations are an important part of our 'inner' life as well as playing a major role, perhaps *the* major role, in our 'outer', public life. Might dialogue constitute sociality as such? I am suggesting that this is the case and I've tried to show this in my several accounts of British Quakerism (see, for example, Collins 2002a, 2004). It is  no surprise, then, that ethnography has always been dialogic and storied but in recent years has become methodologically less conservative, due to changes in the moral, ontological and epistemic climate. Anthropologists are increasingly likely to enter into a more equal dialogue with others in the field, and this is increasingly reflected in their writing too. This is especially so as research is increasingly carried out at home – and I don't mean to suggest an overly simplistic, homogenising idea of 'home' here.

Is a Dialogic Anthropology Necessary?

The idea of dialogic anthropology certainly isn't new. Kevin Dwyer (1977, 1979, 1982) was advocating its adoption as long ago as the 1970s, and in 1979 he wrote: 'anthropologists, perhaps sensing that to expose the self is necessarily to place it in jeopardy, have for the most part been unwilling to take such a gamble. Avoiding this risk with unusual virtuosity, they have refused to admit that the very possibility of dealing squarely with the Other is tied to the capacity to put the Self at stake' (1979: 205).

What, then, is dialogic anthropology? First, according to Dwyer, it involves a 'wager' – it means accepting the possibility of failure in the fieldwork encounter; it demands that the anthropologist's talk draws on his own experience; and that the field engagement allows for the other to talk back: crudely, the anthropologist continues to 'fish for data' while remaining open, herself, to being fished. Dwyer begins one conversation by asking Faqir Mbarak, 'What do you think I am doing here?'

How often do research participants have the opportunity to ask questions of us? How much do we 'give away'? Fieldwork remains a matter of give and take, but hopefully not in the sense that we take while others give. In participant observation, this mode of conversation is almost always an option, in so far as the anthropologist is directly or at least indirectly involved in 'the action'. The 'good conversation' is a more or less (though never quite) equal exchange; and there is a moral imperative that we accept the complexity of others as we would expect others to accept our complexity.

There is a further issue here concerning what Strathern (1999) calls the anthropologist's two fields: dialogic anthropology started in the field, continues in the study.[12] If dialogue is at the centre of social life, then surely it should be at the centre of ethnography? The matter hinges not only on one's practice in the field but also on the extent to which others' voices are represented in the final account as well as the degree to which they are involved in its construction. We should perhaps be a little less inclined to demand the 'final word', and it's no longer unusual for anthropologists to engage in dialogic ethnography, for instance, by foregrounding the voice of the other, by sending transcripts back to research participants for further comment, and so forth.[13]

To deny the self as a resource in conducting fieldwork would be to deny the centrality of dialogue in human sociality, and thereby to deny the humanity of those among whom we live in the field. However, the question that remains is the extent to which the anthropologist can use her self as a resource where fieldwork is not reflexive, where a non-storied self is assumed and where dialogue is precluded by the mode of fieldwork. I would say, of course, that in such circumstances the self remains largely dormant as a resource and that a less humanistic (and therefore less convincing) anthropology is the likely result. However, Dwyer's work remains important because, in positioning his work at one end of the spectrum, that is, by emphasising the voice of the other, he provides us with an opportunity to consider both the theory and practice, the strengths and weaknesses, of a dialogical anthropology. While I am not convinced that giving way entirely to the voice of the other is necessary, I am sure that, for moral as well as epistemological and ontological reasons, dialogue must be central to the ethnographic and, *pari passu*, the (sociocultural) anthropological enterprise.

Conclusions

In this chapter I have brought together a number of interconnected processes that necessitate the self as ethnographic resource: self, story, memory and dialogue. My argument is that, if we are to engage in humanistic ethnography (and therefore anthropology), we must accept the importance of the self as a resource in our work: both in the field and in the study. Although I happen to agree with those who argue for a multiple rather than a single self, this has little bearing here. What I do wish to make clear is that the self is, in any case, thoroughly storied. Furthermore, it is likely that we sort these stories and sometimes hold them in novel juxtapositions – sometimes consciously, sometimes below the level of consciousness. Memory is central to all of this and is facilitated by the storage of experiences as narrative. Along with other contributors to this volume, notably Coleman, Kohn and Davis, I want to make clear the crucial role that memory plays during the practice of fieldwork and during its later inscription. Finally, it is primarily (if not entirely) in conversation with others that we constitute our selves. And it should be clear by now that as well as being 'a resource', the self is also extraordinarily resourceful.

To conclude, let us return to the extracts from meeting house conversations presented at the beginning of this chapter. I know that the resonance experienced on these occasions is a common experience in carrying out fieldwork – the resonance is not always powerfully felt but it is often felt nonetheless. Such resonance is the embodied response (there is always a frisson) to the production of a jointly constructed narrative. In this case, the process of construction was not entirely conscious, my narrative self willingly engaged through a prompt of memory in this co-construction. And, although I would agree that the sociocultural and spatial context of the Quaker meeting house facilitates such exchanges, along with the fact that I was not working in a second (or third) language as are many anthropologists, this resourcefulness of self is very likely to be a characteristic of all ethnography. In short, our ethnographic experiences are apprehended and comprehended entirely by virtue of our memory, or facility to recall similar experiences that we have had in the past. As Cohen reminds us (1994: 117), Rorty (in his debate with Geertz) argues strongly that self-consciousness implies our capacity to take moral positions. By foregrounding the ethnographic self as a resource, I hope I make it clear that this practice is a moral as well as methodological necessity.

Notes

1. For further consideration of the senses in anthropology, see Stoller (1989) and Howes (2003, 2005). Also see the journal *Senses and Society*.
2. The terms 'Friend' and 'Quaker' are synonymous.
3. Quakers in Britain meet (and talk) in a variety of contexts other than in meeting for worship – in order to conduct church business ('meetings for church affairs', or business meetings); workshops, both at the meeting house and elsewhere; weekend 'retreats', during peace rallies, in discussion groups, for instance.
4. The editors discuss the issue of reflexivity at greater length in Chapter 1.
5. I discuss this issue further in Collins (2002b).
6. The cooperative nature of self-construction was identified long ago – first by the American pragmatist Charles Horton Cooley, whose idea of a 'looking glass self' (1964 [1902]) heralded the later work of symbolic interactionists such as G.H. Mead, Herbert Blumer and others.
7. For a range of accounts of the centrality of narrative to social life see, for example Bruner (1986, 1987, 1990, 1994, 1997, 1998), Gergen (1988), Kleinman (1988), Britton and Pellegrini (eds. 1990), Nash (ed. 1990), Kerby (1991), Carrithers (1994), Ochs and Capps (1996, 2001), Holstein and Gubrium (2000). See also Webster (1983), who suggests that ethnography itself is a form of storytelling.
8. For an exquisite account of the emergence of selves see Kondo (1990).
9. But see the papers in Neisser and Fivush (1994) for alternative views.
10. These 'scripts' must be, despite Schank's emphasis on language, more or less embodied. Unfortunately, I cannot discuss this issue further here.
11. I might add that I have continued this 'strategy' in recent, interview-based research. See Collins (1998) for further discussion.
12. I might just add that I take the idea of the 'two fields' to mark an existential and dynamic rather than a spatio-temporal and static discontinuity.
13. In my experience it is becoming commonplace in the case of undergraduate and postgraduate fieldwork.

References

Bakhtin, M. 1981. 'Discourse in the Novel', in M Holquist (ed.), *The Dialogic Imagination*, trans. C. Emerson and M. Holquist. Austin: University of Texas Press, pp. 259–422.

Berger, L. 2001. 'Inside Out: Narrative Autoethnography as a Path Toward Rapport', *Qualitative Inquiry* 7(4): 504–18.

Bourdieu, P. 2003. 'Participant Objectivation', *Journal of the Royal Anthropological Institute* 9(2): 281–94

Britton, B.K. and A.D. Pellegrini (eds). 1990. *Narrative Thought and Narrative Language*. Hillsdale, NJ: Lawrence Erlbaum.

Bruner, J. 1986. *Actual Minds Possible Worlds*. Cambridge, Mass.: Harvard University Press.

———. 1987. 'Life as Narrative', *Social Research* 54(1): 11–32.

———. 1990. *Acts of Meaning*. Cambridge, Mass.: Harvard University Press.

———. 1994. The 'Remembered Self', in U. Neisser and R. Fivush (eds), *The Remembering Self: Construction and Accuracy in the Self-narrative*. Cambridge, UK: Cambridge University Press.

———. 1997. 'A Narrative Model of Self-construction', in J. G. Snodgrass and R. L. Thompson (eds), *The Self Across Psychology: Self-Recognition, Self-Awareness, and the Self Concept*. New York: New York Academy of Sciences, pp. 145–61.

———. 1998. 'Narrative and Metanarrative in the Construction of Self', in M.D. Ferrari and R.J. Sternberg (eds), *Self-awareness: Its Nature and Development*. New York: Guilford Press, pp. 308–31.

Carrithers, M. 1994. *Why Humans Have Cultures*. Oxford: Oxford University Press.

Cohen, A.P. 1994. *Self-Conscious Anthropology: An Alternative Anthropology of Identity*. London: Routledge.

Collins, P.J. 1998. 'Negotiating Lives: Reflections on "Unstructured Interviewing"', *Sociological Research Online* 3(3). http://www.socresonline.org.uk/socreson line/3/3/2.html. Accessed April 2007.

———. 2002a. 'Connecting Anthropology and Quakerism: Transcending the Insider/Outsider Dichotomy', in E. Arweck and M.D. Stringer (eds), *Theorising Faith: The Insider/Outsider Problem in the Study of Ritual*. Birmingham: Birmingham University Press, pp. 77–95.

———. 2002b. 'Both Independent and Interconnected Voices: Bakhtin Among the Quakers', in N.Rapport (ed.), *Best of British: The Anthropology of Britain*, Berg, pp. 281–98.

———. 2003. 'Storying Self and Others: the Construction of Narrative Identity', *Journal of Politics and Language* 2(2): 243–65.

———. 2004. 'Congregations, Narratives and Identities: a Quaker Case Study', in M. Guest, K. Tusting and L. Woodhead (eds), *Congregational Studies in the UK: Christianity in a Post-Christian Context*. Aldershot: Ashgate, pp. 99–112.

Cooley, C.H. 1964 [1902]. *Human Nature and the Social Order*. New York: Scribner's.

Dennett, D. 1992. 'The Self as a Centre of Narrative Gravity', in F. Kessel, P. Cole and D. Johnson (eds), *Self and Consciousness: Multiple Perspectives*. Hillsdale, NJ: Erlbaum, pp. 103–15.

Dwyer, K. 1977. 'On the Dialogic of Field Work', *Dialectical Anthropology* 2: 143–51.
———. 1979. 'The Dialogic of Ethnology', *Dialectical Anthropology* 4: 205–24.
———. 1982. *Moroccan Dialogues: Anthropology in Question.* Baltimore: Johns Hopkins University Press.
Gergen, M. 1988. 'Narrative Structures in Social Explanation', in C. Antaki (ed.), *Analysing Everyday Explanation, a Casebook of Methods.* London: Sage.
Harre, R. 1994. *The Discursive Mind.* Thousand Oaks: Sage.
Holstein, J.A. and J.F. Gubrium. 2000. *The Self We Live By: Narrative Identity in a Postmodern World.* Oxford: Oxford University Press.
Howes, D. (ed.). 2003. *Sensual Relations: Engaging the Senses in Culture and Social Theory.* Ann Arbor, Mich.: University of Michigan Press.
———. 2005. *Empire of the Senses: The Sensual Culture Reader.* Oxford: Berg.
Kerby, A.P. 1991. *Narrative and the Self.* Bloomington: Indiana University Press.
Kleinman, A. 1988. *The Illness Narratives.* New York: Basic Books.
Kondo, D. 1990. *Crafting Selves. Power, Gender and Discourses of Identity in a Japanese Workplace.* Chicago: Chicago University Press.
Nash, C. (ed.). 1990. *Narrative in Culture: The Uses of Storytelling in the Sciences, Philosophy, and Literature.* London: Routledge.
Neisser, U. and R. Fivush (eds). 1994. *The Remembering Self: Construction and Accuracy in the Self-narrative.* Cambridge and New York: Cambridge University Press.
Ochs, E. and L. Capps 1996. 'Narrating the Self', *Annual Review of Anthropology* 25: 19–43.
———. 2001. *Living Narrative: Creating Lives in Everyday Storytelling.* Cambridge, Mass., London: Harvard University Press.
Rapport, N. 1987. *Talking Violence: An Anthropological Interpretation of Conversation in the City.* St Johns, Newfoundland: ISER Books.
———. 1993. *Diverse World Views in an English Village.* Edinburgh: Edinburgh University Press.
Schank, R.C. 1990. *Tell Me a Story: A New Look at Real and Artificial Memory.* New York: Scribner's.
Stoller, P. 1989. *Taste of Ethnographic Things: The Senses in Anthropology.* Philadephia: University of Pennsylvania Press
Strathern, M. 1999. *Property, Substance and Effect: Anthropological Essays on Persons and Things.* London: Athlone Press.
Strawson, G. 2004. 'Against Narrativity', *Ratio* 17(4): 428–52.
Vygotsky, L. 1962. *Thought and Language.* Cambridge, Mass.: MIT Press.
Webster, S. 1983. 'Ethnography as Storytelling', *Dialectical Anthropology* 8: 185–206.

Chapter 15

EPILOGUE: WHAT A STORY WE ANTHROPOLOGISTS HAVE TO TELL!

James W. Fernandez

I expect that most readers, like myself, have found themselves stimulated and instructed by the special insight and intuition into the human condition present in this self-directed and self-oriented collection of essays. Their authors tell us much about the fabulating ways (Lévi Strauss 1963) that we humans capture each other's imaginations, that is our imaginative selves, and the ways that we do or don't make music together (Schutz 1977).[1] There are, in brief, many riches in this collection, and perhaps, something of a Pandora's box as well. For this collection and its contributors' venturesome mettle do, after all, raise challenges to the ego strength, the secure selfhood, of those of us who may have come to depend upon a readily applicable and practicable research protocol. It asks of them, as it asks of us all, that, by reflecting on our self-involvement more deeply and honestly we come to recognise the pros and cons, the successes and failures, of our fieldwork experience. It asks of us, and perhaps sometimes painfully, to probe the adequacy and inadequacy, the superficiality or percipience of our interpretations and understandings.

To be sure, fieldwork that puts the self front and centre, as this collection does, is very likely to be faced with the many awkwardnesses that arise out of the idiosyncrasies of individual selves. Such waywardness inevitably arises and is regularly involved in communicative interaction. And this is not to speak of the always possible solipsism of self-immersion and of being, at times, one's own informant which is also advocated here. But the reader will find that, by reflecting deeply on the fieldworking self and upon the cross-currents of memory and narrative in which it is enmeshed, this collection gains a very certain strength. It anchors itself securely by making more explicit these difficulties and, by not avoiding them, becoming the more directly knowledgeable about them ... these ever possible waywardnesses of self oriented but poorly self-aware ambitions.

To be sure also, the featured self, embodied as the brow of Athena infusing our discipline with new sensitivity to the currents of social life for some (including this reader), can be a Medusa's head for others, stultifying anthropology's practitioners with multitudinous challenges, not the least of which is the serendipities involved in the self's negotiation of everyday life. For the self in its always present and ever possible idiosyncrasy is not the easily constrained and sharply honed instrument of enquiry customary in the social sciences! Just consider its capabilities as presented in these pages and the challenges to the ethnography of field and study that the putting into practice of self-awareness represents. We see, as offered for us by Rapport, for example, the self's reflective capacities for skilfully and sensitively parsing the moral dynamics of field interaction, an interaction involving the obligations recognised or neglected in the emerging social relations of fieldwork; we see, as offered by Collins, our narrativising capacities to take the humdrum of everyday interacting humanity and give it episodic character and climactic suspense; we see, as Phipps puts it, the self's ever inventive use of language and languaging which is constantly present in making or breaking human relations through communicative interaction; we see the self's dependence on the its body's agility and balance and coordination. Skinner makes this very clear in his dance floor ethnography, as does Dyck in respect to studying, by also necessarily bodily participating in, children's sport. We see (in Kohn and Amit) the self's pliant, often enough compliant, ability to deal with the challenge of serendipitous reroutings of our informants' and our own expectations in interaction. And then there is, finally, the ineradicable idiosyncrasy and incipient individuality as manifested even in the most identical of identical twins (as related to us by the Davis twins), indeed the impossibility, amidst all our efforts at symbiosis, of absolute identification with the other.

By thus focusing on the self we are necessarily focused on the constancy of ambiguity and idiosyncrasy in human relations, which is intensified by the associated and ever accompanying possibility of serendipity in these relations. The presence of these 'disconcerts' in the field is something any grounded anthropological enquiry will readily recognise, although they may often be ignored in the rush to ethnographic order. We have only to read the field accounts of Šikić-Mićanović, of Larsen and of Gallinat to see the workings of unexpected disjunctions in the identity of 'self and other', at times with awkward or distressing consequences; in Šikić-Mićanović's case it is the distress of being perceived as a careless mother and hence finding herself, an observer herself painfully observed by her interlocutors; with Larsen it is the 'disconcert' of finding herself as an unattached young woman a natural object of, perhaps prurient, interest in local storytelling – as she says 'Whose story is it anyway?'; and with Gallinat it is the ambiguity of playing the native card of privileged local memory only to find distinct differences in *Ostalgia* between herself and other former East Germans according to generation and according to identification with the former East German regime. Gallinat, in particular, raises several important questions as regards the self: the difference in the social anchoring of self and its social perception as between memory and that kind of memory known as nostalgia; or the impact upon the self consequent to a (or its) society's having undergone a drastic change (in this case *die Wende*) in political economy, passing all too quickly from a communalist to an individualist self-actualising evaluation of self. A collection of essays that puts the self and self-awareness at the centre of inquiry is bound to be revelatory in these and other ways about the fundamental awkwardness of participant observation. It is bound to be also a challenge, surely at the grounded level of its enquiry, to the confidence of any science-like report of validity and verifiability of result.

This collection, of course, has its predecessors, as is recognised by both its editors and its contributors. Still, it may be useful and certainly appropriate here to recall and salute a previous collection of essays in which the self-aware ethnographer as writer of *Fieldnotes* was put front and centre (Sanjek 1990). Influenced, to be sure, by the 'Writing Culture' movement, *Fieldnotes* was an important complement to it, anchoring that movement more firmly in the original 'writing down' of the field moment, that is in the field notes themselves and in the field memory, the 'headnotes', which together are the source, after all, of the final writing up. Similarly the collection we have at hand here anchors more firmly in the idiosyncratic self the gradual movement in anthropology away from the constraints of Durkheimian exteriorities to the interiorities, the psychosocial 'secret lives', as it were, of social interaction in the field. The *Fieldnotes* collection also gave us a useful vocabulary to parse the complexities of the writing down and the preserving process, not only the distinction between field notes and head notes, but also scratch notes, organised notes, archived notes, field-path notes, autochthonous texts, journals and diaries, reports home and finally home notes verging into final ethnography. Thus this collection gives us, particularly in the editors' introduction and in Collins's resourceful chapter, the various vocabularies of memory and narrative that can enable us to better focus upon and grasp how the self comes to terms with itself by seeking anchorage in the remembrances of the past melded into its present powers of self and other narrative.

And here I might, in the same vein and in something of an indulgence of self, reflect upon a previous struggle of my own to grasp the dynamic of selves in social interaction. This bringing of my own ethnographic sense of self and selves into play, this self-indulgence, is after all both stimulated by and licensed by the orientation and subject matter of these essays. My particular disposition of understanding[2] was influenced by Victor Turner (1957) and Kenneth Burke (1989) and their disposition to understand fieldwork and its writing up in dramatistic terms, that is, to understand both the selves of one's interlocutors and one's own self as dramatis personae. These dramatically constructed and narratively understood persons were mutually and actively engaged in seeking emergent understanding of each other and of the groups and subcultures to which they, including the ethnographer, belonged and who were inevitably brought into play in the ongoing, so readily construed as episodic, scenarios of fieldwork (Fernandez 1982). In a shorthand way, I treated these various interacting selves of the field as inchoate pronouns in dynamic emergent interaction, seeking to predicate upon themselves both in singular and plural appropriate identities. I felt that among the ethnographer's first tasks was that of registering revelatory moments or dramatic episodes of social life, where some percipience is offered into the dynamics of emergent selves and emergent others in the context of local cultural circumstance.

The anchoring of social life in the interaction of inchoate pronouns engaged in seeking emergent understanding, at once called pronominalism by insightful, if captious friends, is surely reductionist in the extreme and would seem to be the very opposite of the enrichment of self-social awareness that is offered and encouraged in this collection. It would seem a strategy of understanding that essentialises the self or society of selves to the point of disappearance. But I might argue that the intention is rather to put forth a template of enquiry that is, or should be, very much 'selves oriented' and is hence congruent in its way with what we are offered here. It was intended not as a self-sufficient framework but as an impetus to enquiry into the way that any culture is, in fact, a society of selves seeking to escape inchoateness in the various scenarios of interaction. For me it was and should be a pronouncedly inductive plan of work. It was a plan to make fieldwork and the resultant ethnography more sensitive to these revelatory moments or scenarios where the engagement of selves –of the inchoate pronouns if one wishes – is susceptible to narrative presentation to the reader's imagination. It called for the formatting of ethnography through the narration of the revelatory incidents found in field notebooks, in which the ethnographer is in some way involved, actively or as an observer. The role of these narrations was to launch each and every chapter and to ground subsequent discussion.

However one might formulate, and formulate it was, the basic vectors of field awareness, in seeking to make more percipient our study of the dynamic of selves in society, it risked being too formalistic. And it risked being insufficiently transitional in registering the sea change over the decades from the Durkheimian emphasis on the discovery of controlling externalities to the increasing emphasis on internalities and the complex percipience present in the selves' internal registry of experience. There are many ways to put this sea change. There is the shift from the pre-scripted and essentialised actor to the more freely scripted and polyvalent self holding a more complex and even conflicted view of human nature, not just *Homo faber* or *Homo ludens* or *Homo economicus*, but a fully invested and difficult to essentialise *Homo sapiens*, a disambiguating animal with a truly multiplex sapient grasp of the world. Or the sea change can be seen as the shift from a purely instrumental agent focused on real-world manipulations to a much more emotionally expressive and morally involved self in truly ambiguous and ambivalent relation to that 'real world' which is the field situation … only saved perhaps, and at that only momentarily, by his or her powers of disambiguation. In that sense, the pronominalism I proposed was, for its time, but one of these initiatory disambiguations of fieldwork that worked for me but may not have worked for thee! This present collection, in any event, focusing on the selves of fieldwork, attentive as it is itself to the tension between the resonance of memory and the needs of current narrative, possesses, I would say, a natural nominalism. And it is one that goes further into the interaction of selves. It hardly needs a rubric summarised in a key term and evoking an arid anchoring armature to recommend it.

Be the various precedences of this volume as they may, what in the end is the story that anthropologists have to tell? The rhetorical narrative of our heroism that came to us, but especially to Lévi-Strauss, from Susan Sontag (Hayes and Hayes 1970; see also Hartman 2007)[3] in the 1960s and 1970s seemed a bit over the top as a description of the particular way that we anthropologists quietly, and hopefully unobtrusively, stepped over into the unknown, 'taking our lives' into our hands in making our particular kind of, often quite humdrum, enquiry and interpretation. And, for these present times, in which we so often work at home, the sobriquet seems especially far-fetched.

And yet anthropologists do still go out to the unknown, even at home. We do go out to work in other's families, moving from the familiar to the unfamiliar in that sense, even when so much of such home work is said to be 'familiar'. Focusing on the vicissitudes of the self in this adventure makes that clear. If we lead with the self and centre on the self's reactions and reflections, we do put our 'lives on the line', to say it figuratively, and in a way that is uncharacteristic of most members of our species, in general and in disciplinary particular. While perhaps not heroic or melodramatic in the life or death sense, anthropology in this way becomes the story of an especially alert and self-sensitive creature doing the unusual by putting that exposed self into the company of barely known others. And not only that but exposing that self for extended periods of time in such unfamiliar circumstances. It is a 'calling' that most of our fellows would hardly think of heeding. To understand what that sort of 'heroism' amounts to one has only to read the accounts of Rapport or Larsen, to name only two of the venturesome contributors here. Even one's own garden, familiar as it is, when brought into play with other gardens and the gardening impulse generally can be an adventure in discovery from season to season, from year to year and from neighbour to neighbour (Nadel-Klein).

Of course, for a long time and for many anthropologists, we have protected ourselves against the hazards of our calling of exposing the self by following scientistically a defining and tightly guiding methodology, a strict commitment to the validity and verifiability of a questionnaire, notes and queries kind of approach. But none of the practitioners whose chapters we contemplated in these many exercises in the reflecting self, reflecting upon its long enquiry among distinct others, seeks to protect themselves in that way. In carrying themselves to the field as the main bundle of 'instruments', the principal 'resource' of their enquiry, they also offer, as we said to begin with and reaffirm here at the end, revealing intuition and insight into the many natures of the human condition. They call us to be present at its and our endless, if often enough failed, efforts at truly communicative interaction, at mutual narrative enthralment, at the resourceful capturing each others' imagination, in short at our making or not making music together. Such revealings are no small thing. I can hardly thank the contributors enough for the many diverse understandings of the human condition that they, that is to say their selves, and their editors offer us here.

Notes

The subtitle of this chapter is with apologies to Miles Richardson (1975) and his memorable reminder to us of the many stories of the human career and the human condition that anthropology is, uniquely among the disciplines, enabled to tell.

1. In general, for Schutz's phenomenology of the social world, see *The Structures of the Life World* (1975).
2. I am talking about 1970s work largely, in which I formulated this pronominal perspective.
3. The book by Hayes and Hayes (1970) is a study-collection on Lévi-Strauss' work, evoking in its title the 1963 essay of the same name by Susan Sontag in *The New York Review of Books*. Interestingly, as far as our discussion here is

concerned, for Sontag, writing as she felt at a time, the 1960s, in which modern selves were seeking identification with 'the truly other', it was only the anthropologist who could truly achieve that heroic loss of self in the other.

References

Burke, K. 1989. *On Symbols and Society*, edited and with an introduction by J.R. Gusfield. Chicago: University of Chicago Press.

Fernandez, J.W. 1982. *Bwiti: An Ethnography of the Religious Imagination in Africa*. Princeton: Princeton University Press.

Hartman, T. 2007. 'Beyond Sontag as a Reader of Lévi-Strauss: the Anthropologist as Hero', *Anthropology Matters Journal* 9(1): 1–11.

Hayes, E.N. and T. Hayes. 1970. *Claude Lévi-Strauss: The Anthropologist as Hero*. Cambridge: MIT Press.

Lèvi Strauss, C. 1963. 'The Sorcerer and His Magic', in C. Lèvi Strauss (ed.), *Structural Anthropology*. Basic Books: New York, pp. 167–85.

Richardson, M. 1975. 'Anthropologist – the Myth Teller', *American Ethnologist* 2 (3): 517–33.

Sanjek, R. (ed.). 1990. *Fieldnotes: The Makings of Anthropology*. Ithaca: Cornell University Press.

Schutz, A. 1975. *The Structures of the Life World*. Evanston: Northwestern University Press.

———. 1977. 'Making Music Together: a Study in Social Relationships', in J. Dolgin, D. Kemnitzer and D. Schneider (eds), *Symbolic Anthropology: A Reader*. New York: Columbia Press, pp. 106–20.

Sontag, S. 1994 [1963]. 'The Anthropologist as Hero', in S. Sontag (ed.), *Against Interpretation*. London: Vintage, pp. 69–81.

Turner, V. 1957. *Schism and Continuity in an African Society: A Study of Ndembu Village Life*. Manchester: Manchester University Press.

NOTES ON CONTRIBUTORS

Vered Amit is Professor of Anthropology at Concordia University, Canada. Her research has focused on various forms of transnational mobility and has interrogated the attendant disjunctures, desires, networks and links that arise through or are attenuated by movement across space and time. Of particular interest have been efforts to carefully ground and build on anthropological conceptualisations of community and sociality. She has conducted fieldwork in London (UK), Montreal, Vancouver and the Cayman Islands. She is the author or editor of ten books.

Simon Coleman is Professor of Anthropology at the University of Sussex, UK, and Editor of the *Journal of the Royal Anthropological Institute*. His interests include charismatic Christianity, pilgrimage, hospital ethnography and chaplaincies, and friendship. Among his books are *The Globalisation of Charismatic Christianity* (Cambridge University Press, 2000), *Reframing Pilgrimage: Cultures in Motion* (with J. Eade, Routledge, 2004) and *Locating the Field: Space, Place and Context in Anthropology* (with P. Collins, Berg, 2006).

Peter Collins is Senior Lecturer in the Department of Anthropology, Durham University. His research interests are religion, space and place and narrative theory. He recently co-edited *The Quaker Condition: The Sociology of a Liberal Tradition* (with P. Dandelion, Cambridge Scholars Press, 2008), *Locating the Field: Space, Place and Context in Anthropology* (with Simon Coleman, Berg, 2006) and *Reading Religion in Text and Context* (with Elisabeth Arweck, Ashgate, 2006). He has carried out fieldwork among British and Kenyan Quakers, among local government employees in the North of England and in NHS acute hospitals.

Dona Lee Davis is Professor of Anthropology at the University of South Dakota in the USA. Her research interests include medical anthropology, cultural psychology, and maritime anthropology. She has conducted fieldwork in Newfoundland, Canada and North Norway as well as at home in the United States. She recently co-edited *Mutuality and Empathy: Self and Other in the Ethnographic Encouter* (with Anne Sigfrid Gronseth, Sean Kingston Press, 2010). She is currently completing a book on identical twins.

Dorothy I. Davis is a lecturer in the Department of Anthropology at the University of North Carolina in Greensboro, North Carolina. For the last decade the focus of her research has been the study of research pedagogy in anthropology with a special emphasis on introductory-level classes. This research continues to test the implementation and effectiveness of educational innovations in the classroom. Recently she has participated in a research project on twins directed by her twin sister, Dona Davis. The sisters have collaborated on several papers on identical twins and identity issues. Major publications include *Cultures in Contact* (as editor) (Kendall Hunt, 2008), *A Study Guide for Contemporary Non-Western Cultures* (Kendall Hunt, 2006) and *Readings in Non-Western Cultures* (Dorothy Bruner (ed.), Simon and Schuster, 1998).

Noel Dyck is Professor of Social Anthropology at Simon Fraser University in British Columbia. The author of several books on relations between aboriginal peoples and governments, he has subsequently conducted field research on sport, childhood and youth mobility in Canada. Recent volumes that he has edited include *Exploring Regimes of Discipline* (Berghahn, 2008), *Sport, Dance and Embodied Identities* (with Eduardo P. Archetti, Berg, 2003) and *Games, Sports and Culture* (MacMillan, 2000). He is currently completing studies of the social construction of children's sports.

James W. Fernandez is Emeritus Professor of Anthropology, Chicago University. He has carried out fieldwork in various parts of Africa (most notably among the Fang) and in Spain. His interests include trope theory, religious movements and art and architectonics. Among his many publications are *Irony in Action: Anthropology, Practice and the Moral Imagination* (ed. with Mary Taylor Huber, University of Chicago Press, 2001); *Beyond Metaphor: The Theory of Tropes in Anthropology* (ed., Stanford University Press, 1991); *Campos Léxicos y Vida Cultural n'Asturies* (Academia de la Llingua Asturiana, 1996); *Persuasions and Performances: The Play of Tropes in Culture* (Indiana University Press, 1986); *Bwiti: an Ethnography of the Religious Imagination in Africa* (Books on Demand, 1982).

Anselma Gallinat is a lecturer at the School for Geography, Politics and Sociology at Newcastle University. She has conducted several periods of fieldwork in eastern Germany focusing on questions of sociocultural change in post-socialism, the self, identity, public discourse, suffering and the past. Her research expertise concerns ethnography, narrative and life stories. Her most recent work explores the social construction of memory and questions of morality. She has published on narratives of former political prisoners in *Ethnos* and *Anthropology Today*, on questions of belonging in *Identities* and on morality in fieldwork and in memory in *Anthropology and History*.

Tamara Kohn is Senior Lecturer in Anthropology at the University of Melbourne. Her field research experiences in Scotland, Nepal, California and Japan are linked by common interest in migration, identity and transnational communities of embodied practice. Publications include *The Discipline of Leisure* (Berghahn, 2007, ed. with S. Coleman), *Extending the Boundaries of 'Care'* (Berg 1999, ed. with R. McKechnie), 'Becoming an Islander through Action in the Scottish Hebrides', *JRAI* 8(1) (2002), and 'Creatively Sculpting the Self Through the Discipline of Martial Arts Training', in N. Dyck (ed.), *Exploring Regimes of Discipline* (Berg, 2008).

Anne Kathrine Larsen is an associate professor in social anthropology at the Norwegian University of Science and Technology. She has conducted fieldwork in Norway, Malaysia and the United Arab Emirates on issues ranging from local community dynamics, world views, development discourses, cultural heritage and perceptions on well-being. Larsen has written about discourses on development in Malaysia, in S. Abram and J. Waldren (eds), *Anthropological Perspectives on Development. Interests, Identities and Sentiments in Conflict* (Routledge, 1998) and on tradition as reflexive project in Norway and Malaysia, in U. Kockel, N.M. Craith (eds), *Cultural Heritages as Reflexive Traditions* (Macmillan, 2006). She also has an interest in questions pertaining to methodology.

Jane Nadel-Klein is a professor of anthropology at Trinity College in Hartford, Connecticut. She is the author of *Fishing for Heritage: Modernity and Loss along the Scottish Coast* (Berg, 2003), the co-editor (with Dona Davis) of *To Work and to Weep: Women in Fishing Economies* (ISER 1988). She has now turned her scholarly attention inland and is engaged in a comparison of gardening as a social practice in the United States and the United Kingdom. During her most recent sabbatical, she studied to be a Master Gardener.

Alison Phipps is Professor of Languages and Intercultural Studies and Director of the Centre for Studies in Faith, Culture and Education at the University of Glasgow, where she teaches modern languages, comparative literature, anthropology and intercultural education. Her books include *Acting Identities* (Lang, 2000), *Contemporary German Cultural Studies* (Arnold, 2002), *Modern Languages: Learning and Teaching in an Intercultural Field* (Sage, 2004) with Mike Gonzalez, *Critical Pedagogy: Political Approaches to Languages and Intercultural Communication* (Multilingual Matters, 2004) with Manuela Guilherme, *Tourism and Intercultural Exchange* (Channel View, 2005) with Gavin Jack and *Learning the Arts of Linguistic Survival: Tourism, Languaging, Life* (Channel View, 2007). Her first collection of poetry, *Through Wood*, was published in 2009 with Wild Goose Publications.

Nigel Rapport is Professor of Anthropological and Philosophical Studies at the University of St Andrews, Scotland, where he is Director of the Centre for Cosmopolitan Studies. He has also held the Canada Research Chair in Globalization, Citizenship and Justice at Concordia University of Montreal. His research interests include: social theory, identity and individuality, consciousness, conversation, liberalism and humanism, and links between anthropology and literature and philosophy. Among his recent books are: *'I am Dynamite': An Alternative Anthropology of Power* (Routledge, 2003); *Social and Cultural Anthropology: The Key Concepts,* 2nd edition (Routledge, 2007); *Of Orderlies and Men: Hospital Porters Achieving Wellness at Work* (Carolina Academic Press, 2008); and (as editor) *Democracy, Science and the Open Society: A European Legacy?* (Transaction, 2006).

Lynette Šikić-Mićanović is a research associate at the Institute of Social Sciences Ivo Pilar in Zagreb, Croatia. She received her Ph.D. in anthropology and her research focuses on rural/farm women, Roma women and children and the homeless in Croatia. She is the author of numerous articles and book chapters in Croatian and English on gender, domestic labour, domesticity and rural development. She is co-editor of *New Countryside: Culture, Local Governance and Sustainability in Rural Development* (Alutus, 2005).

Jonathan Skinner is a lecturer in social anthropology at the School of History and Anthropology, Queen's University Belfast. His main interests are in tourism and dance in the Caribbean, the UK and the US. He is author of the book *Before the Volcano: Reverberations of Identity on Montserrat* (Arawak Publications, 2004) and co-edited *Managing Island Life* (University of Abertay Press, 2006). He is a former treasurer of the Association of Social Anthropologists, and former editor of the journal *Anthropology in Action*.

INDEX

Lightning Source UK Ltd.
Milton Keynes UK
UKOW04f2209280214

227368UK00005B/107/P